STANDING MY GROUND

Over
my lifetime I've
witnessed continued losses
of a wide range of our unique natural
heritage, from ocean depth to mountain
top, and can see that nature conservation is
increasingly challenging for us. Sadly conservation
seems mostly involved in reducing the rate
of loss of our precious heritage. Real
gains are the exception, therefore
ecosanctuaries are important
for conservation and
for education.
Support for
our Orokonui
Ecosanctuary
is essential to help turn the tide.

ALAN MARK

Statement by Alan Mark for the Place exhibition of sculptures by Louisa Baillie, Dunedin, February 2012.

STANDING MY GROUND
A voice for nature conservation

Alan F. Mark

OTAGO UNIVERSITY PRESS

Published by Otago University Press
Level 1, 398 Cumberland Street
Dunedin, New Zealand
university.press@otago.ac.nz
www.otago.ac.nz/press

First published 2015
Copyright © Alan F. Mark
The moral rights of the author have been asserted.
ISBN 978-1-927322-04-8

A catalogue record for this book is available from the National Library of New Zealand. This book is copyright. Except for the purpose of fair review, no part may be stored or transmitted in any form or by any means, electronic or mechanical, including recording or storage in any information retrieval system, without permission in writing from the publishers. No reproduction may be made, whether by photocopying or by any other means, unless a licence has been obtained from the publisher.

Editors: Richard Reeve, Jane Connor
Design/layout: Jane Connor
Index: Diane Lowther

Printed in China through Asia Pacific Offset Ltd

Cover photograph: Bridget Mark. Frontispiece cartoon: Murray Webb

CONTENTS

Foreword: Sir Geoffrey Palmer 9

1   FORMATIVE YEARS 13
Early years and school 13
New Zealand tertiary education 18
The USA: Postgraduate studies and marriage 22
Initial employment: Otago Catchment Board 32

2   RESEARCH FOR THE HELLABY TRUST 38
Snow-tussock grassland: A burning issue 38
Snow tussock and water production 46
What's in a fog? 51

3   THE SOUTH ISLAND HIGH COUNTRY 63
Maungatua: Battle for a boundary 63
Black Rock Scientific Reserve 67
Pukerau Red/Copper Tussock Scientific Reserve 69
Gorge Hill Red/Copper Tussock Conservation Area 72
A proposed Central Otago conservation park 74
Eyre Mountains land allocation 79
The Hocken Lecture 81

4   THE NARDOO TUSSOCK GRASSLAND DEBATE 82

5   SAVE MANAPOURI – AND BEYOND   94
Resolution of the issue and establishment of the Guardians of Lakes
    Manapouri and Te Anau   107
1987 and beyond   118
A second tail-race tunnel for West Arm   126
Manapouri saved   128

6   QUANGOS I HAVE KNOWN   132
Technical Advisory Committee on Reserves and Scenic Amenities,
    Dunedin Regional Planning Authority, 1968–78   133
Scientific Co-ordinating Committee on Beech Research, New Zealand
    Forest Service, 1973–83   134
New Zealand National Parks and Reserves Authority, 1981–90   137
Land Settlement Board, 1984–86   141
Task Force on Wetlands, New Zealand Environmental Council,
    1982–83   147
New Zealand Mountain Lands Institute, 1989–92   150
Otago Conservation Board, 1990–2001   154
Fiordland Marine Guardians, 2001–13   161
New Zealand Conservation Authority, 2001–   166
Review Panel on Flora, Fauna and Land Use, Ministry of Research,
    Science and Technology, 1992–93   168

7   ROYAL FOREST AND BIRD PROTECTION SOCIETY OF
    NEW ZEALAND   171
Diversification of society activities   173
Protection for West Coast indigenous forests   178
Credible conservation   181
Timberlands: A postscript   184
Hurunui water project   187
Save the Denniston Plateau, 2011–13   189
Dunedin branch activities   193

8 OTHER RESEARCH ACTIVITIES 199
Secretary Island: The impact of deer-browsing 199
Vegetation succession: Changes along environmental gradients 202
Vegetation survey and monitoring of Mount Aspiring National Park 204
Southland ecology and conservation 209
Ecological studies of the Waitutu marine-terrace sequence 211
Ecological studies in South Westland 213
Nokomai patterned wetlands 218
Ecology of mānuka 220
New Zealand alpine vegetation in a global context 221

9 ENGO AND LOCAL GOVERNMENT INVOLVEMENTS 226
Native Forest Action Council: The Maruia Declaration, 1975 227
Save Aramoana Campaign, 1974–84 230
Otago Catchment Board, 1974–86 235
Save Central, 2005–13 242
Wise Response, 2011– 248
Future prospects 254

Epilogue: Rewards and Recognitions 258
Appendix: Wise Response Inc. Oral Submission to Finance and Expenditure Select Committee, 1 July 2015 260
Acknowledgements 267
Notes 269
Bibliography 281
Index 292

FOREWORD: A LIFE IN SCIENCE FOR THE PUBLIC INTEREST

Sir Geoffrey Palmer

The University of Otago's Emeritus Professor of Botany, Sir Alan Mark, stands out as a remarkable New Zealander and he has written a book like no other I have ever read. It contains a meticulous account, written in clear, unemotional prose, of many great struggles to preserve New Zealand's incomparable environment, particularly in the south. Sir Alan is certainly 'a voice for conservation', as the book's subtitle attests, and what a powerful, influential and persistent voice his has been.

The title, 'Standing My Ground', appears to me a polite reference to the consequences New Zealanders often suffer for speaking out on public issues, especially conservation. Development in New Zealand has exacted a heavy toll on the environment, and the issues seem to recur in every generation.

The great struggles over the National Development Act 1979 and its fast-track development finally led to the Resource Management Act 1991. But there are no final victories in politics: efforts to tilt the balance away from the environment and toward development have been persistent. In recent times the intensification of agriculture, especially dairying, has raised serious issues for water quality. Sir Alan has championed the environment throughout these struggles, raising the voice of scientific reason. For this he has often been attacked by those who favour economic gain above all things.

The internationally accepted principle of sustainability teaches that development must take place within the capacity of ecosystems to support life. As the Rio Declaration declared in 1992: 'In order to achieve sustainable development, environmental protections now constitute an integral part of the development process and cannot be considered in isolation from it.' In New Zealand we need new mechanisms of ecological governance that aim to improve the management of natural systems, not degrade them. A human right to a clean and healthy environment is likely to arrive as a legal principle sooner than we think.

Alan Mark is a loyal son of the south. Born in Dunedin and brought up in modest circumstances in Kaikorai Valley, he was invested at an early age with a love of the outdoors through his father's activities: shooting, camping in the Catlins and elsewhere. At Mosgiel District High School he was the only sixth-former in his year but he went off to Otago University and studied botany, zoology and chemistry, achieving an MSc (first-class honours) in plant ecology.

A Fulbright Travel Grant enabled him to study for a PhD at Duke University in the United States, and while there he married fellow Otago botany student Patricia Davie. After extensive fieldwork in challenging environments, including encounters with black bears in the Great Smoky Mountains National Park, Alan Mark returned home to work at the Otago Catchment Board, of which years later he would become an elected member. His first research project focused on the tussock grasslands of the Otago high country, which were to remain an abiding interest.

Sir Alan's published research on snow tussock upset some high-country runholders and hydrologists. He stood his ground in the face of attacks by one particular runholder, and the controversy simmered for many years. As a result of his efforts much tussock has been preserved. The South Island high country has benefitted enormously from Sir Alan's copious research.

Perhaps his most famous victory was the campaign to preserve Lakes Te Anau and Manapouri, a conservation battle that lasted 13 years. The

FOREWORD

issue revolved around a proposal to raise the lake levels in order to feed a hydro-electric plant that would smelt aluminium at Bluff. In those days the Ministry of Works and the New Zealand Electricity Department carried out no environmental impact assessment. The Botany Department at Otago University was approached by the DSIR. Sir Alan was tasked with carrying out a survey and some of his public comment incurred the wrath of officialdom. Today, New Zealand universities have a statutory duty to act as a critic and conscience of society, and they cherished those values even before the law was enacted.

A massive public petition to parliament to save the lakes gathered 264,000 signatures. Manapouri became a significant issue in the 1972 general election, and the many twists and turns are all carefully set out in this book. In the end the lake levels were preserved, and the government established the Guardians of Lakes Manapouri and Te Anau.

Sir Alan remained one of the guardians until 1999, and even after that he continued to publish research on the subject. His conclusion is arresting: 'My greatest satisfaction, however, has been being able to convey to the wider public the value of natural areas and the significance of integrating ecological principles with the sustainable use of our natural resources.'

Sir Alan has served on at least 10 quangos (quasi non-governmental organisations). His chapter on these organisations offers many insights into their curious and byzantine interactions with the political establishment in Wellington, including the ways in which the policy-making process may be influenced. The methods used by public servants to shield ministers make up a fascinating sub-text.

Sir Alan's involvement with the Royal Forest and Bird Protection Society of New Zealand was driven by the conviction that scientists on their own are often politically impotent when it comes to conservation issues. Yet, mobilising support for these issues in New Zealand is difficult because commercial and farmer organisations work hard to get their own way within the councils of the government, and they frequently succeed. The methods of science are rigorous and subject to peer review, but the question of who pays for the research can influence both its content and its reception. There are many illustrations of this tendency in the book.

Most recently Sir Alan has masterminded the establishment of Wise Response Inc., which has called for a national risk assessment of economic security, energy and climate security, business continuity, ecological/environmental security and genuine well-being. The aim is to develop and implement cross-party policies that will identify and avert threats to future generations of New Zealanders. It will be interesting to see if anyone is listening. These days it is harder to secure public support for environmental issues than it was in the days of the southern lakes controversy. And that is strange, since we now have MMP and a Green Party. Go figure.

Attacking the man rather than the science is common in New Zealand, and it often works, at least in the short term. Prejudice is never far from the surface in many New Zealand public debates, so that achieving public policy founded upon rational analysis is not easy. Cutting down tall poppies has always been popular here and intellectual analysis is not valued as highly as it is in many other societies. The life of a New Zealand intellectual who enters areas of public controversy can be difficult and his future fragile.

It is a tribute to Sir Alan that, despite his close and heavy involvement with numerous conservation issues over many years, his reputation remains high. It is because he has kept to solid science in all he has done.

The contribution of scientists to the vexed issue of climate change is indispensible. It is a pity the science is not heard to a greater degree by the policy-makers. Climate change is the biggest environmental issue the world has ever faced and we are not doing well. It will not be for want of trying on Sir Alan's part if we fail.

Here is a man and a career New Zealanders should celebrate.

1

FORMATIVE YEARS

EARLY YEARS AND SCHOOL

I was born the second child and only son of Cyril and Eva Mark in June 1932 – towards the end of the Great Depression – to a low-income Dunedin family who were strongly affected by the Depression. As work picked up, Dad was employed as an electrician with A & T Burt and worked both locally – particularly on post-War government houses – and further out on country jobs.

Cyril left A & T Burt in 1957 and went to work for the Dunedin City Corporation's Transport Department. In 1959, just after he finished wiring my older sister Elaine and her husband Keith's new house in Hocken Street, Kenmure, Dad suffered a stroke and never worked again. My early years were modest, to say the least, but living near the edge of town in Mulberry Lane, off Kaikorai Valley Road, and with loving parents and three doting grandparents nearby, I could have had a much worse life.

A two-kilometre walk to Mornington School took me past the Roslyn Woollen Mills where, each day, the Kaikorai Stream was crossed at Stone Street just below the mill's dye-house discharge. There was an almost daily change in the colour of the stream, depending on the most recent batch of dyed wool, so there was no playing in this stream except at weekends, when it sometimes ran clear; not surprisingly, it was lifeless.

During the week, Elaine and I usually had our midday meal with our grandparents, the Marshalls, who lived within easy walking distance at 32 Beaumont Road. Grandad Frank was a retired watchmaker-jeweller who had owned a shop in Oamaru before retiring to Dunedin. He used to spend much of his time at the Athenaeum, a rather fusty spot in the lower Octagon, where he mostly played chess with friends and read. Mum would join us for midday dinner on Fridays before she went to town for the week's shopping with Grandma Jane. Afternoon tea at the salubrious Savoy tearooms between the Octagon and Moray Place South was usually included, an event that Elaine and I also shared during school holidays.

Dad's mother, Emma, lived alone in Gamma Street, Roslyn, having come to town from Lawrence, where Grandad Tom had been a miner at Blue Spur gold mine. He died before I was born, and we usually visited his grave in the Lawrence cemetery at Easter when we drove up and stayed with Dad's cousins, Mabel and Bob Walker, who lived near the edge of town in Whitehaven Street. Easter frequently involved a day at the Beaumont races, doing the round of Uncle Bob's rabbit traps on the hills about town, and a visit with Jimmy Chou Shim, the last of the Central Otago–Tuapeka full-blooded Chinese gold miners.

Jimmy Chou Shim had worked with Grandad Tom at Weatherstons gold mine and Blue Spur, where he was co-owner of a claim. Apparently gold was found at this claim shortly after it was sold. When I visited Jimmy he was living alone in a small galvanised-iron hut with a mud floor, not far from the Walkers' house, and worked his adjacent market garden. Jimmy died in 1945, aged 96.

Some of Dad's country electrical work and most long holidays took us a modest distance into the country, first in the 1925 Chevy Tourer and later in the much-prized 1932 Chrysler, with our limited camping

CLOCKWISE FROM TOP LEFT: *Grandad Tom Mark in Lawrence in 1920; Elaine and Alan at home in Mulberry Lane, Kaikorai Valley, during the pre-school years,* ca. *1934; Frank and Jane Marshall at their Beaumont Road home* ca. *1940; Grandma Emma in The Octagon, Dunedin,* ca. *1938.*

FORMATIVE YEARS

gear, including a standard 9 x 9-foot tent. Our Christmas holidays were mostly spent alongside one of Dad's favourite trout-fishing rivers, most often the Catlins or Owaka rivers, with a five-gallon keg of Speight's draught picked up from the open goods shed at the nearest railway siding. Occasionally we ventured as far as Omarama in the Mackenzie Basin to fish the Omarama Stream and Ahuriri River, and to Garston in northern Southland to fish the still-famous upper Mataura River. Fly fishing had its frequent rewards, and many a trout breakfast was enjoyed under canvas. Rabbits shot with the family's .22 Winchester repeater were also regularly on the field menu.

There were shooting trips once or twice a year, usually to rough farmland at Tuapeka West, but occasionally across the other side of the Clutha River to the Blue Mountains. Here, as a nine-year-old, I was given my first shot from a .303, a BSA sporting rifle, one of Dad's most-prized possessions. I dropped a young fallow stag with that first shot along one of the many firebreaks in the plantation forest there. My first rabbit

LEFT: *Alan and Elaine at home in Mulberry Lane* ca. 1950. RIGHT: *Mum and Dad in the lounge at our Mulberry Lane home,* ca. 1954.

Dad, Elaine and Mum with the 1932 Chrysler at Monkey Flat, upper Hollyford Valley, in the late 1940s.

had been shot at a somewhat earlier age – my interest in and love of the outdoors began early in life, even if the terrain was modest. Frequent shooting companions were Dad's close friends Harold Fountain, Bill Crowe and Ralph Allan, after whom (plus Grandad Frank) I was named.

A growing interest in farming and the outdoors was kindled by these many enjoyable times spent camping in various parts of the southern South Island – particularly on farmland in the Catlins – and shared with my folks and sister. When it was time to choose a high school in 1945, I was easily persuaded by the agriculture-horticulture courses being offered at Mosgiel District High School on the Taieri Plain. Commuting daily by bus or train was free to any townie who had made this choice – we amounted to about a busload, most but not all of us boys, over each of the six years when I attended. I was allowed to ride Dad's ex-racing 1926 Rudge Whitworth motorbike, and regularly rode it to Roslyn to catch the bus or train to Mosgiel. I even took the bike to school on rare occasions.

Low levels of academic achievement were accepted for those of us doing the rural courses at Mosgiel, so by the time I passed School Certificate in 1947 (with good passes in agriculture, horticulture and chemistry, but a pathetic 34 in English), I had come to the end of the available training for these courses. But my teachers – notably Jim Cumberbeach and Jack Davis for agriculture-horticulture, as well as Ted Farrant (chemistry), Alan Sewell (English) and Frank Gaston (geography) – persuaded me to join the sixth-formers at Otago Boys' High School the year after to progress my secondary education.

In the event, this proved too much for an ex-MDHS pupil. The several new subjects, as well as all the new teachers and classmates, and a 'Colditz Castle' atmosphere, were more than I could handle at this time. So in desperation, after just three days, I returned to discuss prospects with the teachers at Mosgiel District High. I was not disappointed, and they willingly accepted me back as their first and only sixth-former.

It was decided I could register with correspondence school (and catch up on some courses that I had to date avoided, notably mathematics), but continue attending Mosgiel District High and receive personal tuition and direction from some of the teachers. Alan Sewell in particular, aware of my needs in English, was most generous with his time. Meanwhile, I enjoyed the company and sports offered by the school, despite my diminutive size associated with late maturity, and was given the responsibility of head prefect for the year. I finally made it to the First XV as hooker, and even played one match on Carisbrook, against John McGlashan (which we lost), as a curtain-raiser to an eventful Otago versus Auckland game. I also managed to win the cross-country in my final year. Even though I qualified for Endorsed School Certificate at the end of the year and was accredited for University Entrance in English, chemistry and botany (all with A passes) in 1949, I was not well prepared for the next major step in my education.

NEW ZEALAND TERTIARY EDUCATION

An agricultural course at Lincoln College was out of the question in terms of costs to my struggling family. Nevertheless, my teachers strongly encouraged me to proceed to tertiary-level study. Otago University in my home town was the only viable option, but the liaison officer, Basil Howard, was anything but encouraging during our opening discussions. He strongly advised an additional upper-sixth-form year at high school to better prepare me for my first-year university courses. To me it was Hobson's choice, and I decided on the university courses that most interested me: botany, zoology and chemistry.

These subjects were all absorbing, and living at home allowed me to devote the time I knew they demanded if I was to have any chance of success. Surprise, surprise – I passed all three courses that year, even managing an A pass for the plant course. With first-year geology in my second year, I continued with botany and zoology to third year, enlightened and encouraged by the heads of these departments, professors Geoff Baylis in botany and Brian Marples in zoology.

Despite my initially greater interest in zoology, particularly in wildlife management, which I had always idealised as my vocation, I was led into plant ecology for several reasons: the lectures, labs, field trips, my fellow students – one of whom was my wife-to-be, Patricia Davie – and a sense of the increasing importance being ascribed to this subject. With several other students, I managed to get summer work assisting the Forest Service on their National Forest Survey, based at Bell Hill near Greymouth over the first summer and at Maungarakau near Collingwood in Golden Bay during the second. By this time I had bought a new 500cc BSA motor cycle – though I can't recall the source of funds – which was my means of transport to the West Coast and also for my M.Sc. fieldwork that was to follow.

My folks had to be convinced that two more years of postgraduate research towards an M.Sc. degree was both within my grasp and in my long-term interest. I remain forever extremely appreciative of the efforts that Geoff Baylis made in visiting home and talking them through their general ambivalence and reluctance to let me follow such an option. My father, in particular, was keen to see me usefully employed and earning my keep as soon as possible.

With fellow student Peter Wardle already a year into a plant ecological survey of the higher hills north of Dunedin (Mount Cargill, Flagstaff,

My two supervisors, Professors Geoff Baylis of Otago University and Dwight Billings of Duke University, with Shirley Billings, on Dwight's second study leave in New Zealand, 1982.

Swampy Summit and Silver Peaks) under Geoff Baylis's supervision, Maungatua (Maukaatua), the 900 m-high range to the west of the Taieri Plain was suggested for my complementary research project. This was a great choice, aided financially by a university senior scholarship and a Blair Trust fellowship (eligible through my secondary schooling on the Taieri Plain). The Maungatua area turned out to have a wide range of indigenous vegetation types and ecological issues: podocarp–broadleaved and beech forests with different regeneration patterns, mixed shrublands, tussock grasslands and low-alpine cushion bogs that appeared to be encroaching on the snow-tussock grassland; two permanent quadrats established in 1953 and resampled at decade intervals later confirmed this.[1] There were also palaeoecological issues in the form of remnants of an earlier forest and woodland cover. These included totara logs scattered among the tussock grassland, and tangles of bog pine and pink pine dead stems in areas of exposed peat on the summit, as well as localised areas of beech stumps and numerous 'forest dimples' (small mounds and adjacent hollows where trees had been wind-blown in the past) on the tussock-clad western slopes. There were also clusters of moa gizzard stones (gastroliths) of polished quartz pebbles located among the peat and woodland remains on the crest. Various impacts of pastoral farming – burning and grazing by sheep – also presented themselves, with some distinctive fenceline contrasts of vegetation to explain, and so the dynamics and varying vulnerability of upland tussock grassland and shrubland communities became patently obvious. The local farmers, particularly Bill Kofoed in the south and the Reid brothers, Archie, Ken and Ron, in the north, were most helpful, providing encouragement and information on their past farming practices, which assisted my understanding of the distinctive vegetation patterns.

This project was a wonderful introduction to many of the ecological issues of the day, both in New Zealand and abroad. In particular, it gave me a much clearer insight into the strongly prevailing view of the Forest Service's Chief Ecologist, Jack Holloway, following analyses of records of the National Forest Survey that I had been employed on in the West Coast and northwest Nelson during the long vacations.

During the May vacation, I was entrusted with Dad's Chrysler to drive to the road-end in the lower Hollyford Valley with fellow student Bill Croxford for a deer-stalking trip. We climbed into the upper Olivine Valley via Lake Alabaster and Alabaster Pass, returning laden with skins, which were fetching premium prices at the time, in demand for use as self-sealing fuel tanks in American planes during the Korean War. I also borrowed the family car for an equally successful deer-shooting trip in the upper Dart valley, where the herds were even larger.

The encouraging results of my M.Sc. project (First Class Honours), and publication of the main findings,[2] sustained my enthusiasm for the subject. Peter Wardle had headed to England, as was traditional for New Zealand graduates at this time, for a Ph.D. research programme at Cambridge University. Fortuitously, world-renowned biogeographer Professor Pierre Dansereau was visiting his colleague Geoff Baylis in the Botany Department during my final M.Sc. year in 1955. I spent some time with Pierre on Maungatua and in other parts of the southern South Island, during which he encouraged me to continue with my studies, but in the United States, which he knew well, rather than in England.

Again chance played its hand. Fulbright Travel Grants – an American scheme proposed by Senator William Fulbright for funding educational exchanges with allied countries as a means of repayment for World War II surplus goods left there – had just been initiated. The grants were being advertised and candidates advised to attempt to secure adequate financial support from an academic institution for the costs of residence and study. For New Zealanders like me, the grant would cover only return travel to the US. My offer of a Fulbright Travel Grant, however exciting, was conditional on obtaining the necessary further support.

My original prospect, the University of Michigan, was no longer eligible for financial support as Pierre was transferring to the University of Montreal in Canada. He suggested that I apply to both the University of California at Davis, to study under world-famous evolutionary plant geneticist G. Ledyard Stebbins, or to Duke University in the southeastern state of North Carolina, to work with Professor Dwight Billings, an up-and-coming community and physiological plant ecologist.

Responses from both Davis – which had received my application but no supporting references – and also the University of California at Los Angeles – which had received references but no application – arrived some days before an offer from Duke University of a graduate assistantship, which I accepted immediately. I reluctantly declined a somewhat more generous offer from Davis when it arrived a few weeks later. As it turned out, I made the right decision; I've had no regrets.

THE USA: POSTGRADUATE STUDIES AND MARRIAGE
Highly excited but rather nervous with my first venture abroad, and sad to leave my family and friends, particularly my fiancée Pat, I left with a dozen other New Zealand Fulbright fellows on the M.V. *Rangitane* for a leisurely cruise across the Pacific to Panama. Here we were all thoroughly examined by US officials, an ordeal that included a full-size

FORMATIVE YEARS

The Duke University Chapel, centre of the university's west campus, showing the distinctive Gothic architecture and bluestone construction, October 2009.

chest x-ray, before taking a flight to Miami. One of our contingent was rejected in Panama on the basis of his suspect chest x-ray and so had to re-embark for Southampton.

From Miami we went our individual ways, and I traded an air ticket for the option of seeing some new country with a Greyhound bus ride (and eventually recovered the balance in cash) non-stop over two days to Raleigh, the capital of North Carolina, some 40 km from Durham, where Duke University and the Leggitt & Myers Tobacco Company both had their homes. While waiting to be met in Raleigh by another Kiwi, Patricia Roberts, ex-Canterbury University, who had been in the Botany Department one year earlier, I was traumatised by the display of live snakes at the Raleigh Museum, where I filled in time before being met. Among the 'Poisonous Snakes of North Carolina' were some very impressive anacondas from the coastal plain, as well as several rattlesnakes and copperheads from the mountain region where I was hopeful of spending some time, if not most of my field time, on my main research topic.

The collegial welcome at Duke was equally warm, but dormitory life was an entirely new experience that took some adjustment. The campus was most impressive, with its main (west) campus buildings strongly reminiscent of Otago University, being of similar gothic design and built of bluestone (basalt). The university grounds and gardens were extensive and immaculate, particularly the main campus, thanks largely to the cheap Negro labour. The Botany Department was housed in a separate red brick (east) campus some 2 km distant. Traversing the campus drive between east and west campuses by bicycle (or bus) along with many other students allowed me to adjust to the new road rules before venturing into four-wheeled transport.

Life in the university system at Duke was full of challenges, enjoyment and satisfaction. Different from the traditional Commonwealth system that Peter Wardle was experiencing at Cambridge, where the Ph.D. programme involved only the research topic, Duke's graduate programme, as with the American system generally, involved two years of virtually full-time course work. A wide selection of courses both within and outside one's major department was available, and the choices were made to plug perceived gaps or weaknesses in the main subject and pursue one's main interest in the field.

The calibre of the large Duke botany staff was awesome, and virtually all aspects of the subject were available, mostly from recognised leaders in their fields, as separate post-graduate courses. Equally impressive was the large number of graduate students, many pursuing courses in ecology but conducting their field research across much of the country. Indeed, very few were working within North Carolina itself, despite a wide range of opportunities here. Weekend camping trips to the mountains with students and staff were a traditional feature of life in the Botany Department. Those first trips to the mountains, down the Blue Ridge Parkway and through the Great Smoky Mountains during the height

FORMATIVE YEARS

Three Duke ecology graduates celebrate Professor Dwight Billings' retirement, here on the edge of Duke Forest, left to right: Larry Bliss, Bob Linn, Dwight and me (the one who travelled furthest), April 1980.

of the fall (autumn) colouration of the mixed deciduous forests, were unforgettable experiences. Impressive too was the number of visitors to the department from within and outside the US, most of whom gave guest lectures, and the wide range of research projects being conducted by graduate students, staff and visiting overseas research fellows.

Correspondence with Peter Wardle at Cambridge revealed some interesting contrasts in our respective Ph.D. programmes. While Peter was full-time on his research topic, the ecology of the English ash, without diversions, my time was almost fully committed to course work and the associated exams for which my earlier broad training at Otago had prepared me very well. My deficiencies were clearly less pronounced than those of most of my fellow American students, whose earlier course work had been more narrowly focused. Thus the general 'preliminary' exams at Duke at the end of my second year were completed without a hitch, allowing me to proceed full-time with the research project.

Selecting a research topic was a challenge. I was keen to select one of general relevance and interest but funding was a major limitation. Had more generous funding been available, my chosen topic may well have been subalpine forest on Libby Flat in the Medicine Bow Mountains of Wyoming, where local destruction of forest some decades earlier had resulted in the area reverting to alpine tundra vegetation rather than regenerating forest.

Not only had this situation interested Dwight Billings, who had several other on-going projects nearby, but it also offered scope for a research topic not dissimilar to an ecological issue, then current in New Zealand, raised by forest ecologist Jack Holloway. Holloway had claimed that extensive areas of our podocarp–broadleaved forest had failed to regenerate their podocarp component, presumably because of an earlier climate change. He considered this podocarp component destined to be replaced eventually by some alternative broadleaved forest type, a belief consistent with the earlier views of Leonard Cockayne. For this reason, Holloway was not opposed to its being logged. He also considered that extensive replacement of forest by tussock grassland in the South Island rain-shadow region, usually aided by fire, could be partially explained by the same climatic change.

However, an alternative project in the mountains of western North Carolina proved to be equally appropriate and considerably less expensive and time-consuming. Many of the hilltops on the mountains of the Southern Appalachians and Blue Ridge, extending northwards into southern Virginia and southwards into northern Georgia, were covered in native grassland or mixed shrub–grassland, rather than the forest that was generally the natural cover in these mountains. Mixed deciduous forests covered the lower slopes and merged into evergreen spruce–fir conifer forest on the upper slopes above about 1550 m. Hilltops in the zone of transition between the deciduous and coniferous forest, however, were often treeless, being covered instead by indigenous grasses, herbs and scattered shrubs, mostly blueberries, azaleas and rhododendrons, and were referred to generally as 'grass balds'.

FORMATIVE YEARS

An ecological study of the Southern Appalachian grass balds turned out to be a fantastic project in all ways. It took me into some of the most spectacular mountain country in the eastern US – the Great Smoky Mountains National Park and the Blue Ridge of the Southern Appalachian Mountains as well as the *Rhododendron catawbiense* natural gardens on Roan Mountain located on the North Carolina–Tennessee state border. The Smoky Mountains, in particular, had the added excitement of a thriving population of black bears. These animals frequented the open cabins along the Appalachian Trail and also the highway across the park from Cherokee in North Carolina to Gatlinburg in Tennessee (where the park headquarters was located).

Being mostly on my own while working in the park, I had several encounters with bears. I felt quite vulnerable at night, sleeping on the benches provided in the open shelters while bears lurked around, showing particular interest in my food even when it was stowed outside or in the special cubicles provided in most shelters. Shouting seemed to be the best method of discouraging them, but it generally had only short-term effects. The few cases of mauling I heard of while there (usually about 12 each year) resulted from people offering food out of car windows. 'Bear jams' were not uncommon along the highway; any stopped car was usually indicative of a bear in the vicinity. Park rangers were forever dispersing these bear jams. The closest encounter I had with a bear was when I had special permission to stay overnight at the parking area on Clingman's Dome, close to one of my study sites on Andrew's Bald. A large paw appeared on the back window of my Pontiac Coupe, right over my head, when the animal climbed aboard while I was asleep on the rear seat. It was obviously sniffing for the food stored in the boot. By yelling I again succeeded in warding it off, until the bear finally gave up, presumably frustrated. I did get some sleep, I recall.

There was much local interest in the grass balds, and this initiated many friendly acquaintances and also an opportunity to obtain a scholarship from the Highlands Biological Station in western North Carolina to use it as a base, when needed, during the first summer's fieldwork. The

US Forest Service provided a rent-free house trailer on Roan Mountain for the second summer's intensive phase of the study. The project also allowed me to spend part of the second winter in the highest farmhouse east of the Rocky Mountains, on Roan Mountain, where the farmers Rex and Winnie Peake were not only interested and extremely hospitable but also provided the venue for my marriage, on 28 June 1957, to Patricia, who ventured alone from New Zealand for this occasion.

Patricia Kaye Davie – Pat – my wife-to-be and eventually the mother of our four children, was born in Caversham, Dunedin. The oldest of three, she was the daughter of Ivy and Arthur Davie. Arthur was born in Scotland and emigrated to Dunedin with his parents and eight siblings. Unable to afford a secondary education, he became an insurance clerk with a good head for figures, impeccable handwriting and a joy of walking, which included managing a few rounds of golf aged 90. Ivy, born in Dunedin, the oldest of five and also lacking a secondary education, worked in a bookstore till her marriage. Both parents fostered a love of learning and reading, and also community involvement.

Pat and I met at Otago University, where we shared several biology classes, and were engaged before I left New Zealand in September 1958. (Pat would later join the DSIR Botany Division in Christchurch, and has been a member of the Mount Aspiring National Park Board, its successor the Otago Conservation Board and the Yellow-eyed Penguin Trust, among other organisations). We kept up a steady correspondence during my first two years at Duke, and finally decided to wed in the US and perhaps go on to Europe before returning home. Pat ventured as far as Tennessee on her own, travelling on Greyhound buses to Johnson City, where we finally met up just a few days ahead of the wedding.

Our wedding on Roan Mountain in the Southern Appalachians was a unique event. No family members were present, Pat being 'given away' by our adopted father, Rex. The wedding ceremony was held in the Peakes' farmhouse on Roan Mountain's mid-slopes. Best man and matron of honour for the occasion, Tommy and Patsy Gilbert, were from Gatlinburg, Tennessee; I had befriended the Gilberts through my work

FORMATIVE YEARS

Wedding day on Roan Mountain, 28 June 1957, with Patsy and Tommy Gilbert.

in the Great Smoky Mountain National Park, where Tommy, a ranger-naturalist, also had an interest in the grass balds of the region (he had researched them for an M.Sc. project at the University of Tennessee). Several friends, mostly students from Duke University, as well as some locals, were entertained to a pre-wedding luncheon at the nearby summer cottage of the Peakes' neighbours, the Durhams. The ceremony, conducted by a local Episcopal priest, coincided with the summer season's first hurricane, Audrey, which added a certain drama to the day. The daily newspaper, *The Durham Sun*, gave some publicity to our wedding under the heading 'New Zealand Natives Wed on Roan Mountain'.

While on Roan Mountain, I was invited to sip the locally distilled mountain corn liquor or 'whaat laatnin' (white lightning) from a communal 'mason jar' (preserving bottle) under spruce trees on the roadside at

Carvers Gap on the state border. I also met a number of keen amateur naturalists who frequented the Roan Mountain area, particularly Fred Behrend, a birdwatcher who visited most weekends from his home in Elizabethton, eastern Tennessee.

Following one summer's extensive field survey of 61 sites that had been designated 'balds' on topographic maps – as well as other grassy areas suggested for study in the Southern Appalachian Mountain region – my second summer was spent on more intensive studies on Roan Mountain. (This also better suited plans to 'tie the knot' with Pat that summer.) The writing-up phase back at Duke was facilitated by my amateur typist wife who, unable to earn ready cash because of her foreign citizenship, proved willing and able to learn typing in order to hasten completion of the thesis. My income had increased courtesy of a prestigious James B. Duke fellowship, which allowed me to work full-time on the writing-up phase rather than continue as a teaching assistant in undergraduate classes, though this had itself been an enjoyable and rewarding experience.

With the thesis completed early in the summer of 1958 and submitted for publication,[3] we were keen to see more of the renowned natural features of the US, particularly the many famous national parks. Pat and I left as soon as the thesis had been completed (and examined – successfully; I later graduated 'in absentia') for a circuit of the US in our '41 Pontiac Club Coupe. This had already done yeoman service in the North Carolina mountains during two summers and a winter. It had about paid for itself (US$115) with an $85 reimbursement from a fellow student's insurance company following the loss of the rear door ('deck lid') soon after purchase in a minor prang while the vehicle was parked one night on campus. The replacement door, bought from one of the many local junk yards, cost $5, which, plus $2 for a spray can of matching paint, netted a $78 profit and a significant contribution to the original purchase price.

Our planned, mostly camping journey was sweeping in its range. Beginning in early summer, we toured west across the southern states of Tennessee, Arkansas and the Ozarks in Oklahoma, onwards through the Texas panhandle and New Mexico, then to Flagstaff, Tucson, and the Grand Canyon in Arizona, and northwards through Bryce and Zion canyons in Utah. From here we drove westward to Las Vegas and Reno in Nevada, New Mexico, across Death Valley to the Sequoia and Yosemite national parks, before heading to California. Our route led north from San Francisco into Crater Lake National Park in Oregon and on to the Olympic Mountains in Washington State. Then we turned eastward to the Grand Coulee, 'Going to the Sun' Highway and Glacier National Park in Montana, further east to Yellowstone National Park and the Grant Tetons in Wyoming, and on through the Black Hills of South Dakota. From the Black Hills we drove east again, this time through Minnesota and Wisconsin to Sault Saint Marie on the Michigan–Canadian border. Here our plans to enter Canada were thwarted by a possible re-entry visa problem, so on 4 July 1958, we were forced to head southeast rather than north as we had planned, eventually to New York City.

Here, we thought our luck was running out. The Pontiac had developed engine problems among the very congested traffic of Fifth Avenue. However, a 'missing' motor – a valve stuck open through wear and tear, according to a local garage mechanic – freed up overnight, and next day the same helpful mechanic came to our aid. On learning we planned to sell the car when we returned to Durham, he suggested our luck might hold with a can of upper cylinder lubricant ($5) rather than a much-more-expensive engine-head removal and valve grind. This proved to be good advice and made no difference to the price we ultimately received for our Pontiac back in Durham. When I bragged to a second-hand car dealer that our '41 Pontiac Coupe had just done a trouble-free circuit of the outer states, he replied that he wouldn't even drive this car the 40 miles to Raleigh. So with 25,000 mostly trouble-free miles more on the odometer than when I bought the car for a paltry $115 – from well-known Australian ecophysiologist Ralph Slatyer, who had been researching plant-water relations with Paul Kramer in the Botany Department – I had to settle for a mere $25. I decided the car would be worth no less without its excellent radio, which formed part of our limited luggage on

Our families gathered together to celebrate our first daughter, Jenifer's, baptism in 1959, left to right: Ivy Davie, Pat, her youngest sister Helen, Arthur, me with Jenifer, Cyril and Eva Mark.

our return journey to New Zealand, where it gave years of trouble-free service installed in my field vehicle.

Homeward bound via San Francisco and the M.V. *Oronsay*, we recrossed the Pacific. A job offer was waiting in Dunedin – a newly established position with the Otago Catchment Board. Settling back in Dunedin was not difficult, with several family reunions, including an 'at home' wedding reception. We moved into a rental house at Sunnybrae on the Otago Peninsula. Jenifer, the first of our four children, arrived a few weeks later on 2 January. With most of my work being in the field in Central Otago, family life for much of the next year was unfortunately largely restricted to weekends.

INITIAL EMPLOYMENT: OTAGO CATCHMENT BOARD
My work with the Catchment Board was as part of a newly established two-person High Country Research Team. John Hill, an Otago geology B.Sc. graduate, was the earth scientist and other member. Advertised

as offering opportunities for 'long-term fundamental research into the tussock grasslands of the Otago high country,' the positions involved undertaking land inventory and land-use capability surveys of much of the Central Otago high country. Our work was designed to extend the board's earlier surveys of the Shotover, Arrow and Nevis catchments. These had been conducted during the mid-1950s by teams comprising board and non-board staff. The botanical component had been conducted by colleague Peter Wardle, recently returned with a Ph.D. from Cambridge.

Beginning on the Old Man Range, we surveyed in detail the Fraser catchment and Mount Benger district. The Fraser catchment showed itself to be a significant water-production area for both hydroelectricity and irrigation but providing too little water in late summer and autumn to satisfy demand. The Benger district was seen as an area of high country where the local farming community might be able to manage their own burning programme. Keen to follow up our completed surveys with research into the impacts of burning and grazing as separate aspects of high-country pastoral farming, we proposed our course of study but, sadly and unexpectedly, this was firmly rejected. We managed to get approval for an elementary study of the Old Man Range climate and how this related to the vegetation patterns and, in turn, the area's water-production potential. In relation to the obvious loss of water-resource from the upper Fraser Basin as wind-driven snow across the crest of the range in winter – a phenomenon we observed on several occasions when servicing the climate stations – we were also permitted to build an experimental snow fence on the upper eastern slope of the basin near the Obelisk.

Apart from this, our future role with the Catchment Board was clearly to involve further land condition/capability surveys, but without any follow-up research to provide direction and insight for improved, hopefully sustainable management of their generally depleted tussock grasslands and associated mountain lands. Our proposals were to no avail. Indeed, to clarify our role with the board, our title was formally changed from High Country *Research* Team to High Country *Survey* Team – but not without considerable protest from John and myself. We were accused of attempting to have the tail wagging the dog by the then chairman Len Ireland. Moreover, we received no support from the senior staff – neither from Alan Greenall, Chief Soil Conservator, nor from the board's secretary and CEO, the strongly autocratic Jack McCrae.

Despite our frustration with the board, we did get 15 climatic stations established on three altitudinal transects up the Old Man Range: from Waikaia Bush Road in the south, the Fruitlands–Obelisk four-wheel-drive track in the centre, and Blackman's Gully–Earnscleugh Station Road in the north. Stations were arranged at about 1000 ft (330 m) intervals to record air- and soil-temperature extremes and rain/snowfall on a monthly basis throughout the year; evaporation and soil moisture were also recorded at all 15 sites over the snow-free period, and wind speed was recorded at one site on the main crest. All sites could be visited within a six-hour period without snow, but two days were needed in winter. With this exercise I was ably and keenly assisted by Stan Taylor, the Catchment Board's hydrologist/engineering assistant, who was based in Alexandra. Stan also meticulously recorded daily weather conditions on the Old Man Range over the first two years (1959–60) of this study: days of rain and snowfall, snow-lie and fog cover, plus wind direction. Long-term estimates of temperature and rainfall were made for each of our sites. These estimates were based on deviations from long-term values that were recorded over the same two-year period at the official station in Alexandra, where we had installed a set of the improvised equipment to compare records.

These were the first climatic records from any Central Otago mountains, and there were several surprises in our results, sufficient to raise some eyebrows. Very strong altitudinal gradients in both precipitation and temperature were perhaps less surprising than the actual values recorded for the upper slopes and summit region. Rather than a 30–35 in. (750–890 mm) rainfall on the summit, as was shown on climate maps of the time, long-term estimates for seven sites above

4000 ft (1220 m) at the centre and southern end of the range varied from 40.4 in. (1026 mm) to 97 in. (2477 mm), but this was reduced to 27 in. (693 mm) at the 1220 m site on the northern end, reflecting the very strong moisture gradient from south to north along the range. Air temperatures on the crest were certainly much more severe than had been assumed, with an annual mean value close to freezing (0.2° C) and monthly means ranging from -7.5°C for the coldest month (August) to 5.3°C for the warmest months (January and February). Equally striking altitudinal and seasonal gradients in soil temperatures were recorded, while summer (December to March) evaporation and potential evapotranspiration (PE) rates,[4] relative to those recorded simultaneously at Alexandra, ranged from 1.67 in scabweed vegetation at 1100 ft (370 m) to 0.58 in the upland snow tussock grassland at 4050 ft (1230 m) on the southern end of the range. Soil moisture was found to be generally deficient in the scabweed communities at the northern end of the range, sometimes deficient in the low-altitude short-tussock grassland but only rarely deficient in the higher-altitude grasslands. Also surprising was the relatively high incidence of fog observed on the upper slopes of the range: up to 75% of the days in some months, and no less than 38% of days in any month averaged over the two years of observation.

Our results for these first two years created considerable debate, particularly among the Catchment Board's engineers and hydrologists, who were concerned with our precipitation records from the higher altitudes, where generally high winds make measurements difficult and probably unreliable.[5] This difficulty is most pronounced during winter when measuring gauges may be covered with snow and unable to record new falls, or uncovered and thus able to receive both snow that is falling for the first time (primary snow) as well as that which is being subsequently shifted by strong winds (secondary snow). An attempt by the board's engineers to address this issue – using a series of improvised paired pipes of requisite diameter, 6, 8 and 10 ft tall, with one of each pair fitted with a standard Alto windshield to reduce wind speed around the top of the gauge – added nothing to the debate since anti-freeze was not used to prime these gauges through winter. As a result the taps fitted at their base yielded no liquid during the crucial winter months! These pipes, prominently painted in red, yellow and black bands, are still in place but have never yielded any records.

Precipitation on the upper slopes of the Old Man Range and other ranges in the Central Otago region thus remains speculative because high winds both drive the rain and mobilise the settled snow. The precise amount, however, is in any case perhaps only of academic interest and value. More relevant to the valuable water production from the mountains is the size and content of the late spring snow pack during the thaw. Stan Taylor obtained several measurements of this with conventional snow-sampling tubes.

The snow fence also aroused debate. Built out of heart rimu to a conventional design (upright battens covering 50% of the area) and some 12 m long, it drew criticism from the Catchment Board engineers, who claimed they could build an equally effective but much cheaper fence from used steel boiler tubes and cyclone wire. This they constructed alongside the initial fence. Despite being later reinforced with hardwood battens, their attempt proved nowhere near as effective or durable as our wooden fence, which had been bedded in with angle iron and concrete. Still standing 56 years later (2015), this fence has consistently accumulated snow in a regular pattern in its sheltered lee, which has in turn resulted in snowbank plant communities – a snowbank characterised by cushions of *Kelleria childii* and *Phyllachne rubra*, plus the cosmopolitan snowbank indicator species *Carex pyrenaica*, with a surrounding early snowbank community indicated particularly by *Craspedia lanata* and a notable dearth of the prostrate brown shrub *Dracophyllum muscoides*, which remains dominant in the surrounding exposed cushionfield.[6]

It became clear within the first year that the Catchment Board work was not likely to satisfy either member of the team. There was clearly no long-term future or satisfaction to be had in the extensive surveys of the Central Otago high country. The board was unwilling to approve any applied research that might lead to more sustainable farming practices

FORMATIVE YEARS

The snow fence built in 1959 near the crest of the Old Man Range, which collects snow to leeward during the snow-free season and which periodic sampling (in 1986, 1991, 2002, 2003 and 2011) has shown is sufficient to develop a snowbank community from the original cushionfield that characterises the exposed crest of the range.

in respect of the obvious land degradation that had occurred. Moreover, the board had difficulty coping with two full-time research staff whose work was almost entirely in the field during the snow-free period. Standard allowances for camping or staying in musterers' huts close to the work sites were not only substantially reduced but also applied retrospectively and without consultation. We adopted the only option available to us, which was to use the nearest hotels, thereby significantly diminishing our time in the field while also increasing costs through more expensive accommodation, much greater vehicle usage and substantial travelling time. Allowances for our own field equipment were also reviewed and reduced. This, together with the board's insistence on changing our name from a 'research' to a 'survey' team, clearly put the writing on the wall.

2

RESEARCH FOR THE HELLABY TRUST

SNOW-TUSSOCK GRASSLAND: A BURNING ISSUE
John Hill left the Catchment Board for a state-government job in Tasmania. I had almost accepted a lectureship in botany at Canberra University College, forerunner to the ANU, when the newly established Hellaby Indigenous Grasslands Research Trust made me an irresistible offer. Professor Geoff Baylis from Otago University, one of three

Otago University Botany Department in the 1960s; it was mostly housed in the Otago Museum (right) basement, with a garden and glasshouse in the foreground and a seminar room above the workshop in the background. Botany Department archives

RESEARCH FOR THE HELLABY TRUST

Members of the Hellaby Indigenous Grasslands Research Trust on their first visit to Central Otago in 1966, left to right: Dr Eric Godley, Lily Hellaby, Arthur Hellaby, Professor Geoff Baylis and me, the first fellow. Bem Hellaby.

governors on the trust, offered me their first fellowship to initiate the trust's operation. Lily Hellaby of Auckland funded the trust to encourage basic and applied ecological research into New Zealand's native grasslands as a basis for their sustainable management, a field long neglected by the bureaucracy despite its obvious importance. The job description entailed a comprehensive review of the limited literature in this field plus initiation of some relevant research. The offer of a three-year fellowship was highly tempting but lacked the long-term job security I sought, and which the Australian offer provided. Professor Baylis immediately addressed my concern by arranging, through the university's Vice-Chancellor, Professor Frederick Soper, my appointment as lecturer in botany, with three years' leave to work full-time for the trust.

It soon became obvious when I delved into the sparse literature that the most pressing research needed was on snow tussock, the dominant species of upland tussock grassland on the Crown pastoral leasehold lands of the South Island high country. Given my earlier involvement with the Maungatua and Old Man ranges, these areas seemed ideal candidates for an east–west transect across Otago. I chose Coronet Peak for the western area, being the only mountain in the Lakes District with reliable winter (skifield) access. All the runholders I approached were supportive and encouraging – Archie Reid on Maungatua, John McCambridge on the Old Man Range and the Dagg brothers on Coronet Peak. I started a series of studies including environmental recording, examining the growth and reproductive behaviour of snow tussocks across their wide altitudinal range, and looking at the effects of burning and grazing. I had low-, mid- and high-altitude sites on all but Maungatua, and to collect environmental data I used methods similar to those I had used earlier on the Old Man Range.[7]

I published the results of my initial studies in a series of papers between 1965 and 1974.[8] These revealed that there were two, not one, species of snow tussock in the Otago high country: narrow-leaved snow tussock, *Chionochloa rigida*, at low to mid-altitudes, and slim snow tussock, *C. macra*, at higher altitudes.[9] I found that, rather than being relic species out of tune with the present environment, as had been recently suggested by a committee of government ecologists (based entirely on observations), both species were well attuned to their environments, particularly to differences in temperature and length of the growing season experienced at the different altitudes. Their growing season varies from about eight months at low elevation to only five months at their upper limits, and it was temperature that proved to be the main determinant of tussock growth and intermittent flowering.

A reciprocal transplanting of snow tussocks between the three sites on the Old Man Range (910 m, 1220 m and 1590 m) and the Botany Department garden in Dunedin (10 m)[10] was most revealing. For this I cut tussocks with a spade into sections and so could have the same plant growing in different places. I was therefore able to show that, while a tussock could grow and survive at any of these sites, their behaviour varied according to both their place of origin and their new location. In terms of leaf elongation, tussocks grew more, and for longer, the lower the altitude at which they were replanted. But there were also significant

TOP: *Tussock reciprocal transplant 'garden' at 1590 m on the crest of the Old Man Range, soon after transplanting; left to right are tussocks from this site, 1220 m and 910 m and Maungatua (800 m), May, 1961.* BOTTOM: *The same tussocks growing in the Botany Department garden, Dunedin, all flowering heavily, December, 1965.*

growth differences between the three altitudinal populations at each of the garden sites. Tussock pieces originating from lower elevations grew more, and for longer periods, than those obtained from higher elevations. I was interested to find that, near sea level in Dunedin, the two lower-altitude populations from the Old Man Range grew throughout winter, whereas the highest-altitude population (slim snow tussock) ceased to grow for about two or three months in mid-winter, even though temperatures during this period in Dunedin were higher than what prevailed at their home site at 1590 m on the Old Man Range during mid-summer. This indicated a genetically (rather than environmentally) imposed mid-winter dormancy for slim snow tussock plants, which may aid their survival when growing under severe conditions on upper mountain slopes. This was the first indication of a separate, high-altitude snow tussock species.

There were many more surprises. The transplant experiment showed that flowering of both snow tussock species was irregular from year to year and that this irregular flowering (masting) is triggered by above-normal temperatures during the long days of summer (mid-November to mid-February) in the season *prior* to flowering. I was able to induce flowering artificially using long days (exceeding 14 hours) combined with warm temperatures in a glasshouse. What's more, in a separate study, transplanting whole tussocks to the Botany Department garden in Dunedin at intervals over a summer showed that the intensity of flowering in a tussock increased with a longer duration of high temperatures during this critical long-day period. Of the reciprocal transplants, only those plant pieces that were shifted to lower elevations flowered during a natural non-flowering year. The pieces that had been replanted at their home site or shifted to higher altitudes, like the rest of the snow tussock plants on the mountain that year, did not flower. Plant pieces shifted to lower (warmer) sites experience a warmer than average summer every year compared to their home site and thus flowered annually, whereas those shifted to higher (and colder) sites never experienced a warmer-than-average summer and so never flowered. But those replanted to their home site behaved just like the local population, flowering only in a flowering year.

This pattern of flowering showed that flowering years are not only controlled by the temperature of the previous summer, they are equally influenced by genetics. Populations of plants growing at different altitudes have genetically adapted to the average conditions at their site (driven largely by the altitudinal gradient of temperature; about 6°C lower for each 1000 m increase in elevation). This was another indication of two separate snow tussock species – *Chionochloa macra* at high altitudes and *C. rigida* at mid to low altitudes. Even this latter species was found to have genetically distinct populations related to altitude to suit the natural temperature gradient. All you actually see out in the high country in summer, however, are plants either non-flowering or in full bloom covering vast hill slopes every two or more years – responding to the warmer summer that affected the whole region one year earlier.

This explanation of the synchronous flowering and non-flowering of snow tussocks was also consistent with the effects of burning on snow tussock flowering. When snow tussocks were burnt in spring, they flowered prolifically in summer a year later. By studying burnt tussocks, I found that it was not the actual burning that caused the subsequent flowering but the relatively warm summer that a burnt tussock experiences in the months following a fire, because of the blackened tussock bases that absorb and hold more heat, and the loss of an insulating cover of leaves and litter. After a fire, a tussock always experiences a summer warm enough to induce flowering, even if the summer is relatively cool. A burnt snow tussock will thus flower heavily in the following season, even if non-burnt plants don't. This flowering response within a year of burning ensures that a bumper crop of snow tussock seed is always produced when there is the best chance for seedling establishment – with dead leaf litter removed and some bare soil exposed. Tussock seed that could have been lying dormant for a year or more below leaf litter can also be stimulated to germinate by the heat generated with a tussock fire.[11]

Fire stimulates the growth of snow tussocks, particularly in the first year or two following fire, with substantially increased leaf growth, new leaves and stems (tillers). Perhaps not surprisingly, it was also found that the usual practice by high-country runholders of grazing livestock

A fenceline boundary at ca. 900 m on the St Bathans Range, north Otago, which differentiated grazing following a recent fire. Sheep dispersed widely over the large burnt area to the left of the fence, where the snow tussocks are recovering well, but they concentrated on the small area burnt on the right and have killed or severely damaged the tussocks here, February 1959.

on snow-tussock grasslands in the first year or two after fire is highly detrimental to the tussocks, particularly heavy grazing in the early period of recovery from fire. The burnt plants transfer much of their limited nutrient reserves from their stems and roots into the recovering foliage,[12] which makes it much more palatable and nutritious to stock than that of unburnt plants, but the cost to recovering tussocks can be major and often permanent. This was probably the main reason for the serious degradation of snow-tussock grasslands over much of the South Island high country in the early decades of pastoral farming.

These responses of growth, flowering and germination in snow tussocks seem clear adaptations to periodic fire, which had been a feature of New Zealand grasslands since long before human settlement about 1280 AD. Natural fires, however, were much less frequent than those post-settlement. The human-induced fires allowed the grasslands to expand in the central and eastern South Island as woody vegetation was usually destroyed by these fires. Recovery of woody plants was probably prevented by the periodic burning, whereas grasslands could tolerate this in the absence of grazing mammals.

Ian Payton, a Ph.D. student funded by the Hellaby Trust, followed up my tussock-burning plots on the Old Man Range and uncovered some of burning and grazing's longer-term effects. We investigated the fate of nutrients in the decades following fire,[13] and the intriguing long-term impact of fire on tussock growth, flowering, and the very slow recovery of above-ground biomass.[14] We found that leaf growth declined after the first year's increase, but four to five years later it was back to 'normal' (what the unburnt plants in the area were achieving). Recovery of a tussock's total leaf mass after a fire, however, may take up to two decades, even without grazing. Similarly, a tussock's flowering behaviour also requires about the same period to return to normal. Snow tussock flowering is sparse for many years following the one prolific season after a burn. This inability of plants to flower normally is now known to be due not to depleted energy (starch) reserves but to the very slow rate at which new stems (tillers) mature to the stage where they can flower in response to a warmer-than-normal summer. It seems to take more than a decade for tillers to mature; hence, a single fire has a prolonged impact on a snow tussock's behaviour.

Slow growth rates and recovery are a natural feature of these long-lived tussock plants. Botanist Lucy Moore alluded to their great age when she suggested, in 1955, that 'tussocks have more of the characteristics of forest than short-rotation pasture and, like forest, are much easier to destroy than rebuild.'[15] There is no way of determining the age of a snow tussock as they do not produce anything like the annual growth rings of most trees. Their method of perpetuating their stems (tillers) by initiating new ones as old ones flower and die (or perhaps die without flowering) may render the snow tussocks potentially immortal. Other ecologists have claimed that snow tussocks, like most other plants, go through a staged life cycle from seedlings to juveniles to adults, then to a state of decadence – a concept to which I do not subscribe. Unlike

Healthy snow tussocks beyond a wetland at 1090 m, opposite the Mountain Hut site on the Lammermoor Range, where I challenged those on a field trip to find a dead tussock – there were none!

a mixed-age natural forest – where such life stages can be obvious and recently dead trees usually remain standing for a few years at least – no comparable situation occurs in a healthy snow-tussock grassland, where I challenge people to find a dead tussock.[16] Only in degraded tussocklands that have been burnt and grazed repeatedly can one easily find dead plants and bare ground.

SNOW TUSSOCK AND WATER PRODUCTION

While still with the Hellaby Trust, I took study leave in 1966 and, among other travels, visited the Scottish highlands. There I was impressed by a simple but effective method used by F.W.H. Green of the Nature Conservancy in the Cairngorm Mountains to measure the water produced from these uplands. I was keen to apply the same method to snow-tussock grasslands since water is a major and valuable product of these uplands but the yield had never been quantified. Apart from recording a general increase in precipitation and a steady decrease in temperature with increasing altitude on some Otago mountains, we had no other information on water yield and how it might vary with differences in plant cover. Given the increasing demand for water in the adjacent lowlands, it seemed desirable to try and quantify water production in relation to differing plant cover on the upper slopes.

Later that year, Jennifer Rowley (an M.Sc. student) and I initiated the first study of water yield from snow-tussock grasslands on Doug Matheson's Kilmory Run, at 1000 m, on the eastern slopes of Central Otago's Rock and Pillar Range. We installed 15 lysimeter (water-measuring) tanks made from 44-gallon drums cut down to 60 cm, tarred inside and with an outlet drain fitted at the base. The tanks were dug into the ground in five groups of three tanks, spaced out along the contour. Polythene tubes were fitted to the tank outlets and run downhill in covered trenches into reservoir tanks. The collected water would be surplus to evaporation and plant transpiration (ET) losses from the lysimeter tanks and represent the water yield from each. Nine mature snow tussocks of similar size were selected from the locality and carefully dug out to fit snugly one to a tank. A filter of quartz pebbles and then subsoil was used to fill the base of a tank so that its rim was slightly exposed above the soil when the tussock and its sod of soil were snugly fitted. This was to prevent surface water from washing into or out of the tanks. The cross-section area of these tanks (0.25 m^2) was only slightly less than the area that an average snow tussock has to itself (0.34 m^2); there are three tussocks per square metre at this relatively undisturbed site on the Rock and Pillar Range and elsewhere in the high country.

One group of three tanks with snow tussocks was burnt, another severely clipped, while a third group was left unmodified. In another set of three tanks, we placed turfs of short (10 cm) blue tussock (*Poa colensoi*) – which often replaces mismanaged snow-tussock grassland in the region) – while the remaining fifth set was left with bare soil. All but the unmodified snow tussocks had the tussocks around them clipped so as not to shelter these tanks with surrounding tall tussocks.

We were very surprised at the differences in water yield, which were consistent over the six years of this study. The tanks containing unmodi-

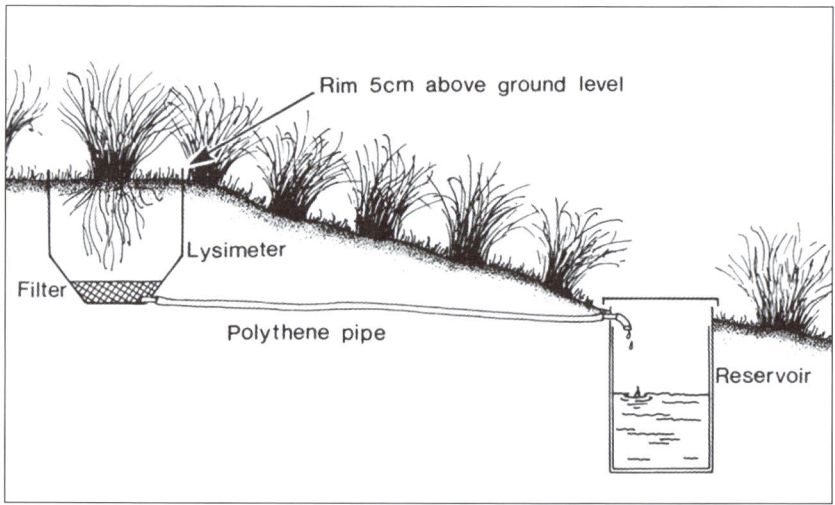

TOP: *A water yield study site at 980 m on the Lammerlaw Range, showing the 10 x 10 m area of clipped vegetation to remove any shelter from the area surrounding a lysimeter containing short blue tussock in the centre. Another clipped area shows beyond and the unmodified area between contains a tussock lysimeter. Instruments to record some climatic factors show in the centre, 31 August 1977.* ABOVE: *A cross-section of a lysimeter tank with a snow tussock, and its reservoir*

Water droplets accumulated from fog, which is efficiently intercepted by the long fine foliage of a snow tussock. These droplets run down the leaves into the soil at a rate of up to half a litre an hour for a single tussock when negligible rain can be measured in a conventional gauge.

fied snow tussocks produced the greatest water surplus, with an annual yield of 63% of the measured precipitation of 1350 mm. This was significantly more than from any of the other four treatments. The blue tussock cover yielded only 49% of the precipitation, while bare soil yielded slightly more, 56%. The snow tussocks that had been either burned or severely clipped yielded intermediate amounts of water (60% and 54%, respectively) over the six-year period and, interestingly, the yield from these treatments increased over the six-year period as the tussock canopies recovered from their initial defoliation. We had predicted that the lysimeters with the largest plants, in this case the unmodified snow tussocks, would have lost the greatest amount of water through transpiration and therefore yield the least water, but we showed subsequently that the long fine foliage of snow tussocks is very efficient at intercepting or straining water from wind-driven fog, which is not uncommon on these uplands.[17] Moreover, we showed that transpiration of water from snow tussock leaves is very low because of their distinctive anatomy.

Our results caused much discussion among some runholders – probably concerned about its implications for land use – and professional hydrologists, who preferred whole catchments rather than small tanks to measure water yield. This doubtless prompted the paired catchment studies that soon followed in the region, one by the Forest Research Institute (FRI) and another by the Ministry of Works (MOW) Water and Soil Division, both on the nearby Lammerlaw Range.

In 1980, at Glendhu in the upper Waipori basin, FRI initiated a paired catchment study to compare water yield from a snow-tussock grassland (218 ha. catchment) with that of an adjacent catchment (310 ha.) where the Forest Service had plans for a *Pinus radiata* forest. Over the initial three-year calibration period, the water yield from the tussock grassland was 64% of the 1305 mm annual precipitation, a remarkably similar value to what we had obtained with our lysimeters on the Rock and Pillar Range. The Glendhu study also revealed much lower rates of evapo-transpiration from the snow tussock cover in summer than had been predicted from empirical formulae, and led the hydrologists to conclude that snow tussock was likely to produce more water than any other vegetation. Water yield from the pine-forest catchment began to decline in comparison with that from the snow-tussock catchment after about six years and continued to decrease as the trees grew. This reduction reached 31% only nine years after planting, and by 2004, with the trees 22 years old, the yield was 41% less than from the snow-tussock catchment. It continues to decline in other than drought years.

In 1977 David Holdsworth extended our lysimeter studies with his two-year Ph.D. study. He had seven snow-tussock grassland sites, three on the Rock and Pillar Range (including the initial study site) and four on the Lammerlaw and Lammermoor ranges, 40 km to the southwest. Funding for this study from the Dunedin City Council and the Water Resources Council allowed lysimeter tanks to be built with a surface area of 0.34 m^2, matching a unit area of snow tussock in these grasslands. The set-up was otherwise similar to that used in Jennifer Rowley's project.

Only three cover types were used: snow tussock, blue tussock and bare soil, each replicated four times at a site. A *Celmisia viscosa* (alpine daisy) herbfield was added at the highest site (1340 m) near the crest of the Rock and Pillar Range, and a pasture grassland turf at the lowest site (490 m) on the Lammerlaw Range, where land was being developed at the time.

Snow-tussock grassland again yielded the most water at all six sites above 700 m. Water yield ranged from 80% of the measured annual precipitation (1372 mm) at 870 m on the southern Lammerlaws to a mere 12% (of 510 mm precipitation) at the lowest site, at 490 m on the northern end of the range. Water yield from blue tussock and bare soil (and the *Celmisia* herbfield) ranged considerably between sites, from 16 to 62% of the measured annual precipitation. The site with the highest water yield on the southern Lammerlaw Range actually produced a higher yield during the snow-free six months (86% of the precipitation) than for the full year (80%). We attributed this to the interception gains of water from fog, which is common in this area (but not trapped when the tussocks are under snow or replaced by bare soil or a blue-tussock turf). In publishing our results,[18] we estimated that the water gained through the tussock interception of fog may increase water yield up to 25% from the most fog-prone sites on the Otago uplands.

WHAT'S IN A FOG?
Our results continued to concern some runholders and hydrologists. When we submitted a paper in 1979 to the Tussock Grasslands and Mountain Lands Institute, with our results summarised for publication in their journal *Review* (which had a wide circulation among runholders), its release was apparently delayed until 1980[19] to await a paper commissioned from John Hayward of Lincoln College, who was undertaking hydrological studies in the Torlesse catchment below Porters Pass in mid-Canterbury. The contrasting messages between these two papers was striking. Our paper of course, concluded that the type and condition of the plant cover could greatly affect water yield, with snow-

Rock and Pillar Range, 1140 m, showing the devices designed to catch fog and rain. The fog-catcher (left) is a fine nylon mesh screen, 0.16 m^2, mounted vertically over a buried collection flask, and perpendicular to the prevailing fog-bearing southwesterly wind. The screen is protected from most rain with a 1.6 m diameter metal umbrella. The rain-catcher (right) is a 10 cm diameter plastic funnel (red) mounted over a buried container. Both containers have paraffin oil added to prevent evaporation.

tussock grassland in good condition yielding significantly more than a short turf of blue-tussock grassland or even bare soil. We attributed such findings largely to low water use by the tussocks plus interception gains from fog. This, we had shown with a study on fog-prone Mount Cargill near Dunedin, could result in a single snow tussock trapping up to half a litre of water per hour from dense fog, which registered negligibly in a rain gauge. By contrast, Hayward concluded that water yield does not vary significantly with the type of ground cover. His take-home message, which seemed clearly aimed to demolish our conclusions, was: 'If we want water from our mountain catchments we should pray for rain.'

Runholders were not slow to respond to these opposing viewpoints. Soon afterwards, Hayward and I were invited to Alexandra to address a High Country Federated Farmers meeting on the issue, and it was not difficult to see where their support lay. Some runholders went much further to undermine the credibility of our findings, presumably concerned with their implications for future management of the high country, since most of the water used in the eastern South Island falls

RESEARCH FOR THE HELLABY TRUST

on these snow-tussock uplands as rain or snow. In August 1988, I was alerted by a friend to a session that had just been aired on Radio New Zealand's 'Rural Report' programme regarding a report by two Department of Scientific and Industrial Research (DSIR) hydrologists, Morrie McSavaney and Ian Whitehouse, entitled 'Snow Tussocks and Water-yield: A review of the evidence'. Apparently, the report had been highly critical of our results, and of me in particular. Not having heard the programme, I was naturally keen to follow it up, so I visited the local Radio New Zealand office and talked to the reporter, who showed me the items. I had a quick look at the report, particularly the summary, and was generally satisfied. It read:

1. Streams draining the dominantly snow-tussock-covered Otago uplands appear to yield unusually high proportions of rainfall as runoff, and sustain moderate flows longer than streams draining uplands of similar rainfall elsewhere.
2. Narrow-leaved snow tussocks control water loss by furling their leaves in drying wind, and the resulting low evaporation leaves a high proportion of rainfall to appear as runoff in streams.
3. The ability of the Otago uplands to sustain moderate stream flows for long periods probably is due to the many bogs and ponds, and the widespread thick coarse debris mantle found there.
4. Snow tussocks collect water from fog, but the amount appears to be very small. They collect very much more from wind-driven rain. All of the rain and probably much of the fog would fall to the ground if not first caught on tussocks.
5. Snow tussocks trap snow, and can extend the period of snow lie by several weeks. There is little data on the effects of tussock density and stature on snow storage.
6. The eastern Otago uplands have the lowest erosion rates of New Zealand's steeplands. The rates are so low because of a very low frequency of heavy rain: the lowest in New Zealand.
7. Current knowledge and understanding suggest that maintenance of the snow-tussock cover under a regime of conservatively moderate grazing provides a practical management to maximise water-yield from the Otago uplands.[20]

The only item I seriously disputed was point 4, particularly the claim that 'much of the fog would fall on the ground if not first caught on tussocks.' I have frequently observed fog shrouding a mountain range and moving along with the air mass, then eventually dissipating as the air mass moves on beyond the range. If not caught by tussocks (or whatever), as it moves over the ground surface, I believe that the moisture droplets in fog are unlikely to 'fall to the ground'.

Of much greater concern was a one-page press statement accompanying this report in the name of one of the authors, Ian Whitehouse. It created a very different impression. Headed 'DSIR refutes water conservation theories', it stated:

> The Fog Theory that snow tussocks filter significant amounts of water from fog gets almost no support from DSIR hydrologists in a special report just released. The Fog Theory has been advanced by Professor Mark of the Botany Department, Otago University, to justify the establishment of further ecological reserves of tussock. He maintains that more water would be harvested by tussock country whose streams feed hydro-lakes and water reservoirs ... The report by DSIR scientists M.J. McSaveney and Ian E. Whitehouse showed that Professor Mark used an invalid method of measuring the amount of water filtered from the fog. More water droplets caught by tussock means less fall on the ground as rain further on ... [21]

I had difficulty reconciling the press statement with the actual report, so I phoned Whitehouse in Christchurch. He said that high-country runholder John Miller, who had commissioned the report, had written the press release and conveyed it to him by phone. Whitehouse apparently had strongly advised Miller not to release his statement since it was both misleading and inconsistent with their report. When I told Whitehouse the press release was in his name, he was immediately apologetic. I told Whitehouse I would write to the director general of DSIR and lodge a formal complaint. This I did shortly thereafter, with a comprehensive three-page letter to Dr Jim Ellis outlining my concern with the overall situation. The reply from Ellis advised that DSIR had no control over how its clients used its information and that any recourse I wished to seek would need to be with Miller directly.[22]

I decided not to take action against Miller, even though the *Otago Daily Times* and *Central Otago News* both ran rather incriminating stories, mostly on the basis of his press release. The headlines were 'Fog theory disputed', 'Snow tussock and water-yield: A different assessment', 'DSIR refutes fog theory' and 'Runholders delighted'[23] and the criticism was highly personal in nature. Although I was given the right of reply by the press, some runholders obviously thought that they had scored a major victory and undermined my professional credibility. But that was not all. There was at least one formal letter to the university's vice-chancellor following this event, recommending that he dismiss me on the basis of my professional credibility having been undermined. I was encouraged that this recommendation was not seriously entertained by the university administration.

Though I intended to let the situation rest, it resurfaced in May 1992 at a hearing of the Otago Regional Council in Alexandra, where I was an objector to four applications to burn high-country tussock grassland. This was the first (and only) hearing on such applications under the new Resource Management Act (RMA). Runholders took the hearing very seriously and mounted a major campaign to challenge the objections, assisted by lawyer John Williamson and advisors John Allan and Rodney Patterson. Patterson, lessee of Longslip Station in the Lindis Pass, had a written submission, attached to Allan's report, that among other things stated:

> I am not against the principles of conservation it's just that 'greenies' are a narrow-minded pack of ignorant and arrogant bastards because 'greenyism' is a fanatical religion, not objective science. The 'greenies' bend and distort the truth to support their own arguments. In fact, there will be no need to remind you that Alan Mark's pseudo-scientific work on snowgrass as uncovered by the McSaveney and Whitehouse report, has hardly increased public support in this emotive and subjective arena.[24]

He and Williamson produced a copy of the distinctive yellow-covered report by McSaveney and Whitehouse and asked if I would comment on the criticism levelled in it at our studies of water yield. Infuriated by this situation, I stated that the document was not in serious conflict with the results of our studies but that there was a press statement of a very different nature mounting a personal attack on my integrity and, furthermore, that the author of this press statement, who was present at the back of the room, may wish to identify with that particular statement. Miller did not respond, but I formally requested the council to remove their fallacious and incriminating statements from the record.

As a result of this potentially embarrassing situation, I contacted Whitehouse soon afterwards, informing him of my continued concern with the situation and my objection to being ridiculed in public on the basis of a statement bearing his name. Although he sympathised, he was reluctant to write a new statement clarifying the authorship of the press release. He was finally persuaded to write such a statement and copied it to Miller. In his letter to me, dated 17 December 1993, as general manager of Landcare Research's Land Management Division, he stated:

> I am committed to, and with my staff [am] working towards, reducing land use conflicts in the high country. I do not wish to exacerbate the conflict in any way by dredging up issues of the past. We need to move forwards. However, I accept you believe you have legitimate reasons for wishing to revisit circumstances surrounding the release of the findings of a 1988 contract that was prepared by Dr. M. McSaveney and myself on snow tussocks and water-yield. I acknowledge that the press release of 18 August 1988 titled 'DSIR refutes water conservation theories' was not prepared by me. The press release was prepared by the client for whom the report was written. My name appears on the bottom of the press release as the contact for enquiries as it was thought that enquiries may have been of a technical nature. I provide the above statement on the understanding from our telephone conversation that it will not be used in an adversarial manner. I believe that open exchange of information and opinion is an important part of reducing and avoiding conflict. I have

RESEARCH FOR THE HELLABY TRUST

copied this letter and related correspondence to Mr John Miller. I would welcome the opportunity to work with you both to develop solutions for sustainable management of the tussock grasslands.

Yours sincerely,

Ian E. Whitehouse [25]

While I have not had occasion to use Whitehouse's statement, it did bring closure.

Professional debate over the contribution of fog to water yield from the upland snow-tussock grasslands has been ongoing, particularly after results from a one-year study using a large weighing lysimeter at Glendhu. Although the results confirmed several aspects of our findings, they indicated that only a negligible component of water yield came from fog (about 1.2% of the annual yield). To me, this was not surprising, given the relatively low altitude of the site and the rarity of fog at such altitudes. But even when transferred later to Swampy Summit (730 m), a near-coastal, more fog-prone upland site above Dunedin, the lysimeter indicated that fog contributed less than 2% of the measured precipitation.[26]

A more detailed assessment of fog interception was made in conjunction with our water-yield project at a new site in the Lammerlaw Range's upper Deep Stream catchment. At the highest site (1100 m), a snow tussock was simulated using 40 mature tussock tillers coated in silicone to retain their form and mounted in wire mesh on top of a standard rain gauge. This simulated tussock was set among the natural tussocks and, together with the rain gauge, was monitored hourly using a data logger over two snow-free (November to April) periods. Fog was recorded for about 29% of the time, mostly associated with cold fronts from the west or southwest. During light fogs (measuring less than 0.1 mm/hr of water), the simulated tussock intercepted 1.5–4 mm/hr. Heavy fogs (defined as depositing 0.1–1.0 mm/hr) contributed an estimated 154 mm of intercepted water to a unit area of snow-tussock grassland over the 306-day period of study. Heavy fogs were much less common than light fogs but, together, were estimated to contribute a total of about 166 mm of water over the six-month snow-free period. This would represent an addition of 22% to the precipitation recorded for the six-month period at this site.[27]

Neil Ingraham, appointed to Auckland University's Geology Department in 1995 as a specialist in geo-hydrology, heard about the continued debate over fog and water yield, and contacted me to offer his expertise. According to Ingraham, it was possible to differentiate water derived from fog (as distinct from rain) by analysing the stable heavy isotopes of oxygen and hydrogen it contained. A measurable proportion of the stable heavy isotopes of oxygen (^{18}O) and hydrogen (Deuterium; ^{2}H) is mostly present in the first products of condensation from saturated air (fog). Rain, which condenses later, has relatively low proportions of these two isotopes.

I was keen to try Ingraham's suggested method. At two of our earlier lysimeter sites on the Rock and Pillar (1140 m) and Lammerlaw ranges (870 m), as well as at Swampy Summit, where the large weighing lysimeter was still located, we installed equipment to collect samples of fog, rain and ground water. In the Otago high country, fog tends to precede a rain storm, occur alongside it, and often persists for some time after the rain ceases. Fog was collected with a fine nylon mesh screen about 0.16 m^2. This screen was mounted vertically at right angles to the prevailing fog-bearing wind and sheltered from rain with a large (1.6 m diameter) umbrella-shaped metal dome just above it. Fog water on the screen was caught in small gutters at the base, which drained below ground into a bottle containing some mineral oil to prevent evaporation. Rain was caught with a plastic funnel within 10 cm of the ground, mounted on another collection flask. Samples of ground water were collected from lysimeters at the Rock and Pillar and Swampy sites, and from a nearby minor stream on the Lammerlaws. Water samples were collected at about monthly intervals from November to April and, depending on the weather, through to June.

Our results showed that rain water at all three sites was generally more depleted in the two stable isotopes than the fog. Conversely, values for ground water were intermediate, indicating that this was a mixture of fog and rain, according to Ingraham, in 'rather sub-equal proportions'. We concluded, therefore, that our results 'support the claim for the important contribution of the dominant tussock cover through interception gains from the deposition of fog on its foliage.'[28]

Despite our apparently convincing results, publication was less than straightforward. When we submitted our findings to the *Journal of Hydrology*, a leading American publication, as 'a new direction in attempting to answer questions of a long-standing debate on the contribution of fog deposition on snow tussocks to water-yield on the Otago uplands,' the editor sent our paper to two reviewers, one of whom was obviously a New Zealander. This became apparent when we received the editor's response. Our paper received reasonable and helpful comments from the overseas reviewer – who identified himself – but the other, anonymous referee stated, among other things, that 'the overall standard of the paper is deplorable.' Needless to say, the editor rejected our paper.

Having had earlier papers published in the *Journal of Hydrology*, Ingraham was devastated by this rejection. Nevertheless, he accepted my suggestion that we submit the paper to a different journal with a network of referees who might more fairly assess our contribution. It was reassuring that the Australian Ecological Society, following double-refereeing, accepted our paper with minimal changes for *Austral Ecology*.[29] As I later stated in a note to the New Zealand Ecological Society's 2001 newsletter, under the heading 'Issues in ecology: Open debate or anonymity', 'Our innovative approach and its results [would now] be open for assessment by a wider audience and, hopefully, will contribute to an eventual resolution of this long-standing debate.'[30]

This article put paid to the debate for six years, apart from some exchanges in the monthly current affairs magazine *North and South*. Ex-runholder Arthur Borrell, of Queenstown – a long-time opponent of tussockland conservation and sceptic of the role of fog in water yield

– was responding to an article by deputy-editor Jenny Chamberlain in the April 2003 issue on the pending opening of Te Papanui Conservation Park. Chamberlain had referred to Otago Conservator Jeff Connell's observation that Te Papanui's tussock cover was ideal for water yield since 'it prevents excessive water loss in summer and intercepts moisture during foggy conditions – channelling it down its tightly furled needle leaves and returning it to the soil.' Borrell's letter included the comment, 'Jenny's fog story was discredited years ago. It did not hold water.' Describing our isotope study under the heading 'What's in a fog?', my reply stated that 'our latest research on this issue … showed that fog makes a significant contribution to the water yield here.'[31]

In 2006, Tim Davie, Barry Fahey and Mike Stewart published a paper in the *New Zealand Journal of Hydrology* with the title 'Tussock grasslands and high water-yield: A review of the evidence' – curiously similar to that of the earlier McSaveney and Whitehouse paper. They argued that our isotopic analysis[32] of the water yield was flawed and that low evaporation from the snow-tussock grassland, especially during dry periods, is much more likely to explain the high water yields than fog interception. The paper acknowledged the contribution of the late high-country runholder Arthur Borrell (who had been presumed drowned in the Shotover River in June 2006) but made no other mention of the earlier debate. Suspicious, I enquired of the authors and was told Borrell had commissioned their study and been supplied with a separate report. They were unable to release this, and the Borrell family also refused, but I did obtain a copy from Landcare Research (Tim Davie's employer) under the Official Information Act (OIA).

There was some surprising additional information in this unpublished report. Of particular interest is the claim that I had criticised the earlier McSaveney and Whitehouse paper in a note I published in the New Zealand Ecological Society's newsletter 'for having been contracted by runholders, and for having a perceived political flavour'. Neil Ingraham and I, assisted by isotope chemist Russell Frew of the Otago University Chemistry Department, published a rebuttal of this paper.[33]

RESEARCH FOR THE HELLABY TRUST

Healthy snow tussock grassland in the upper Deep Stream at ca. 900 m in the Te Papanui 'Waterlands' Conservation Park on the eastern Otago Lammerlaw Range; some 60% of Dunedin City's water supply comes from this area.

Our rebuttal prompted a further response (without any prior communication). This time, the same trio invoked a water-balance model developed for the Otago uplands and designed to assist with decision-making as to the effects of land-cover changes on catchment runoff. Since the model made no allowance for fog input, the authors assumed that 'any excess in measured over modeled water yield may at the outset be assigned to fog.' Two of their catchments did show such an excess, and in the one with the highest overall elevation – upper Deep Stream, at 750–1150 m – this averaged 230 mm a year over a seven-year period (or about 15% of the catchment-area rainfall). The authors, however, suggested that the excess could be attributed, at least in part, to 'rain gauge under-catching and suppressed transpiration' rather than to fog. Indeed, they even stated that 'no long-term measurements of fog frequency or duration are available for upland east Otago,' thereby ignoring results of a study discussed in our 2008 paper from the adjoining Deep Creek catchment, where we recorded a detailed assessment of the fog that had 'occurred on c. 29% of the 306-day recording period'.[34]

I suspect that there may be more than passing concern for the implications of our water-yield studies on future high-country land-use options. Along the way, I learned that Arthur Borrell was also party to commissioning the McSaveney and Whitehouse report and that there was a serious effort to discredit at least this aspect of my snow-tussock grassland research.

Meanwhile, my successor and colleague Katharine Dickinson and I had a review paper, 'Maximizing water-yield with indigenous non-forest vegetation: A New Zealand perspective', published in the Ecological Society of America's prestigious new journal *Frontiers in Ecology and the Environment* (2008). In this paper we highlighted the value of the upland snow-tussock grasslands for water production, compared with possible alternative types of land cover – this issue is not in dispute – and emphasised the need to secure these grasslands for the long term through land-use planning by government agencies. Our New Zealand situation is placed in a global context, with reference to several other countries in respect of water yields and alternative land uses as well as the implications of predicted climate change.[35]

The *Frontiers* paper resulted in my being invited to the society's first Millennium Conference at the University of Georgia on 'Water: Ecosystem services, drought and environmental justice'. We presented our New Zealand information as a poster: 'Maximising water yield with indigenous tall tussock (bunch) grassland on New Zealand uplands and trade-offs with alternative land uses'. An excellent conference with almost 100 invited participants, all but four attendees were from the US. Katharine and I were later invited to collaborate with four others in publishing a distillation of the conference as acknowledgment of the financial support of the Environmental Protection Agency (EPA). Our New Zealand studies also featured in this comprehensive publication.[36]

3

THE SOUTH ISLAND HIGH COUNTRY

It became obvious during my M.Sc. project on the Maungatua range in the mid-1950s – and more so when working for the Otago Catchment Board and Hellaby Research Trust – that the lack of any tussock grassland reserves in the entire South Island high country meant a serious absence of any baseline reference areas. Because all of the high country had been allocated for pastoral farming, it was impossible without any representative, non-farmed areas to assess objectively the impacts of the various aspects of pastoral farming, particularly stock grazing at different intensities and/or seasons, combined with burning at different intensities, frequencies and times, and particularly the post-burn management. The numerous protected areas along the axial ranges of both islands, many incorporated in national parks and the extensions of protected forests administered by the Forest Service, were clearly inappropriate to serve as such reference areas. I took it upon myself to attempt to correct this serious situation, and the first opportunity came with the area I knew best, Maungatua.

MAUNGATUA: BATTLE FOR A BOUNDARY
In the early 1960s, Alan Weatherall, having failed to achieve his ambition of establishing ryegrass–white clover swards up to the Maungatua summit, decided to relinquish his pastoral lease on the upper central slopes when it came up for renewal. I suggested to the Lands and Survey staff in Dunedin that this area of narrow-leaved snow-tussock

grassland, mixed shrubland and cushion bog would be highly valuable as a reserve. Not only was there a wide variety of native vegetation in relatively good condition, but the biological values were also important as the area was the 'type locality' for several native plant species. They agreed to investigate the proposition but meanwhile the Forest Service, which was active with exotic forestry plantings in the region, also expressed an interest in the block. There were a few years' delay while the area was assessed for its forestry potential, but I wasn't surprised to learn of their decision not to proceed with afforestation on this inaccessible upland block.

I discussed my aspirations for the reserve with two of the adjoining runholders, Archie Reid of Allendale Station and Ken Reid of Horsehoof, who were sons of the original occupier. They were both enthusiastic to the point of offering to contribute adjoining parcels of their leasehold land to make the Weatherall block more representative of Maungatua's upper slopes and summit. The existing boundary fences between the three properties at this time were derelict to the point of needing replacement (which they were both planning to do). They each suggested new boundaries, while requesting no reduction in their lease rentals for the land being relinquished to a reserve.

I thus presented Lands and Survey with a formal proposal for up to 600 ha. of reserve on Maungatua, with three options. My preference was for all of Weatherall's relinquished lease plus the areas offered by Ken and Archie Reid. Weatherall's block would take in extensive cushion bogs and mixed snow tussock–shrubland along the crest, while the Reids' areas would add a large rock tor and nearby cushion bog, and also a westward extension across the gentle crest of the range to the upper western slopes. This would include most of the remaining cushion bog and also the largest area of exposed sub-fossil woodland of bog pine and pink pine on the range. My second option was to exclude the smaller area offered by Ken Reid, and the third was to proceed only with Weatherall's surrendered lease. Lands and Survey requested that I join reserves ranger Colin Bassett on a site visit, which I did. Since Bassett

Maungatua Reserve of mixed shrub–snow-tussock grassland, which was established in 1967, with the inclusion of an area of Ken Reid's Horsehoof Station, containing the only sizeable rock tor (top) plus an area of sub-fossil bog pine–pink pine woodland contributed from Archie Reid's Allendale Station (above).

was obviously impressed with the proposal, I was hopeful of a positive outcome before departing on my first overseas study leave early in 1966.

On visiting Maungatua soon after my return in September, I was dismayed to see not only a new fence along the Weatherall–Archie Reid boundary but also serious damage to the vegetation on Archie's property. Cattle had pugged the cushion bog, grazed the large mountain daisies (*Celmisia semicordata*) and damaged the large inaka (*Dracophyllum longifolium*) shrubs.[37] Ken Reid's new fence was also in place, but along a new alignment to incorporate the cushion bog and prominent schist tors from his lease into a reserve, as previously agreed.

Both Reids indicated their frustration with Lands and Survey staff's failure to act, Archie particularly so since he had little choice but to construct his new fence along the original (legal) boundary. He admitted surprise and concern at the damage his cattle were causing to the native plant cover along the crest, even to the point of offering to remove the cattle until February and allow the fence to be shifted by Lands and Survey staff to the boundary on which we had all previously agreed. He indicated some urgency with this proposal since his property was now for sale.

Lands and Survey staff were apologetic for the lack of progress. They also expressed a willingness to retrieve the situation when I told them that the Reids were still keen to fulfil their offers, with Ken Reid having already fenced the proposed area from his run. Further delays with the department, however, meant that there had been no progress by early February. Finally, when Archie offered to remove his cattle for a further month, action began. I rejected a request from the department to arrange student labour to relocate the fence some 200 m distant, whereupon fencing contractors moved it. I had been invited by Archie Reid to mark the new boundary with reserve ranger Bill Hislop shortly before his property was sold, and so, thanks largely to the enthusiasm and support of the Reid brothers, and the availability of Alan Weatherall's relinquished lease, a 553 ha. Maungatua Scientific Reserve was finally established in 1967.

My plea for a scenic rather than scientific reserve on Maungatua was to no avail, since it was claimed within Lands and Survey circles that there were no values in the area that justified such a status. Scenic reserve would presumably imply scenic values while also allowing public right of access. Lands and Survey, however, claimed that there were no such values at Maungatua and so insisted on scientific-reserve status. While this recognised its scientific value, it apparently involved some limitation of access and probably also made it less appealing to the general public. But there was an unexpected bonus since, in a subsequent country-wide reserve classification exercise as to local, regional or national significance, it was decreed that all scientific reserves would automatically achieve 'national reserve' status. Later, when Maungatua Reserve was extended to connect with forested scenic reserves at Woodside in the north and Mill Creek–Waipori Gorge in the south, the Maungatua Reserve finally received scenic status.

Since then, under the terms of the Ngāi Tahu Settlement Act of 1997, the reserve's name has been changed to Maukaatua Scenic Reserve and the upper slopes designated a Tōpuni – a special status providing an overlay of tangata whenua values on an already-protected area that has particular significance to Māori. More recently, in 2007, a wind farm was proposed for the upper western slopes on private land adjacent to the reserve boundary. Windpower Maungatua Ltd staff had several discussions with me and others, even offering a consultancy contract in mid-2008, which I respectfully declined. They originally planned to apply for a resource consent by the end of 2008, but a shortfall in funding and environmental issues put paid to the project.

BLACK ROCK SCIENTIFIC RESERVE
Following the Maungatua Reserve success, I became aware of active farmland development on the eastern Otago uplands by the Land Settlement Board arm of Lands and Survey. This development was rapidly foreclosing options to protect representative areas of low- to mid-altitude snow-tussock grassland in the Lammerlaw–Lammermoor region.

I discussed the issue in the late 1960s with departmental staff, who suggested I visit the Black Rock area on the Lammerlaw Range and identify a few 4–8 ha. areas that might be suitable as reserves. A visit soon revealed the urgency of the exercise. I requested a minimum of

The western entrance to Black Rock Scientific Reserve 30 years after its establishment in 1972, when it was predicted that the area would develop into a hebe-dominated shrubland if the farming practices of burning, grazing and topdressing were curtailed. This is implied in the message at the bottom of the sign. Monitoring has shown the tussocks continue to increase in both height and cover.

200 ha. in a single block, necessary for a representative reserve on the gently rolling terrain. My case was not helped by advice the department had received from their formal advisor on reserves at the time, Lance McCaskill of Lincoln College. McCaskill claimed the reserve would have little long-term value, predicting that the snow-tussock grassland would soon be succeeded by a shrubland, dominated by the native *Hebe odora*, once burning, grazing and topdressing ceased. Rejecting this claim, I offered to monitor the area if it was reserved.

In 1972 Black Rock Scientific Reserve (144 ha.) was established as the first low- to mid-altitude (690–770 m) tussock grassland reserve within the South Island high country pastoral lands. Again, I had to concede to the reserve being designated 'scientific', although it was quite different from Maungatua and, to many people, much less scenic, being more uniformly tussock grassland. Botany student Bruce Bulloch established monitoring here as his Honours B.Sc. project, on four representative 1 ha. sites (using a modification of David Scott's height-frequency method, developed particularly for tussock grasslands)[38]. Contrary to McCaskill's prediction, a resurvey 16 years later showed that the snow tussock continued to increase significantly in biomass through gains in both height and cover, whereas shrubs showed no obvious change. Two more monitoring sites were established, one in 1988 to follow establishment of *Dracophyllum longifolium* (inaka) shrubs on a hilltop, and another in 1991 to track a very minor presence of the aggressive mouse ear hawkweed (*Hieracium pilosella*). A later resurvey, 30 years after the establishment of the reserve, showed snow tussock continuing to increase and dominate.[39]

Of the most common shrubs from the first resurvey, *Dracophyllum* alone showed any increase but remained a minor component. The low (subdominant) shrubs *Coprosma cheesemanii*, *Acrothamnus* (*Leucopogon*) *colensoi* and *Gaultheria macrostigma*, plus the moss *Hypnum cupressiforme*, had all become prominent, and the grassland habitat had become much moister. There had been some loss in diversity among the small herbs, but the exotic hawkweed was barely persisting. In the longer term, we predicted development of a mosaic pattern of snow tussock and woody vegetation pockets, related to local topography, which may reflect the pre-human situation in this region.[40]

Black Rock has proved to be very important in understanding the longer-term dynamics of low- to mid-altitude snow-tussock grassland under conservation management. Like all reserves, its ecological value should increase with time. To date, the reserve does not support the prediction of several contemporary ecologists, consistent with that offered earlier by Lance McCaskill, that such areas will soon revert to a dominance of woody cover.

PUKERAU RED/COPPER TUSSOCK SCIENTIFIC RESERVE

In the late 1970s, at Pukerau in South Otago, on State Highway 1 between Clinton and Gore, a 2 ha. private reserve of copper-tussock (*Chionochloa rubra* subsp. *cuprea*) grassland was to be sold along with the rest of the farm. I was aware of its ecological values, including buried wood remains of a podocarp forest, having supervised David Caldwell's Honours B.Sc. project there in 1974.

I alerted Lands and Survey staff to the sale because I was anxious not to lose one of the few remaining areas of what had once been extensive copper-tussock grassland in the south-central South Island. Invercargill staff undertook to negotiate for the area to be excluded from sale and purchased by the department. These negotiations, however, failed. Soon afterwards, while passing by en route to Secretary Island with Geoff Baylis and others, we saw the northern end of this reserve being burned. Later discussions with the new owners revealed their intention to 'develop' the area, though they were aware it had some ecological value because it attracted an annual biology class visit from Gore High School. There was obvious sympathy and willingness to contemplate a sale – which Lands and Survey staff later negotiated at my request. Told the area could be bought for $900, I was asked, 'Was it worth it?' The answer was easy and the area duly purchased.

Some time later, an impressive sign was erected – 'Pukerau Red Tussock Scientific Reserve',[41] – which I suspect cost considerably more than the land. Again, my plea for scenic rather than scientific status – it is after all the only patch of native vegetation adjacent to the highway between Dunedin and Invercargill – was unsuccessful.

More recently, following successful negotiations with the multinational enterprise Tasman Agriculture, I managed to facilitate acquisition of an additional larger area (7 ha.) of copper tussockland bordering the highway to the south. When Chris Bycroft, in 1993 researching the ecology of copper-tussock grassland for his Ph.D., was looking for a site for some modest experimental burning, we approached staff, who responded, 'burn the bloody lot!' I had further discussions with field manager Dave Yardley on site and he agreed that the area had little potential for dairying. He said his company would gift the area to the Department of Conservation (DOC) and hopefully gain 'brownie points' in the process. The formal hand-over was in August 1997 (recorded with a front-page photo in the *Otago Daily Times*) and a day's effort by three supporters and DOC staff was all that was required to rid its road frontage of broom. This addition provided a second significant reserve of copper-tussock grassland alongside State Highway 1, but as yet there is no sign to inform the public.

Even though these areas are, by general standards, relatively small for protected areas, they are the last remaining patches in a reasonably natural state in the district; only isolated tussocks still persist in nearby pasture and roadsides. With occasional clearance of seedling broom (these small areas are probably viable in the long term), such tussock-land remnants are valuable for their biodiversity, their scenic value, and for small experiments such as Chris Bycroft's, which showed that this tussock is less tolerant of fire than the high-country narrow-leaved snow tussock.

GORGE HILL RED/COPPER TUSSOCK CONSERVATION AREA

In 1973, when I first began regular trips to Fiordland for meetings of the Lake Guardians, I became aware of the threat of intensive farmland development – again by the Lands and Survey Department – to the remaining large areas of copper-tussock grassland in the Mavora Lakes–Gorge Hill area of western Southland. These grasslands justified the creation of a reserve of an adequately representative area and, given the rate at which they were disappearing beneath the developers' ploughs, I decided to act.

My written proposal recommended an extensive reserve adjoining the highway. However, the Southland Lands and Survey staff suggested that a narrow strip – a few hundred metres long, close to the highway along Weyden Stream – might be protected from on-going development. In response to this, I advised protection of the entire catchment of Weyden Stream, which was essentially the view north from the highway on the eastern slopes of Gorge Hill, amounting to some 1500 ha. This immediately raised concern in the department, whose staff sought independent advice from the DSIR Botany Division. My colleague Peter Johnson was assigned the task. Not only did he endorse the area I had recommended as

Professor Christian Körner amid the red/copper tussock at the Gorge Hill (Burwood) Conservation Area, western Southland, January 2010.

a scenic reserve, he also suggested that a more-remote and little-modified 100 ha. area, enclosed by beech forest, be created as a scientific reserve.

Southland Federated Farmers must have heard of these proposals and wrote to me, seeking justification for such a large area being reserved. Obviously dissatisfied with my response, the branch organised a roadside debate on the issue and invited me to present the case for conservation. Some 50 people turned out on a clear but cold Sunday afternoon in July 1988. I made the case for reservation, and a senior Federated Farmers representative presented the opposing case for farm development – the prospect for three economic units. When the votes were taken, surprisingly I had a small but significant majority, including unpredicted support from Erskine Bowmar, farmer from the adjoining Burwood Station. The debate had been vigorous, prompting my Chinese student Yin Ronghua, whom I had invited along for the experience, to make two perceptive observations on our return journey to Dunedin: 'In China, farmers very poor; in New Zealand, farmers very rich. In China, nobody argues with professor; in New Zealand, everybody argues with professor.'

Te Anau chemist and debate chair, John Donaldson, conveyed the consensus view to reserve the entire 1500 ha. of tussockland to the Southland Commissioner of Crown Lands, Joe Harty. (Lands and Survey staff had not been present for the roadside debate.) Harty arranged a further roadside discussion with Peter Johnson and me, asking us for suggestions as to how the area might be managed to retain its tussock dominance, preferably with some grazing. We suggested the area be fenced into three equal blocks, each burnt infrequently (every 20–30 years), then spelled for several years before being grazed by sheep only. Unfortunately, our advice was not heeded; much of the area was subsequently burnt and, with minimum spelling, cattle allowed to graze on it. The result was predictable. Large areas of copper tussock did not recover. The several bright-green patches of dominant exotic grasses, which replaced the overgrazed tussocks, still mar this reserve's general appearance and value.

The catalyst for protecting the entire 1500 ha. area was finally provided by the Fauna Protection Advisory Committee. They had been searching for an area of copper tussockland suitable for holding takahē that had been reared in captivity in Te Anau, prior to their release back into the Murchison Mountains, and endorsed the Gorge Hill area as eminently suitable for this purpose. The department agreed with the committee's recommendation, and an adjoining farmhouse and buildings were acquired for the captive rearing facility at Burwood. To my delight, the adjacent and equally large area of mixed beech forest (the future of which was never in doubt) was added to the conservation area, and an 80 ha. area on the tussock–forest margin was predator fenced to protect the juvenile takahē.

The Burwood facility has proved a successful venture for the takahē captive-rearing programme. The area alongside the highway has been

Opening the new takahē captive-rearing area at the Gorge Hill Burwood facility, western Southland, in April 2013. Some 25 chicks were raised on this area in the 2014–15 season, increasing the total population to more than 300 birds for the first time since their management began in the early 1950s. Pat Mark.

signposted as the 'Red Tussock Conservation Area', while the equally extensive area of beech forest beyond is barely visible from the road. Another part of this conservation area has now been dedicated to an updated takahē programme: pairs of birds are being run in several 1 ha. fenced areas in the hope of raising offspring that will breed more effectively in the wild than those raised earlier at the facility. I was invited to launch this new area and release the first takahē at an Easter 2013 ceremony.

A PROPOSED CENTRAL OTAGO CONSERVATION PARK

In 1990 members of the Otago University Geography Department requested that I contribute a chapter to their book *Southern Landscapes*, which was to be dedicated to retiring staff Bill Brockie and Ray Hargreaves.[42] I decided it would be appropriate to summarise the three

Protected Natural Areas (PNA) Survey reports of the Nokomai, Old Man and Umbrella ecological districts, as well as information from a recreation and conservation survey of the adjoining Remarkables District with which I had earlier been involved.[43] I took the opportunity to highlight their conservation values and present the case for a conservation park to embrace their most important areas.[44] The National Parks Authority had unsuccessfully floated the concept of a national park in the area in 1977, but this was a new concept. Conservation parks are generally much easier to achieve than national parks, and I thought one in Central Otago was justified, though it was likely to be controversial in high-country farming circles. This certainly proved to be the case.

The area I proposed for the Central Otago Conservation Park involved 34 pastoral runs and covered some 146,150 ha. of upland, including The Remarkables, the Nevis catchment and eastward to the Old Man Range. It would cover about 30% of four ecological districts: The Remarkables, Old Man, Nokomai and Umbrella. Some 19,900 ha. (13.7%) of the proposed area was already formally protected or committed to protection. The park would include 30 areas that had been recommended for protection in the PNA surveys, which would total 42,980 ha., or 29% of the proposed park. I suggested that covenants over the remaining areas could be more lenient in their formal commitments to protect at least the natural landscape values, perhaps with limited grazing.

The proposed park would thus accommodate conservation goals alongside limited farming, as well as eco-tourism. Importantly, it would have ensured that the regional, national and international conservation values of this extensive upland area were retained in perpetuity for their intrinsic worth. Although I conceded there would be some loss of production, I indicated that a not-insignificant amount of the total area proposed (13.8%) was categorised as Land Use Capability Class VIII land: unsuitable for grazing or other productive uses, but with important hydrological, recreation and/or landscape values. Furthermore, much of the remaining area in the proposed park was Class VIIe land, implying severe erosion or erosion hazards and also limited productive potential. The government policy for such land under pastoral leasehold tenure was destocking, retirement and surrender to the Crown, a policy that continues to be actively promoted through tenure review of the high-country leases (an issue discussed later). Importantly, the area had no serious animal pest or weed problems and, with careful management, should remain so. The tussock cover and vigour could be maintained through infrequent fires and conservative management of stock.

Certain parts of the proposed park contained land that fulfilled the criteria of a 'remote experience area'. Despite this, much of its boundary was readily accessible, with two public roads traversing it, including four-wheel-drive access to higher altitudes. Given this level of access, I considered the area to have significant potential for nature tourism were it adequately protected and managed. Establishment of the park would also have partly addressed the serious under-representation of tussock grasslands in the country's reserves network.

My chapter produced a greater outcry than expected, given my widespread consultation with DOC staff, runholders and others. John Miller, on behalf of the Tussocklands Resource Users Association, wrote a highly critical letter to the vice-chancellor, condemning me for using the university's 'good name' to further my own political aspirations. He claimed I was promoting a national park, designed to displace many lessees from rightful occupation of their leasehold properties. He also requested that I be directed to desist from using the university's name in any publications that were not peer-reviewed. I responded to the VC that most claims were erroneous, particularly references to a national park. My proposal had been for a *conservation park*, which provides for multiple uses and requires much less protective management than a national park. Moreover, not only had my chapter been peer-reviewed – but by University of Otago staff. I was encouraged by the support of the university on this issue, and the tone of the registrar's letter rejecting the complainant's requests.[45]

THE SOUTH ISLAND HIGH COUNTRY

Despite these and other efforts by a group of runholders who formed the so-called High Country Trustees (successor to the Tussocklands Resource Users Association), I have always tried to maintain dialogue with them. This has included supplying copies of my publications, either voluntarily or on request. I have also extended invitations to them to attend conferences or Botany Department seminars of particular relevance or interest. Following the first occasion when some members attended a seminar given by another staff member on a high-country topic, the following letter by G.M. Eckhoff of Coal Creek, Roxburgh, appeared in the *Central Otago News* (30 May 1991) under the title 'Degradation':

> Sir, the two fashionable buzz words, sustainability and degradation, often used to describe high country farming, apply equally to other aspects of life in New Zealand. Having visited the Botany Department of the University of Otago on two occasions during the past year, I was appalled at the degradation that has taken place ever since the area was first inhabited by homo sapiens. The habitat has suffered a gradual decline from its once pristine condition to its present unsightly state brought about, in my opinion, by years of misuse and bad management. I was particularly upset by the condition of the fragile upper areas of the Department [referring to the seminar room at the time, shown on p. 38], indeed even the walkway to this area showed signs of neglect. Is this area the best of what remains? If so, should this area be declared a P.N.A. so as to halt the further degradation of this important natural area? Should the D.O.C. not regard the area as important? I would suggest a timely fire through the building between the months of June and September (preferably with snow on the roof) so that a new and vigorous Department, better suited to the needs of the inhabitants, will arise in due course. Future generations may well be interested in how the current flora and fauna survived in this fragile ecosystem. I would respectfully suggest the human species sustainability come from areas like the South Island high country whose productive capacity enables large salaries to be paid to a few of the more 'important' species who frequent this habitat.[46]

So, my Central Otago Conservation Park did not eventuate as such. Instead, in 1998 a series of somewhat smaller conservation parks was proposed in the Otago Conservation Management Strategy (CMS), produced by DOC in collaboration with the Conservation Board. Of the six proposed parks – Te Papanui, Oteake, The Remarkables, Pisa, Kopuwai, and Rock and Pillar – the first was formalised as a 20,590 ha. park in 2003, while the second listed (64,815 ha.), plus Hawea Conservation Park (105,260 ha.), were formalised in 2010 and 2009, respectively. Kopuwai, which would likely embrace much of the area outlined in my proposal, as well as the others identified for Otago, awaits completion of tenure review.

Meanwhile, important conservation parks have been gazetted in other South Island conservancies. They include: in northern Southland, Eyre Mountain/Taka Rā Haka (65,160 ha.) in 2005;[47] in Canterbury, Korowai/Torlesse (20,328 ha.) in 2000, Ahuriri (46,655 ha.) in 2005, Ruataniwha (37,221 ha.) in 2006, Hakatere (39,138 ha.) in 2007 and Te Kahui Kaupeka (93,800 ha.) in 2009; and in Marlborough, Ka Whata Tu o Rakihouia/Kaikoura (88,066 ha.) in 2008. These collectively have contributed to a government policy of creating up to 22 conservation parks throughout the South Island high country. In addition, Molesworth Station, formerly managed by Land Information New Zealand (LINZ) for cattle grazing, was in 2005 transferred to DOC to be managed for conservation and recreation (with continued localised cattle grazing under licence to LINZ). Another major conservation achievement was the government's purchase in October 2008 of the country's largest pastoral leasehold property, St James Station (78,196 ha.) in southern Marlborough and northern Canterbury. With a wide range of vegetation types and very high conservation–recreation values, St James Station achieves a continuous corridor of conservation lands from coast to coast at a latitude of about 42°S.

Never in my wildest dreams, while struggling to defend Maungatua and Black Rock from development in the 1960s, did I dream of seeing so many magnificent areas of high country managed and cherished for their natural-heritage values.[48]

EYRE MOUNTAINS LAND ALLOCATION

In 1986, pursuant to the division of Crown lands between the soon-to-be-established Department of Conservation and SOEs Forestcorp and Landcorp, a limited period was allowed for public submissions. This was following the major land-allocation exercise by Lands and Survey and Forest Service staff. Crown lands with significant conservation values were to be allocated to the new Department of Conservation, while productive pastoral and forested lands would be split up between, respectively, Landcorp and Forestcorp.

In northern Southland's rugged Eyre Mountains there appeared to be a major discrepancy, with two pastoral farming blocks, abandoned in the 1960s as uneconomic leases, now being conservatively farmed by Landcorp. The Cainard Block in the upper Mataura Valley and the adjacent Eyre Creek block occupying the upper Eyre catchment both extended to the crest of the Eyre Mountains at altitudes of 1800–2028 m. It seemed

Eyre Mountains core study team, 1987, left to right: Katharine Dickinson, Graeme Loh, Susan Timmins, Barbara Simpson, Neil Simpson, Gerry McSweeney and me.

inexplicable to me, based on the criteria for the land-allocation exercise, that these two blocks could be assigned in their entirety to Landcorp for continued pastoral farming. After all, most of their upper slopes were still recovering from serious degradation associated with earlier pastoral farming and, moreover, were mapped as either Land Use Capability Class VIII (land without productive potential) or Class VIIe land (eroding or potentially highly erodible land with very limited productive potential). These areas, clearly mis-allocated, should have been consigned to DOC for soil and nature conservation (and recreation) purposes.

My application to conduct an ecological assessment on these two blocks was accepted by Landcorp, conditional on government conservation staff being formally involved. A PNA-type survey was conducted over a 10-day period in January 1987, involving a field team of 13 from DOC, Invermay Research Centre, DSIR Botany Division, the Forest Service, the Otago University Botany Department and Forest & Bird. Our survey covered some 30,000 ha. in the central Eyre Mountains and involved sampling a wide range of indigenous vegetation, including beech forests, shrublands, tussock grasslands, herbfields, fellfields, bluffs, screes and snowbanks. The tussock grasslands and shrublands were in relatively good condition, with burning and stock grazing having been greatly reduced or curtailed since the runs were resumed by the Crown in 1963. Some of the lower-altitude grasslands even had an abundance of the highly palatable native blue wheatgrass (*Anthosachne (Elymus) solandri*), together with the more widespread hard tussock (*Festuca novae-zelandiae*). This situation was considered indicative of a return to more natural composition of these grasslands.

Ten separate indigenous plant communities were identified. These ranged from mixed (silver, mountain and red) beech forest on the lower slopes and valley floors through to mixed shrublands, snow-tussock grasslands, alpine boulderfields and rock bluffs. Among the most distinctive endemic plants were several alpine plants, two alpine daisies (*Celmisia thomsonii* and *C. philocremna*), a recently described scree buttercup (*Ranunculus scrithalis*) and a speargrass (*Aciphylla spedenii*).

We also recorded the easternmost population of rock wren, together with New Zealand falcon and other threatened birds, and many invertebrates, including the rare, locally endemic giant snail *Powelliphanta spedeni spedeni*.[49]

In our preliminary report we recommended that some 20,000 ha. of the 30,000 ha. surveyed be transferred to DOC, based on its negligible productive potential and high conservation values.[50] Initially our report lay in the 'too hard' basket of the Officials Committee: it was referred to the special ministerial committee on Crown land allocation, who agreed with us that all 20,000 ha. should be transferred to DOC for management. This decision obviously delighted our study team. Although the area was transferred to DOC as stewardship land, it was decided that there should be five more years of continued grazing on the valley floors and lower slopes to allow Landcorp to adjust its management. Much later, in 2005, this stewardship land, and adjoining areas of conservation land with very high conservation, scenic and recreational values,[51] were designated part of the 65,160 ha. Eyre Mountains/Taka Rā Haka Conservation Park, the first in Southland.

THE HOCKEN LECTURE
An invitation to present the University of Otago's prestigious Hocken Lecture for 2004 gave me the chance to pursue tussock-grassland conservation issues in a more public context. To satisfy the historical perspective expected of a Hocken Lecture, I chose the title 'Our Golden Landscapes: An historical perspective on the origin and management of our tussock grasslands and associated mountain lands'.[52] The enthusiastic, near-capacity crowd in the Castle Lecture Theatre prompted one member of the audience, DOC's Otago Conservator Jeff Connell, to comment that the topic had obviously 'come of age'.

4

THE NARDOO TUSSOCK GRASSLAND DEBATE

One of two quangos associated with the Lands and Survey Department, the Land Settlement Board was responsible for overseeing government-sponsored land development and managing the Crown leasehold lands, most notably the South Island high country. In 1974 the board purchased Waipori Station (15,625 ha.) on the Lammerlaw Range of the eastern Otago uplands as part of its on-going involvement in land development and settlement, particularly for returned servicemen from World War II. This was at a time when government departments involved with major development projects were required to prepare an environmental impact report for public comment.[53] When this appeared in 1976, some 400 ha. were recommended for reservation, mostly riparian strips and lakeshore verges, but also the only stand of native forest on the property – a 10 ha. area of silver beech in the Nardoo catchment.

Several local scientists, including myself, responded to this report collectively and recommended that much of the Nardoo catchment (some 1050 ha.) be set aside as a representative regional reserve for both baseline research and biological conservation.[54] An audit by the Commission for the Environment (predecessor of the Ministry for the Environment) supported our proposal, as did the department's only scientist. Unknown to us, a number of head-office staff at Lands and Survey had strongly supported a comprehensive scientific assessment of the various environmental impacts of such land development. This was advocated in their paper presented to the 1979 international conference on 'The Agricultural Industry and its Effects on Water Quality and Quantity' at Hamilton, which, by chance, I also attended to present the results of our water-yield studies. Some serious adverse environmental effects of the department's development programme, particularly in the Rotorua district, were admitted in their paper, apparently caused by insufficient attention to preventing soil erosion or relieving the problems of nutrient enrichment of water bodies and changes in water yield.[55]

Based on past experience, the Lands and Survey staff admitted that their planned development for Waipori Station would benefit from being 'carried out in conjunction with a programme of continued monitoring and research to measure the effects of the land development on water-yield, water quality, erosion, flora and fauna'. They also stated: 'research will be undertaken by a number of bodies including the Water and Soil Division of the Ministry of Works and Development, Botany and Zoology Departments of the University of Otago, and DSIR. The greatest barrier to more enlightened land development and farm management is the lack of clear information based on rigorous scientific research.'[56]

As a consequence of this encouraging statement, I became one of a group of nine local university and government scientists, representing all the institutions and research areas listed in the statement, who reassessed the reserve needs. We recommended that virtually all of the Nardoo catchment be reserved, since it fulfilled the criteria for a representative regional reserve of tussock grassland. The Nardoo catchment was a minimum of 1000 ha., with an adequate range of altitude, topography, vegetation and soil sequences, had a compact shape, well-defined natural boundaries, and contained a permanently flowing stream with a series of minor tributaries. It certainly fulfilled the criteria developed for an ecological area by the Forest Service's Scientific Co-ordinating Committee (of which I was a member).

The Nardoo also provided a rare opportunity to study the interaction of native and introduced fish, since an old mining dam a short distance above Nardoo Stream's outlet into Lake Mahinerangi provided a barrier to fish migration. Below the dam there were three introduced and two native fish species, while above it there was only one native species. Also, the water flowing from this catchment, if undeveloped, would provide a valuable baseline reference for the natural nutrient output for comparison with the developed catchments nearby. A 17-year study, by Stuart Mitchell and colleagues from the Otago University's Zoology Department, of the nutrient status of the waters of Lake Mahinerangi and several streams flowing into it had already shown a steady enrichment of the lake waters to a level that was cause for concern. Moreover, Nardoo had an important advantage for scientific research in being accessible by an all-weather road in less than an hour's travel from Dunedin.

The case for reservation of the Nardoo catchment was fully supported in a subsequent independent assessment by a Lands and Survey scientist, as well as by the Royal Society of New Zealand, the New Zealand Ecological Society and the UNESCO 'Man and the Biosphere' programme.

Concern for the reserve proposal, however, was expressed by several development interests, particularly Federated Farmers, who mounted a strong political lobby. In November 1979 the Land Settlement Board decided to reserve the upper 600 ha. of the catchment but exclude the lower 400 ha. because of 'the need for maximum agricultural production from this land'.[57] The board also revealed that, for financial reasons, it was limited in its ability to forego development of land with considerable production potential. Responding to a request for a contribution from the scientific community to compensate for reserving the entire catchment, the Hellaby Indigenous Grasslands Research Trust offered $10,000. The board declined this offer, however, after reconsidering its decision the following May.

In August 1980 our group of ecologists took the Nardoo issue to the ombudsman, Sir Guy Powles.[58] He responded that this was his first request to deal with a conservation matter but that he would undertake an investigation if we could show that we were directly and adversely affected by the government's decision. Clearly, the proposed research

THE NARDOO TUSSOCK GRASSLAND DEBATE

that had been outlined by the Lands and Survey Department would be compromised by the planned development, so the ombudsman undertook his inquiry on the basis that the decision of the board not to reserve the lower 400 ha. of the Nardoo catchment was unreasonable. His grounds were threefold: it would have an adverse effect on the type of research that could be undertaken in the area; the failure to have scientific representation on the board had resulted in a lack of emphasis on the scientific and conservation factors that should be taken into account; and the decision was contrary to the policy statement of the board (published in 1979) concerning the reservation of land for conservation and scientific purposes.[59]

The ombudsman requested a report from the director general of lands. After receiving this in March 1981, he referred certain matters back to us for our 'response and clarification'. In his report, the director general asserted on behalf of the Land Settlement Board that the Nardoo catchment in total had been subjected to occasional fire and some grazing (mainly by sheep) for the past century, and that the 400 ha. area had already been modified by rye grass and white clover such that reversion to an indigenous state would be a very long-term goal. The board's view was that the upper part of the catchment, excluding the lower 400 ha., 'would be a realistic and useful area for research purposes'.[60]

We were aware that a neighbour's out-of-control fire had burnt much of the catchment in August 1977. Following this fire, the department had arranged for oversowing and top-dressing of areas within the catchment, including the 400 ha. now in dispute. Further top-dressing and oversowing was carried out in the spring of 1979 and again in 1980 as part of the department's seasonal maintenance programme. In noting these issues, the department also expressed concern to the ombudsman that, if the area was reserved, it could be difficult to control the spread of noxious weeds from the reserve to adjoining farmland. Moreover, a reserve would cut off access to a large area of land to the north of Nardoo Stream, making farming of this part of the Waipori Block extremely difficult.

The director general conveyed this information to the ombudsman, who responded to us by requesting that we justify retention of the entire catchment as a reserve. We replied that occasional fires and extensive grazing to which the catchment had been subjected were no different from the treatment of other tussock-grassland catchments in the central and eastern South Island. Indeed, the area was probably less modified than most at this elevation at the time of the department's acquisition. While aerial oversowing and top-dressing had occurred, this was not a permanent problem, as long as the treatment was not repeated according to independent advice from an Invermay (AgResearch) grassland scientist. Recovery from the 1977 fire had generally been very good and would be complete within a decade of grazing being terminated. Moreover, there was no significant issue of noxious weeds, given the very limited areas infested. However much a reserve embracing only the upper portion would still have value, the area's potential as a scientific reserve 'would be greatly enhanced if the total catchment was set aside as only then would it be adequately representative of the original tussock grassland ecosystems in this region'.[61]

Concern expressed about access across the lower part of the catchment had been addressed by the provision of a small strip, already fenced and roaded.

I received the final response from the ombudsman in April 1982:

> I am now in a position to report on the decision of the Land Settlement Board to set aside only 816 ha. of land as a scientific reserve in the Nardoo catchment instead of an area of approximately 1200 ha.
> Persuasive arguments have been advanced for designating approximately 400 ha. in the lower Nardoo as farmland and as a scientific reserve. As you are aware the prime objective of the acquisition of Waipori Station by the Crown in 1974 was the development and the ultimate settlement of the Station into economic farms under the Civilian Land Settlement Scheme which a Land Use Committee decided was the best use for the property. It was expected that the Settlement could be developed into 38 economic farm units, but due to the requests of many

organisations for release of part of the land to protect scientific, water, recreational, scenic and historic interests, 3400 ha. of the settlement has now been set aside as reserves of various kinds. This reduced the original 38 to 22 farming units. The Land Settlement Board, while aware of the case for protection of the entire Nardoo Catchment area, nevertheless believes that the decision to set aside 800 ha. in the upper Nardoo is a fair and realistic response to the need to protect scientific values while not prejudicing the agricultural production of the settlement. Furthermore the Board is concerned that because the lower Nardoo has been modified and developed by top-dressing and fertilizing, by a substantial fire which went out of control in 1977 and by the introduction of white clover and rye grass, reversion to its original state will be long delayed and hence its value as a reserve is questionable. As a reserve area, it could present a threat of noxious weed spread to neighbouring farm land and access to a large area of land to the north of the Nardoo Catchment would be severely restricted.

Equally persuasive arguments exist for the designation of the lower Nardoo area as a scientific reserve. The proposal has received a great deal of support from scientists of all the relevant disciplines. Its exclusion from the reserve will prevent the study of a full altitudinal sequence within a single catchment area. I am aware that tussock grasslands are seriously under-represented in the reserves system. The Nardoo Catchment is also ideal for study purposes because of its well-defined boundaries, its adequate size, the fact that it represents a full range of landforms, vegetation, soil, flora and fauna and is readily accessible. I explained to the Department that you, and many other scientists did not accept the development of the area has advanced to such an extent that it is valueless as a scientific reserve. Neither is it accepted that noxious weeds are present in the area with the exception of several small stands of gorse which can be removed without difficulty. In addition, access to land north of the Nardoo Catchment is possible by means of a road across the lower part of the area.

It was conceded during the course of this investigation that the expectation that 38 economic farming units could be developed from the settlement was optimistic and that a more realistic figure would have been 28 units.[62]

The report concluded with the following:

It was established [by the Land Settlement Board] that the loss of the 400 ha. would disrupt the development and settlement of the whole area to the north of the lake. It is proposed to winter 2500 stock units there and if the area was not used in this way the anticipated stock carrying capacity, currently on Waipori of 30,000 su would be reduced to 27,500 su.

The issue raised by the complaint is whether or not the loss of 2,500 su and the development cost of $32,000 which has been expended to date on the development of the 400 ha. outweighs the loss to the scientific community if the area is not designated as a scientific reserve. You contend that the decision to reserve the entire Nardoo catchment would not close its options for future use but that once the lower area is developed as farmland its value as an area for scientific research would be lost. I therefore suggested during the course of a discussion with Mr MacKenzie (Fields Director), who had been closely associated with the acquisition and development of the Settlement, that given the fact that it will take approximately 10–11 years to develop the entire area, the 400 ha. should not be developed any further in the immediate future, but retained as a reserve for a limited period. The area should then be closely monitored to assess whether or not it realises its potential for a scientific reserve. If at the end of a specified period, the area were to exhibit such potential, it could be designated as a scientific reserve. The entire Nardoo Catchment would be subject to a review as a reserve in 15 years time.

Such a proposal would involve:

Defining and fencing the 400 ha. area;
Excluding all livestock;
Precluding any further top-dressing or oversowing;
Annual monitoring of the area to assess vegetation change towards a tussock dominant cover;
Deferring any settlement plans for the area.

The Director General agreed to place this suggestion before the full Land Settlement Board at its meeting in February 1982.

The Land Settlement Board duly considered the matter and resolved: 'to reject the suggestion that further development of the 400 ha. of the lower Nardoo Catchment be deferred and to affirm its earlier decision under Case No. 9433 to reserve for scientific purposes an area of 816 ha. in the Upper Nardoo Catchment which achieves an effective balance between farming and reservation on Waipori Farm Settlement'.

THE NARDOO TUSSOCK GRASSLAND DEBATE

The members of the Board were of the opinion that the addition of the 400 ha. which has already been modified, to the proposed scientific reserve cannot be justified. They believe that deferment would detrimentally affect development plans for this part of the Settlement, would involve substantial costs and cause a significant loss of revenue.

I am satisfied that the Board considered the proposal fully and I am informed that members of the Board had inspected the area before the decision was taken.

The Board is the responsible authority in the matter and I do not believe I could conclude that its decision, which required it to balance competing scientific and economic interests, is unreasonable.[63]

Despite the ombudsman's findings, we felt strongly about our case. I was asked to look for every opportunity to air it in the hope that the decision would be overruled. Jonathon Elworthy was appointed the new minister of lands soon after the findings were released, so I took the issue up with him. He replied that he had studied correspondence between the ombudsman and his department, and believed the board had consulted adequately with scientists and that its decision was a reasonable balance between conflicting interests.

I also decided to take the issue to the National Parks and Reserves Authority, of which I was a member; they in turn referred the matter to the Otago National Parks and Reserves Board. The board would consider the issue under the Reserves Act 1977, which delegated responsibility to it for land administration. Following a May 1982 resolution of the authority, the Land Settlement Board was requested to defer any prejudicial action in the catchment area until the authority had considered the Otago board's report on the issue. However, a failure to communicate this decision from the Lands and Survey Department's head office to its Dunedin office meant that the area in contention was not only bisected by a new road but was aerially top-dressed, apparently just prior to an inspection by a subcommittee of the Otago board on 14 June.

The board's subcommittee of three heard submissions from the department's district field officer, the Federated Farmers' representative, a catchment board soil conservator, an agricultural scientist and myself; it also received fully supportive written submissions from the New Zealand Entomological Society's conservation subcommittee and the Otago section of the New Zealand Institute of Agricultural Scientists. Nevertheless, the Otago board subsequently supported, by a split decision, the recommendation of its subcommittee convenor 'that the Lower Nardoo area be farmed'.[64]

While the Otago National Parks and Reserves Board acknowledged 'that the arguments are delicately balanced', they had difficulty coming to grips with just what the scientists wanted to do with the land if it was given reserve status. Moreover, they were concerned that 'substantial modification of the area [had] already taken place'. Whether the board's decision would have been different if its members had been aware that only one-third of the lower area had been recently top-dressed, in fact just one day before they met and three days after the subcommittee's inspection – a further case of communication failure within the department – could not be determined.

The National Parks and Reserves Authority duly wrote to the minister of lands:

> The Otago National Parks and Reserves Board has studied the situation, but there are aspects of its study on which the Authority is seeking further comment together with consultation during the September meeting of the Authority. Following this consultation the Authority wishes to report further to you. In the light of the position outlined, the Authority requests your deferral of activity or decisions relating to the catchment until its further report.[65]

It remains unclear whether this formal request was acceded to by the Department of Lands and Survey. Shortly afterwards, however, the Land Settlement Board sent me a copy of its new two-page draft policy statement entitled 'Conservation, Education and Research'. I could not fault the statement and, in my unconditional support and enthusiastic response to it, I also suggested that if the Land Settlement Board adopted this policy, they might wish to show some resolve in the matter

THE NARDOO TUSSOCK GRASSLAND DEBATE

Lower Nardoo catchment, Lammerlaw Range, showing the pre-development state (top), April 1982, and after its initial cultivation, October, 1987.

by re-examining the Nardoo issue. I received an encouraging response from the board's secretary indicating that my request was accepted and they would shortly be reviewing the Nardoo decision.[66]

Within two months I was sitting with the board, at the invitation of the minister of lands, along with Allan Evans, president of Federated Mountain Clubs. (How I obtained such status is a story in itself, told in Chapter 6.) Unwilling to raise the Nardoo issue at my first meeting with them, I waited for the next meeting to ask when they were planning to review the decision. I tabled the letter I had received from the board's secretary, to looks of surprise and concern from most members. The board's deputy chair and Lands and Survey Department Director General Bing Lucas responded that the Nardoo issue was 'a hot political potato', particularly with the Labour government (and its policy) having recently ousted the National government, and it would be added to the agenda of the next meeting later in the year.[67]

Enthused by this response, I revisited Nardoo about one week before the third meeting and, to my utter dismay, found that a substantial portion of the lower catchment had been recently ploughed. When I contacted Duncan Sawyer, the department's field officer in Dunedin in charge of the land development, he said that a message had been received from head office requesting deferment of activities but that he was unable to delay the planned development. Furious with this situation, I told him that I would be expressing my extreme disquiet at the board meeting.

Predictably, Nardoo was a hot topic at the next meeting, with the chairman recommending referring the matter, without further discussion, to the new minister, Koro Wetere, given its relevance to the Labour government's policy. Within a month I was invited to accompany the minister and other senior departmental staff to the Nardoo. I was unable to accept this invitation personally because of a prior commitment with the Hellaby Trust, so colleague and co-submitter Peter Johnson, of DSIR Botany Division, represented our group of scientists. A helicopter trip to and around the catchment and discussions with departmental staff obviously convinced the minister that, despite the case for reservation of the whole catchment, the recent development had committed the lower 400 ha. to agriculture. He later wrote to me that, in light of the recent development, he had given his approval for this to continue while also expressing serious reservations as to how the department had handled the matter.[68]

The outcome of the Nardoo issue had major implications for the department's image, particularly its handling of the dual responsibility for land development and nature conservation. When difficult and contentious decisions had to be made between development and conservation, they almost invariably favoured development. This was also the public image the Forest Service had increasingly developed in relation to submissions on publicly notified forest-management plans, something the Land Settlement Board had managed to avoid. The concerned public eventually had their day soon after the Labour government was elected in 1984. Following an 'Environmental Summit' at parliament, the new government announced that the two departments were to be disestablished and replaced by two SOEs, Forestcorp and Landcorp, with the 'green dots' collectively to form a new Department of Conservation.

The outcome and publicity associated with the Nardoo issue, while revealing the political impotence of a small group of scientists, did highlight the parlous state of tussock grasslands. In light of our difficulties in influencing the political process, I decided to join the Royal Forest and Bird Protection Society of New Zealand, the country's largest conservation organisation, where perhaps my conservation aspirations might be assisted with the political clout that such an organisation clearly had. As to the fate of the Nardoo, a small portion of the 400 ha. lower catchment was retrieved for conservation when government lands were allocated between DOC and Landcorp and Forestcorp in 1987. The Nardoo Reserve was later incorporated into the 20,590 ha Te Papanui Conservation Park, established in 2003.

5

SAVE MANAPOURI – AND BEYOND

Lakes Te Anau and Manapouri – the South Island's largest and fourth largest lakes, which form the eastern gateway to Fiordland National Park – were the focus of New Zealand's largest conservation battle, which persisted for some 13 years. With major catchments in one of the country's highest and most reliable rainfall regions, an elevation of approximately 200 m above sea level and a location close to the fiords, they had been eyed by engineers at intervals from the early 1900s. The most significant proposal, however, came in the late 1950s, when a multi-national company then known as Consolidated Zinc Pty Ltd approached the government with a proposal to establish an aluminium smelter on the south coast, using bauxite from Queensland and the hydroelectric potential of these two Fiordland lakes.

Keen to establish a major industry in the south and slow the steady population drift north, the government considered the proposal seriously. It also undertook to fully inform the public of the environmental implications for Fiordland National Park before making a formal decision. However, neither the public nor park management were consulted before the decision was announced in early 1960. The government signed an agreement with the company in January 1960, giving it exclusive rights for 99 years to generate continuous electricity for the smelter it proposed to build at Tiwai Point near Invercargill. The only restriction imposed was that neither lake might be raised so far as to endanger the Te Anau township. This would have allowed Manapouri to be raised some 24 m to the level of Te Anau, creating one large lake.

SAVE MANAPOURI – AND BEYOND

Lake Manapouri from The Monument, with the Hope Arm and a deer-free offshore island in the foregound and the Kepler Mountains in the distance. The glaciated and forested landscape is distinctive.

There was immediate public outcry. However, this was not sufficient to modify the government's stance when, unable to proceed with the full development because of financial constraints, the company negotiated a new agreement with it in 1963. The water rights were exchanged for power rights, and the government agreed to build the power scheme on the same basis as the company had proposed. An aspect of the new agreement, however, was that the government would be entitled to a certain amount of electricity surplus to the company's needs. Perhaps more significantly, the electricity would now be fed into the national grid, which would supply the smelter with its power needs.

Engineering studies soon revealed that Manapouri could not be raised by more than 11 m, and perhaps by only as much as 8 m, therefore the two lakes would not be united as originally planned. Two control structures would now be required, with Te Anau becoming the storage lake and its levels manipulated beyond its natural range so as to retain the maximum head of water possible on Manapouri. Lake Manapouri would fluctuate some 8.38 m, significantly more than its natural range of 4.8 m.

The development was planned in two phases. The first, beginning in 1961, involved constructing an underground powerhouse near sea level below Manapouri's West Arm, plus a 9.8 km tail-race tunnel to the nearest fiord at Deep Cove in Doubtful Sound. Two roads were also required, one of 20 km over Wilmot Pass for access to the portal of the tail-race tunnel, the second of 80 km from the power station to the eastern edge of the park across the Hunter Mountains for construction and maintenance of the transmission lines to the smelter at Tiwai Point. The first of seven generators was commissioned in 1969 and the last in 1971. The second phase of development was to involve controlling the level of Te Anau and raising Manapouri to increase the overall output of electricity. Up to this stage, there had been negligible assessment of the impacts of raising the lake on the shoreline of Manapouri, while the plans for Te Anau had hardly created a murmur since it was assumed to be essentially unaffected by the development.

Prompted by increasing public concern and the lack of any environmental impact assessment on the Manapouri lakeshore, I became embroiled in the issue. In October 1969 the University's Botany Department was approached by DSIR Botany Division in Christchurch about the possibility of conducting detailed environmental assessments, to be funded by the New Zealand Electricity Department (NZED). There were three aspects to this exercise: first, to describe the general vegetation features of the Manapouri lakeshore; second, to describe the vegetation of its several wooded islands that would be submerged, in particular, special orchid communities that were a feature of the ground cover of several of these islands; and third, to describe the micro-environmental conditions that permitted such orchid communities (which normally occur in the crowns of trees) to exist here on the ground.

It was clear that the purpose of the exercise was to record natural features of the lakeshore prior to these being submerged and lost. I invited Peter Johnson – then a promising student with an interest in wetlands who was looking for an Honours project – to select this topic. He did and we visited Manapouri in November to make some initial observations and assess the general scope of the exercise. We first boated around the eastern shoreline as far as South Arm, where a 2 ha. area of lakeshore had recently been cleared by mechanical equipment brought in via the newly constructed transmission-line road. We were anything but impressed with what we saw. The trees had been cut and dropped from a barge into deep water just offshore, and the stumps had been covered with sand that had been bulldozed from the beach to create an artificial batter. We determined the top of this graded batter to be somewhat less than the proposed level of the raised lake, which would extend at least 1 km up-valley through the forest. On the steep rocky slope adjacent to the beach, trees had been cut with a chainsaw over a limited area and dropped into the lake below.

Quizzed by a radio reporter when we returned to the Manapouri township, I was forthright – perhaps naively – in my criticism of this lakeshore clearing exercise. I said it was nothing short of pathetic and in no way demonstrated the feasibility of the proposed lakeshore clearing. The reporter then sought comment from the director general of NZED, Bruce McKenzie, and our strongly contrasting comments were later broadcast together. Concerned with this situation, McKenzie contacted the university Vice-Chancellor, Dr Robin Irvine, to indicate that the environmental assessment contract would be terminated forthwith. My subsequent discussions with the vice-chancellor persuaded him to request that the NZED reconsider their decision because of the importance of the exercise, and to indicate that we would continue with the project unless instructed otherwise. The fieldwork for the project was completed within the next three months, several weeks before the vice-chancellor received a response from the department indicating that the project would not be funded. Being told that the fieldwork had already been completed, the department reluctantly agreed to make payment.

Peter Johnson's comprehensive report was submitted with the Botany Department's endorsement to the NZED later that year.[69] We were fortunate in having a 37-year record of daily lake levels collected by the MWD. This allowed the rather complex zonation pattern of lakeshore vegetation to be interpreted in relation to natural lake-level fluctuations: periodic submergence or, conversely, exposure associated with unnaturally low lake levels. We predicted that this lakeshore vegetation would not survive the proposed lake-raising, even though the engineers claimed the exercise would simply be one of raising the lake level and restoring the status quo, indeed even improving on nature, under their management.

I was invited by the Otago branch of the Royal Society to contribute evidence on lakeshore ecology in relation to the proposed lake-raising as part of the branch's submission to the Manapouri Commission of Inquiry. Branch chairman and physics professor Jack Dodd addressed energy concerns, while geography professor Ron Lister covered social aspects. In combination, we were certainly able to comment comprehensively on the claimed 4.5% increase in annual electricity generation to be achieved with lake raising (an amount not critical for the aluminium smelter) and the predicted damage to the lakeshore. Being my first ever submission to a formal enquiry, I was uneasy with the cross-examination of the Crown's counsel, Solicitor General Richard Savage, who questioned me on the ethics of conveying information to the public that had been obtained with funding from a government department with clearly contrary aspirations. I pointed out that there was nothing in our contract to dictate the outcome of our study or restrict the wider dissemination of information and that we had already supplied it to the NZED. Moreover, the university cherished the principle of freedom of expression and open debate. We felt the public was entitled to our information and could assess it as they wished. My conscience was therefore clear. I was also examined at length by Thomas Eichelbaum QC – who represented Comalco (Consolidated Zinc's rights were transferred in 1969 to Comalco (NZ) Ltd, a subsidiary of the Australian-based Comalco Industries Pty Ltd) – on several aspects of the proposed lakeshore clearing and was relieved at being bailed out by the commission chair James Hutchison in relation to the large area of forest to be cleared at the head of Hope Arm. He confirmed earlier discussions and agreement with

Te Anau lakeshore vegetation survey near the Etrick Burn mouth, showing the surveyor's staff (held by park ranger John Gardner) and level (on the tripod), and a recorder (Conway Powell). The various zones of vegetation were described in relation to the lake levels. The current level, recorded daily, was used as the baseline for each transect. This information was related to that from the Manapouri survey (below).

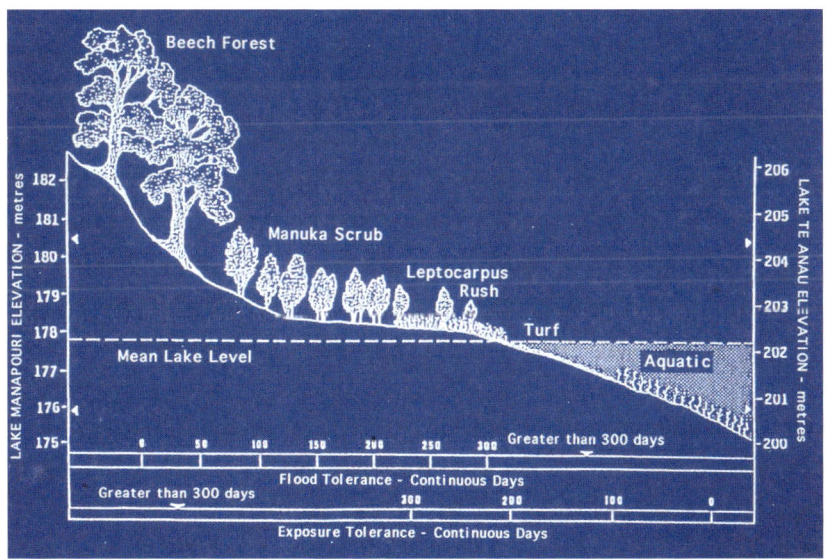

Eichelbaum on the likely difficulty of clearing an extensive area of semi-swamp forest of mataī–kahikatea from this area.

While Manapouri had been the centre of debate up to this time, Te Anau attracted attention when it became known at the commission's inquiry that the proposed maximum operating level would intrude about a metre into the township. This was, of course, contrary to the one formal legal constraint of the whole proposal: that the township of Te Anau not be threatened in any way by the lake-level management. The solution proposed to the commission by MOW senior staff was to build a low masonry wall along the township's lake margin which, they said, would in a modest way resemble the dykes of Holland, behind which vast tracts of land are successfully cultivated. In the unlikely event of water seeping through, the local fire pumps could be used to pump it back into the lake. Not surprisingly, the commission rejected this 'solution' and required a maximum level for Lake Te Anau that would not threaten the township.

Soon afterwards, the Royal Forest and Bird Protection Society's second petition of almost 265,000 signatures was presented to parliament, and the commission of inquiry completed its hearings. With broad terms of reference, the commission sat for 38 days in mid-1970 and received 68 submissions, seven from government departments, one from Comalco, the balance from organisations and individuals. There were conflicting views among the government departments, but only three of the 60 general submissions supported raising the lake. Undoubtedly the most significant aspect of the commission's findings – which was contrary to Prime Minister Keith Holyoake's pre-election reassurance that there was no formal contract requiring lake raising – was that 'the Crown is contractually bound to Comalco to raise the level of Lake Manapouri.' The commission also accepted, however, that:

> ... if the level of Lake Manapouri is so raised: (a) A number of beautiful islands will be submerged, and the appearance of the lake will be to some extent detrimentally affected even after the necessary shoreline treatment is done. (b) Shoreline clearance of trees and scrub to a reasonably acceptable standard is feasible with modern sophisticated equipment. There should be no limit placed on the cost of

this, but we estimate that it would be in the neighbourhood of $10 million if the lake level is to be raised to 610 ft, with an additional $2 million, or $2.5 million, if it is to raised to 620 ft. (c) It will probably take very many years for beaches to be reformed. (d) Certain botanical features will be irretrievably destroyed, and there will be serious damage to bird life and to fishing. (e) It is unlikely that there will be any serious setback to tourism once the shoreline has recovered from the damage done in the clearance of it.[70]

Perhaps one of the commission's most significant statements was: 'One thing that we can say with certainty – because of the loose wording of many aspects of the agreement, much uncertainty remained – is that a considerable and highly responsible section of the community, while accepting that a large-scale aluminium industry in Southland is here to stay, is deeply concerned at the proposed raising of the level of Lake Manapouri.' The commission's findings also strongly discredited the MOW proposal to deal with any threat to Te Anau and recommended that the proposed maximum be lowered to a more appropriate level.

The response of the NZED's assistant general manager, Colin Bambery, in relation to the Te Anau lakeshore issue, was typical of the naivety being expressed by senior government engineers of the time on many ecological aspects. The *Press* quoted him as stating; 'in the absence of scientific evidence as to exactly what will happen when the level of Te Anau is raised, our whole approach is "let's take it quietly".'[71] Dismayed by such an attitude, I expressed my concern to Brian Talboys, minister of science and the local MP, who replied that he was unwilling to take any action since the whole issue was with a select committee. Aware of my correspondence with Brian Talboys, Awarua National MP Hugh Templeton contacted me and shared my concerns. He suggested that a study similar to that which we had completed at Manapouri should be repeated for Te Anau. Rather than adopt my suggestion that such a study might be carried out by DSIR staff, he said he would prefer me to supervise it. He even undertook to arrange funding for it from NZED. I agreed and, to my great surprise, the funding was provided and a contract offered, again without any written constraints as to the subsequent release of information.

Construction of the Te Anau control structure was now beginning so this study was urgently needed. During the May university vacation of 1971, we covered all 520 km of the lakeshore, concentrating on the 20% (106 km) of shoreline forest overlying loose or unconsolidated material in which water-table effects could be expected. Boat transport was provided by Fiordland National Park staff as well as several local residents.

Line transects were run into the forest at right angles from the lakeshore to show how far the forest could be vulnerable to high water tables associated with the proposed lake management. We also recorded elevation along these transects with a surveyor's staff and level, using the lake level as our baseline. On several of the deltas this distance was very considerable. Ten of our traverses took us 300 m from the lakeshore without rising more than 3 m in elevation; on three deltas this distance exceeded 600 m, and the longest traverse, about a kilometre, was on the very extensive flat land alongside the Clinton River, opposite Glade House at the head of the lake. Several of the deltas had storm beaches, built up over centuries of wave action, with areas of often extensive swamp forest, largely out of sight from the lakeshore, that had developed behind them. One of the best examples was at the mouth of the Snag Burn on the south side of the lake's Middle Fiord.

Our study showed that the pattern of vegetation on those sections of the shoreline composed of unconsolidated material was essentially identical to that we had found previously at Manapouri. Moreover, the assumed tolerances to both flooding and exposure based on the historical lake-level records were virtually identical with those we recorded at Manapouri, despite the difference in elevation between the two lakes. This reassured us that the natural variations in lake level were the main determinant for the vegetation pattern on both lakeshores, even though their variation in levels recorded over 37 years was substantially less for Te Anau (3.5 m) than for Manapouri (4.8 m). Our comprehensive results were published in a series of papers in the *Proceedings of the New Zealand Ecological Society* of 1972.[72]

Our report, 'Vegetation of Lake Te Anau shoreline with special reference to the implications of the proposed lake level alterations', written by Peter Johnson, Jim Crush, Colin Meurk and myself, was submitted to the NZED in the month following the survey. It was referred to the Manapouri Officials Committee, who in turn had it appraised by a scientific subcommittee comprising Deputy Director General of DSIR, Ian Baumgart; Director of the Dominion Museum, Robert Falla; Director of the Wildlife Service, Gordon Williams; and Senior Ecologist with the Forest Service, Jack Holloway.

The subcommittee's appraisal, which was conveyed to the Manapouri Officials Committee, endorsed the basis, conclusions and recommendations of our report. They complimented us on the standard of the survey, which gave 'very useful indications', speculating that 'the extent of the area likely to be in the critical zone is not known because of the absence of accurate contour maps' but accepting that '66 miles of shoreline is affected'. They also considered, however, that we:

> ... may not have given full weight to the recovery powers of the forest following the establishment of a new margin consequent on inundation. We consider that this 'unnatural edge' would be ecologically unstable since the tall trees on the margin would be very liable to wind damage. In fact this damage would be the first step in a relatively rapid process of reforming the streamlined edge.[73]

Nevertheless, they were 'generally in agreement with Dr Mark's contention that there is a critical period beyond which trees cannot tolerate inundation and that for beech forests this is about 50 days'.

> Mark's predictions which are based on horizontal projections of lake levels beneath the forest will actually underestimate the water table effect since the water table is always higher than lake level. Hence though an accurate contour map would help to estimate the areas affected, there would still be marginal variations due to the nature of the under-lying sediments, and to the varying tolerance of trees to water levels at different levels of soil fertility.

The subcommittee supported a gradual approach to lake-level management: ' ... *it would be prudent as well as scientifically informative to raise the level of the lake gradually and to continue observance of the effects on water table and vegetation as the water level rises* [their italics].' Further study by the Otago Botany Department was strongly endorsed, with a view to limiting adverse environmental effects of the final control levels of the lake.

On the basis of this official assessment released to us, we wrote an open letter to the general manager of the NZED in March 1972:

> ['I']he Official Subcommittee's report makes it quite clear that there is general agreement regarding the likelihood of forest destruction along about 66 miles of the Te Anau shoreline if the control level is raised above 665 ft [202.68 m].
>
> Moreover, reading paragraph 7 of the Official Subcommittee's report[,] the impression is created that careful studies and observations during the initial period of lake raising will be encouraged in order to minimise damage and further, that such findings 'should be taken into account in determining the final control levels of the lake'. We are encouraged by this approach and endorse this attitude to the question. However paragraph 3 [of the report] insinuates that the Subcommittee is willing to accept extensive destruction of shoreline forests in which instability through wind-throwing and undercutting of trees is seen, not as unacceptable long-term ecological instability but rather as 'the first step in a relatively rapid process of reforming the streamlined forest edge'... We would challenge such an assessment of the consequences.
>
> Because of the apparent inconsistency between these statements in paras 3 and 7, we are anxious to learn the official Government policy regarding Lake Te Anau which should take into account the conclusions of our report and acceptance by Government of our forecast of forest destruction. We anticipate that many other individuals and organizations will be similarly anxious. We would be grateful, therefore, if you would declare the official Government policy, or if you are not in a position to do this, to refer our request to the appropriate quarter in Government.
>
> We would like to obtain an assurance from Government on four aspects, as follows:
>
> 1. That Government's intention is to control the level of Lake Te Anau so as to provide the maximum water use that is commensurate with the conservation of the woody vegetation of its natural shoreline.
> 2. That Government will take all necessary precautions by adopting special procedures during the initial period of lake control, so as to ensure that subsequent damage will be kept to an absolute minimum ...

SAVE MANAPOURI – AND BEYOND

3. That adequate provision will be made for a study period of up to one year (but possibly requiring only a few months) for signs of incipient water table damage to shoreline forest, that it has been assumed will follow retention of the lake at levels above 665 ft for periods in excess of the tolerance limits we have predicted. Such studies should be made at more than one level above 665 ft.

4. That in the early stages of lake control the predicted tolerance limits of the shoreline's woody vegetation will not be grossly exceeded until it has been established that it is safe to do so.

We would point out that this is an open letter that has been widely circulated, together with the official Government reply to our Te Anau report.

As you are no doubt aware, Government's reply to this letter will be keenly awaited by many.

Yours etc.,
A.F. Mark, P.N. Johnson, J.R. Crush, C.D. Meurk[74]

One of the many cartoons depicting various aspects of the Manapouri–Te Anau controversy; this one, by Sid Scales for the Otago Daily Times *of 5 February 1970, was later gifted to me.*

This publicity for the Te Anau situation did nothing to endear me to the NZED, since it emphasised the vulnerable state of the Te Anau lakeshore in relation to the proposals for lake management. It further heightened the debate on the Manapouri–Te Anau issue, particularly with the next general election only a few months away in October. Environmental issues were clearly to become a major focus for this election, most notably the Manapouri–Te Anau controversy but also Lake Wanaka, which had more recently been a focus of public debate with proposals – again by NZED – to raise its water level and bulldoze new beaches around the township to replace those lost. A Hands Off Wanaka Lake (HOWL) committee was making its concerns widely known right up to the election in 1972. In the course of the Manapouri–Te Anau debate, senior NZED staff had aired the prospect of harnessing the Sutherland Falls and/or diverting the Hollyford River if Manapouri was not to be raised. In response, their adversaries accused them of attempting to pressure and mislead an uninformed public.

Leaders of all the political parties visited Te Anau in the run-up to the 1972 election. National Prime Minister Jack Marshall was clearly equivocal on the issue. By contrast, Labour's leader, Norman Kirk, pronounced a policy of maintaining natural lake levels for both Manapouri and Te Anau, and also rejected the proposal to raise Lake Wanaka. The NZED's general manager, Bruce McKenzie, claimed that the cut stumps that Peter Johnson and I had witnessed, still lined up on the lakeshore, were natural phenomena. When taken to inspect the experimental lakeshore clearance at Manapouri's South Arm just ahead of the 1972 election, Kirk apparently responded to McKenzie's assertion by stating that he could believe such a claim since the engineers felt they were so close to God that anything they did could be classed as natural.

The political debate heightened in intensity in August, when major slumping of the lakeshore occurred at Surprise Bay, not far from the Manapouri township. This slumping was associated with the first (and only) occasion when the lake level had been drawn below its natural minimum, in this case a mere 58 cm, much less than was planned over

SAVE MANAPOURI – AND BEYOND

The South Arm clearing rephotographed in April 1971, by which time wave action had excavated the obviously cut beech stumps and littered them along the lakeshore.

the long term. The National government ordered an immediate but confidential enquiry into the slumping by DSIR geologists and ecologists, whereas Labour used the event to confirm its policy of managing the lake levels within their natural ranges. Threats to the security of the Te Anau control structure, then under construction, and also to the transmission lines through Fiordland National Park, added to the controversy. Just prior to the election, and under increasing pressure, the National government undertook to defer for six years its decision on the crucial question of lake-raising, but Labour unequivocally maintained its earlier policy of operating both lakes within their natural ranges. Labour also rejected the government's plans for a wide-based dam at the Manapouri control structure, which would provide for the option of future lake-raising.

RESOLUTION OF THE ISSUE AND ESTABLISHMENT OF THE GUARDIANS OF LAKES MANAPOURI AND TE ANAU

Labour won the 1972 election with significant victories in southern electorates, their conservation policies a major factor in the landslide win. The new prime minister, Norman Kirk, soon confirmed his party's

The initial Manapouri–Te Anau Lake guardians and associates, left to right: Hector Jones (NZED), Ron McLean, Wilson Campbell, me, John Moore, Jim McFarlane and John Gardner (Fiordland National Park ranger, kneeling), at one of the early meetings.
Peter Dyall.

pre-election policy on management of the Fiordland lakes within their natural ranges but then followed a much more courageous path. Early in 1973 I was approached to chair a group to advise on and oversee the management of lakes Manapouri and Te Anau. Shortly afterwards, the government announced its establishment of the Guardians of Lakes Manapouri and Te Anau, a group drawn from those who had led the campaign: Wilson Campbell, a Te Anau motellier; Les Hutchins, general manager of Fiordland Travel (now Real Journeys) from Manapouri; Jim McFarlane, a civil engineer from Invercargill; Ron McLean, chairman of the Save Manapouri Campaign and a farmer from Kennington near Invercargill (Ron had spearheaded the Save Manapouri Campaign with his daughter Jill); John Moore, a medical practitioner from Te Anau, who had driven the Te Anau campaign; and me. In fulfilment of Labour's pre-election promise, Lake Wanaka also had a guardians group appointed under the Lake Wanaka Preservation Act 1973. A Lake Rotorua guardians group followed somewhat later.

SAVE MANAPOURI – AND BEYOND

The Guardians of Lakes Manapouri and Te Anau were given very wide terms of reference in the initial brief from the Minister for the Environment, Joe Walding. These were later formalised in the 1981 Amendment to the Manapouri–Te Anau Development Act and are currently enshrined in Section 6X(2) of the Conservation Act 1987. The functions of the guardians are:

> To make recommendations to the Minister [of Conservation] on any matters arising from the environmental, ecological and social effects of the construction and operation of the Manapouri-Te Anau electric power scheme on the townships of Manapouri and Te Anau, Lakes Manapouri and Te Anau and their shorelines, and on the rivers flowing in and out of these lakes, having particular regard to the effects of the operation on social values, conservation, recreation, tourism and related activities and amenities.
> [...]
> (c) To make to the Minister, and to the Minister responsible for the administration of the Manapouri-Te Anau Development Act 1963, recommendations on the operating guidelines for the levels of Lakes Manapouri and Te Anau, for the purposes of section 4A of that Act.

Subsection (3) states that the guardians 'shall in each year make a report to the Minister on their meetings and recommendations'. To fulfil these functions, we were entitled to receive reports from government on any action relevant to the matters set out above and request any additional information required. A representative of the Electricity Department had the right to participate in discussions but not to vote. The guardians also had the discretion to invite other bodies and government departments to meetings when matters of concern to them were under consideration. We invited a Fiordland National Park staff member to participate regularly on this basis.

While government's decision to operate both lakes within their natural ranges clearly removed the earlier problems, it was evident to me that careful consideration needed to be given to adverse effects accompanying any departure from the maximum durations associated with natural lake-level fluctuations – information that had been derived from our detailed ecological studies of the lakes' shorelines. Initially then, the guardians' main task was to devise guidelines for managing the lake levels to safeguard the natural lakeshore features and stability of the vulnerable shorelines while optimising hydroelectric potential (though this latter aspect was not covered in our brief). We agreed that this complex exercise should be approached scientifically. Annual reports to the minister for the environment were also required and provide a valuable summary of the guardians' main activities from the time of our first report for the year to March 1974.

The early years were particularly busy. In our first year some 13 meetings were held, including one with the new Minister for the Environment, Joe Walding. We also had frequent discussions with staff of NZED, MOW and DSIR, as well as with the chief engineer of the Southland Catchment Board, both at meetings and during inspections. On a visit to Wellington to do the rounds of relevant government departments and officials, John Moore and I were greatly impressed at being met at the airport by delegates who transported us, as required, in a ministerial car.

The August 1972 slumping along sections of the Manapouri shoreline was carefully inspected, and found to be more extensive than first thought. In addition to large rotational slumps in Surprise Bay, Lookout Beach near the entrance to Hope Arm had collapsed into deep water and some adjacent beaches had been partially lost. Our requests to have qualified scientists examine these beaches, along with access to the earlier confidential reports made prior to the election, were readily granted. It became obvious that no permanent reference sites of beach profiles or shoreline vegetation at Manapouri had been established prior to the lake levels being manipulated. We were determined to avert this situation at Te Anau by urgently establishing shoreline monitoring there as well as on the Manapouri shoreline.

In devising lake-level guidelines, the guardians were well aware of the separate problems of high and low lake levels, and of the extremely delicate ecological balance that exists on the shorelines of these two

Lookout Beach near the entrance to Hope Arm, Lake Manapouri, showing its collapse soon after, and as a result of, the lake being lowered 58 cm below its natural minimum in August 1972. The jetty piles (centre) and the bleached area of rocky shore (left) had previously been covered by sand and now indicate the amount of beach lost with the collapse; the lake is at 175.71 m, 14 April 1973.

glacially scoured lakes. However obvious to us, the importance of carefully defining management regimes within the natural ranges of lake levels to conserve natural shoreline features was not widely appreciated. Our earlier ecological studies of the Manapouri and Te Anau lakeshores were clearly relevant to devising management guidelines for the lake levels. I was reluctant to apply them directly, and so sought confirmation from DSIR Botany Division of their relevance in developing these guidelines for both lakes. This was provided, unequivocally.

Problems soon surfaced. Unanticipated friction in the tail-race tunnel reduced the total electricity output by 4.5%, and our lake-management guidelines further diminished energy generation (relative to predicted output with the lake raised). Of the total reduction of about 8.4% reported to us, similar amounts (about 4.5%) were attributed to the tail-race problem and the decision not to raise Lake Manapouri. Interestingly, some engineers apparently referred to the former loss as an engineering quirk to live with, whereas the failure to raise the lake level was avoidable and quite regrettable. A small loss was also attributed to the reduction in storage necessary to 'save' Lake Te Anau. At almost every meeting of the guardians, NZED staff revealed the generation potential of water spilled down the lower Waiau River, such as was necessary to comply with our lake-management guidelines. The guardians were not swayed by such comments and responded accordingly.

Substantial amounts of government information, previously withheld from the public, were released for our use. Only four meetings were held during the second year – one of these involving the ministers for both the environment and electricity, the commissioner for the environment, and Dr Bob Kirk of Canterbury University – to assess the environmental problems associated with low lake levels. We also initiated baseline monitoring of beaches and vegetation at representative sites on the Te Anau lakeshore (under natural conditions prior to the Te Anau control structure becoming operational in April 1974) and also at Lake Manapouri.

In 1974 abnormally low rainfall in the major catchments created a serious electricity shortage. This resulted in a request from the Minister of Electricity, Tom McGuigan, to lower the minimum level on Manapouri by one foot to meet an unprecedented situation of relieving the national grid of its significant contribution to the aluminium smelter's requirement. The minister revealed that this had been occurring for about 10 days. Aware of the likely environmental damage associated with such a draw-down, I reluctantly agreed to half this amount, conditional on the minister's requesting a reduction in demand from Comalco's smelter. The minister agreed but, given the negative response from the company, who rejected the minister's request – plus criticism the guardians sustained from some quarters for compromising their responsibility – we notified the minister that we would be unlikely to concede to a similar request in the future. Fortunately, heavy rain kept the lake levels within our guidelines.

In the third year problems associated with exceptionally heavy rainfall in Fiordland prompted an increase to six meetings. The first storm during Easter spurred local guardian John Moore to enquire as to the reasons for a delay in opening the Te Anau control gates. After contacting the operators at West Arm and Systems Control at Islington without satisfaction, John conveyed his concern to Invercargill Labour MP, J.B. Munro, who advised him to contact the minister of electricity without delay. He did so on Easter Sunday, since the operating rules agreed to by the guardians to meet their high-level guidelines had already been exceeded. In response, the Te Anau control gates were opened wide almost immediately, yet both lakes continued to rise and reached near-record levels in early April. Lake Te Anau exceeded guidelines for its high operating range in early May, due to partial closure of the control gates (in an effort to minimise damage to the vulnerable Manapouri Control Structure then under construction), when further heavy rain again raised the lake to a near-record level on 22 May. Manapouri's level fell more rapidly than Te Anau's because its control structure was still incomplete. There was some immediate and obvious damage to the foreshore of Te Anau township, as well as considerable inconvenience to tourists and lake operators. Preparations were made to sand-bag the main access road into Te Anau, which would have been necessary had the lake risen a further 24 cm. Most boats had to be removed from the boat harbour since the mooring poles were submerged and jetties became generally unusable.

Heavy rain in late July again brought both lakes into their high operating ranges but for a much longer period at Te Anau. The management guidelines for that lake were again exceeded for a considerable period, and there had been some speculation as to the likely impact of this on the shoreline forests. In mid- to late December, some dying off became apparent along parts of the Te Anau lakeshore. By February 1976 it was clear that several hundred trees were dead or dying, particularly on the many deltas around the lake.

We arranged a special survey, which confirmed the death of perhaps 1000 mature trees, mostly silver and mountain beech but also at least 15 other tree species, plus several shrubs and herbs, mostly on deltas and almost certainly because of the unnaturally prolonged flooding of

The Delta Burn beach at the head of South Arm, Lake Te Anau, showing dead beech trees lining the lakeshore as a result of unnaturally high lake levels, 10 April 1976.

the lake.[75] A high incidence of pinhole borer in the affected beech trees was considered a possible cause by NZED staff, but forest entomologist specialist Bob Milligan deemed it to be a secondary effect: the borer was facilitated by the dead and dying trees. Although the loss of these many lakeshore plants was regrettable, it also had its positive side. It was extremely valuable in providing verification of the management guidelines for the high operating range, particularly since the mortality was essentially confined to Lake Te Anau, where the high-level guidelines had been exceeded.[76] Enthusiasm and support for our guidelines increased among our engineering associates as a result.

The guardians were wary about becoming politically active prior to the 1975 general election but were nevertheless concerned for the outcome and at the lack of any formal protection for the lakes at this time. We expressed an interest in hearing the policies of the various political parties in relation to future lake-level management, but did so without promoting our continued role as guardians. Many others were making similar enquiries. The Labour government had announced a clear policy of continuing with the existing situation. This was also the position of the other political parties, except for National, whose leader, Rob Muldoon, refused to respond until 10 days out from the election, when the issue could no longer be ignored. When confronted with it in Marlborough, he announced that the National Party would 'adopt word for word the policy of the Labour Government on Lakes Manapouri and Te Anau'.[77] When asked by the media to respond to this situation, I was happy to state that these lakes were no longer a political issue.

Given National's victory in this election, we were relieved to have such a commitment. The Ministry of Works, however, was soon lobbying the new government to be given responsibility for advising on lake management, thus displacing the guardians. This seemed most likely in mid-1977, when one of our foundation members, Wilson Campbell of Te Anau, resigned. We were reassured to have National MP for Invercargill, Norman Jones – an early Save Manapouri campaigner – appointed to fill this vacancy, an act that clearly confirmed National's support for the guardians' role continuing.

A study was commissioned from Canterbury University to assess in detail the sandy beaches of both lakes, under professor Bob Kirk's supervision. This was conducted largely by Dick Pickrill as a Ph.D. project. Pickrill concluded that 'recommendations for operational control of the two lakes confirmed that the guidelines drawn up by the guardians could not be improved on and if adhered to should maintain stability of the lakeshore beaches'.[78] Pickrill's study was important in further convincing the engineers of the validity of the lake-management guidelines in achieving our prime purpose: safeguarding the natural features and stability of the vulnerable shorelines while optimising the hydroelectric potential of the water resource. With the support of the engineers, we were able to convince the politicians of the new National government to formalise the guidelines, though amendments to the Manapouri–Te Anau Development Act were still some time off.

In December 1977 the government officially accepted the guardians' lake-operating guidelines. In the following January, the minister for the environment confirmed that renegotiation with Comalco meant that 'the Government is no longer under an obligation to raise the level of Lake Manapouri.' The guidelines were ministerially endorsed as:

> ... a sound basis within which the levels of Lakes Manapouri and Te Anau will be operated except when prevented by unforeseeable natural or by emergency situations such as those involving the safety of human life or the integrity of the control structures. They are an acceptable compromise between protecting the unique environmental and ecological features of the lakes system and maximizing the energy output of the Manapouri Power Station ... The development of these guidelines is the culmination of a long period of hard work, careful communication, and improved understanding among scientists, engineers and administrators. It is a real achievement in which opposing views have been brought together and reconciled to a very important end.[79]

There was also an official undertaking by NZED to record in its annual report to parliament the degree of compliance with the guidelines and reasons for any non-compliance. The department further announced that it expected to achieve 93% utilisation of the available water while operating within the guidelines. In October 1979 it commissioned the National Film Unit, under the direction of Greg Stitt, to produce a documentary on the Manapouri–Te Anau controversy, in which the guardians featured. At a meeting in November 1980 the film *A Question of Power? The Manapouri Debate* was shown. There was general satisfaction with this production, including what was seen as objective and unbiased information on a challenging subject.

One concern of the guardians was the diverted Mararoa River. In flood, this was carrying a heavy sediment load (averaging some 30,000 cu. m annually) as well as weeds, particularly gorse, and dead stock, up-river from the control structure into Lake Manapouri. The sediment was being dumped at the confluence of the now-stilled waters of the lower Waiau River, gradually choking its channel to the point where the gates in the control structure immediately downstream would soon serve little purpose. The government agreed that these problems should be

Lower Waiau River, laden with a variety of debris, entering the apparently warmer waters of Lake Manapouri and being submerged, 31 October 1977. Les Hutchins.

urgently addressed. The dirty floodwaters of the Mararoa River were monitored to assess the threshold for its diversion downstream through the automated control gates and on down the lower Waiau River, regardless of the level of Lake Manapouri. In addition, the lower kilometre of the Mararoa River was diverted towards the control gates so that when these were opened during floods, the accumulated gravel would be swept through the gates and so down the channel of this river, as had occurred naturally.

Amendments to the 1963 Manapouri–Te Anau Development Act were finally achieved in 1981, when the lake-raising clauses were replaced. Section 4A(1), the 'Operating guidelines for levels of Lakes Manapouri and Te Anau', was inserted:

> The Minister shall from time to time promulgate by notice in the Gazette, operating guidelines, based on recommendations submitted to him by the Guardians of Lakes Manapouri and Te Anau and the corporation, for the levels of those lakes aimed to protect the existing patterns, ecological stability, and recreational values of their vulnerable shorelines and to optimise the energy output of the Manapouri power station.

We were reassured that the bill, as approved by the guardians, passed unchanged through both the select committee and the House, supported by all political parties. The guardians interpreted this as indicating a general acceptance of the compromise they had proposed, based on detailed scientific evaluation and consultation with all interested parties. A summarised form of the guidelines was published as a notice in the *Gazette* on 3 December 1981, with amended versions on 1 March 1990 and 14 April 1993.

1987 AND BEYOND

In 1987, as part of a wider programme of government restructuring, the operational responsibility for the Manapouri power station was transferred from the MOE's Electricity Department to the Electricity Corporation of New Zealand (ECNZ) under the terms of the State Owned Enterprises Act 1986. An application by Comalco in late March for an interim injunction to prevent this transfer was declined by the High Court. Soon afterwards, certain members of Cabinet commented that ECNZ might sell the Manapouri power station to Comalco or enter into a joint venture with it. The guardians informed seven ministers, including the prime minister, of their concern, particularly at the Comalco spokesman's comment that the company would be interested in obtaining its electrical energy exclusively from the Manapouri power station. The minister of energy responded that 'any possible resale to Comalco (NZ) could have no effect on government control of the lake operating levels and that the Te Anau and Manapouri Lakes would continue to be secure from undesirable environmental damage.'[80]

Our concerns were not fully allayed, however. The pattern of lake management to date had included a safety margin to minimise the risk of exceeding the guidelines, since only 'best endeavours' were required for compliance with the gazette notice. We were concerned that a private company – and Comalco in particular – would minimise the safety margins to maximise its economic return, given the relatively very cheap price of Manapouri power.

SAVE MANAPOURI – AND BEYOND

At the guardians' October 1988 meeting, Comalco's general manager, Kerry McDonald, indicated that the company was interested in having the Manapouri generation and transmission assets owned by a company in which Comalco would have a minority interest. This was suggested at 20%, the balance perhaps to be distributed between its smelter partner Sumitomo (5%), Electricorp and other New Zealand interests. Further,

> Comalco is not interested in purchasing the lake [Manapouri], or land other than that directly linked with the generation and transmission assets. Comalco envisages that the lake will be operated as at present and that the same authorities will continue to operate and guide the operation of the lake. Comalco has no intention to seek any change in the Lake's operating rules and is well aware of the environmental sensitivity associated with the operation of the Lake. Comalco envisages that the generation and transmission assets will continue to be operated by the Electricity Corporation as an integrated part of the system, so that maximum efficiency is gained from their use. In addition it is envisaged that there would be a contractual arrangement between the Electricity Corporation and the smelter to provide additional or make-up electricity when necessary and when the system has such energy available.[81]

The guardians reminded him that the company had showed negligible concern for the welfare of the lakes in 1974 when requested to reduce consumption to avoid lowering Lake Manapouri below its natural minimum. Following the guardians' firm recommendation against privatisating the Manapouri power station, particularly if Comalco were to be the buyer, the minister for the environment, on 28 May 1990, declared: 'no decision has been made to sell all or any part of the generating capacity of Manapouri Power Station to Comalco. I can assure you that if such a sale was to proceed then the Government would ensure that the integrity of the lakes would not be threatened.'[82]

Another major flood in the spring of 1988 produced record high levels on both lakes, higher than since records began in 1926 and the highest since the historic 1878 flood. Lake Te Anau reached 205.11 m (30 cm above its previously recorded natural maximum), while Lake Manapouri reached 181.54 m (1.06 m higher than the previous natural record). Such levels occurred despite both the Te Anau and Manapouri control gates being wide open since early September and the Manapouri power station generating at maximum capacity throughout the period that lake levels were in their high operating ranges. Computer simulations of the events revealed that these lake levels were significantly lower than they would have been without hydroelectric development (Lake Te Anau by 30 cm and Lake Manapouri by 33 cm). Nevertheless, the high operating guidelines were substantially exceeded for both lakes, by up to 56 days for Lake Te Anau and up to 32 days at Manapouri.

As a result of the flood, physical damage around the lakeshores, both to Te Anau township and the forested sections, was conspicuous. However, tree mortality was notably less than in 1975, for reasons that were not obvious. Perhaps the season of flooding is important. A deputation from the local authority, Wallace County Council, indicated they were deeply worried about the situation and unconvinced by the computer simulation. There was concern about Electricorp's management of the lakes, their flood-warning network and procedures for the lower Waiau River, whereas Electricorp considered its warning had been adequate and similar to that of previous floods.

On 4 June 1988 the North Arm of Lake Te Anau suffered a severe earthquake, measuring 6.5 on the Richter scale. Reported on by geologists Sarah Beanland and Ian Turnbull, it triggered appreciable and widespread modifications to beaches of both lakes. However, there was no serious permanent damage.

In 1988, when large catamarans such as the *Fiordland Flyer* were introduced to Manapouri, the guardians commissioned another report from Bob Kirk, this time on the effects of wakes of large boats on the shoreline. According to Kirk, these boats had 'considerable potential to damage shorelines, especially beaches with thin sediment cover in restricted fetches, and adjacent to deep water ...'[83] On the basis of his recommendation, the guardians requested that DOC require all large

SAVE MANAPOURI – AND BEYOND

The original Lake Guardians at the 21st anniversary celebration, West Arm, Lake Manapouri, October 1994, left to right: Wilson Campbell, me, John Moore, Jim McFarlane and Les Hutchins; inset, the late Ron McLean. Christine Henderson.

launches operating on the eastern section of Lake Manapouri to travel more than 500 m offshore, and reduce speed to below 15 knots when within 500 m of the shore. Launches were also required to travel at less than five knots when approaching the lower Waiau River inlet and Pearl Harbour. The guardians also emphasised that speed restrictions for all craft within the lower Waiau River needed to be enforced because of the vulnerable state of the riverbanks there.

Retained at the pleasure of the minister (environment/conservation) during our first 17 years, the guardians were accorded legal status in the Conservation Law Reform Act 1990. While their role did not change for Manapouri and Te Anau, it now also embraced Lake Monowai. With the minister's agreement, the guardians called for public submissions on the present and future use and management of Monowai. Only 10 responses were received. However, these usefully confirmed the recreational importance of the lake and its environs. The fringe of dead trees was generally accepted as a unique historic feature, of both detriment and benefit to lake users but impracticable to remove at this time.

The owners of the Monowai Power Station, Southland Electric Power Supply, agreed to lakeshore surveys of vegetation and beaches by Peter Johnson (then at DSIR) and Bob Kirk. Their reports revealed ongoing slow but steady improvements in the condition of the lakeshore, which had been detrimentally affected by a 2-m rise in lake level in 1926. Based on these reports, the guardians recommended continuing the recent pattern of management. Guidelines for the management of Lake Monowai were drafted on the same basis as for Manapouri and Te Anau but designed to facilitate lakeshore restoration. The company formally adopted these guidelines in 1996, and subsequent owners – first Trust-Power and then Pioneer Generation – have also formally adopted them. Twelve representative transects of the beach and shoreline vegetation used by Bob Kirk and Peter Johnson were permanently marked to serve as future monitoring sites.

During the 1991 winter, the outflow from Te Anau down the upper Waiau was reduced to a mere five cumecs (cubic metres per second) in response to very low lake levels and a statutory responsibility not to exceed the lake-management guidelines. There were no formal guidelines to provide some measure of balance between river and lake management in such circumstances. The period of low flow was fortunately brief because of several requests to increase the river flow. As a result, the guardians – in conjunction with Electricorp, the Southland Fish and Game Council and Southland Regional Council – prepared draft guidelines. Electricorp expressed 'severe reservations about whether it is technically feasible to manage both lakes [Te Anau and Manapouri] and the river without increasing the risk of undesirable effects on the lakes'.[84]

The guardians, however, were aware of their statutory responsibility for advising on the management both of the lakes and 'the rivers flowing in and out of those lakes'. The ecological impact of this event on the upper Waiau seemed relatively minor, mitigated by both its brevity (less than one day) and the time of the year. Even with the increased flow, the lake-management guidelines were not exceeded at this time. The parties agreed to adopt minimum flows of 115 cumecs and, in exceptional circumstances and with consensus, an absolute minimum of 80 cumecs. These limits were implemented on a trial basis, with further work and modelling aimed at identifying an appropriate regime for regulating the rate of change of flows in the river (ramping rates).

In 1994 the guardians celebrated their 21st year. We commissioned Dunedin author Neville Peat to prepare a comprehensive history of the Manapouri campaign and the role of the guardians up to that time. Funding for the exercise was generously provided by Fiordland Travel, DOC and ECNZ, and the book was launched at ECNZ's West Arm hostel. Almost 100 people, including many Save Manapouri campaigners, attended this function. The Minister of Conservation, Denis Marshall, in launching the book, proudly revealed that he had been a Save Manapouri supporter and gatherer of petition signatures during the early 1970s. All five surviving original guardians were present, but unfortunately a family bereavement prevented the family of the other founding guardian and major campaigner, the late Ron McLean, from attending. Les Hutchins and myself, both of whom were foundation guardians and still active, were invited to cut the specially decorated cake provided by ECNZ.

An important development during the 1990s was the modelling of the lake-management guidelines and development of the MANTAray model, specifically to assist with the management of the Fiordland lakes system. This not only improved integration of the Manapouri power generation with that in other parts of the country, it also reduced the frequency of guideline excession through displaying real-time information for each of the two lakes with current levels, the various discharges and any caveats required by the guidelines, for example durations and/or draw-down rates in the high- and low-operating ranges.

A major exercise for the guardians during the early 1990s was their involvement in the Waiau River Working Party. This was established by ECNZ in collaboration with the Southland Regional Council to fulfill

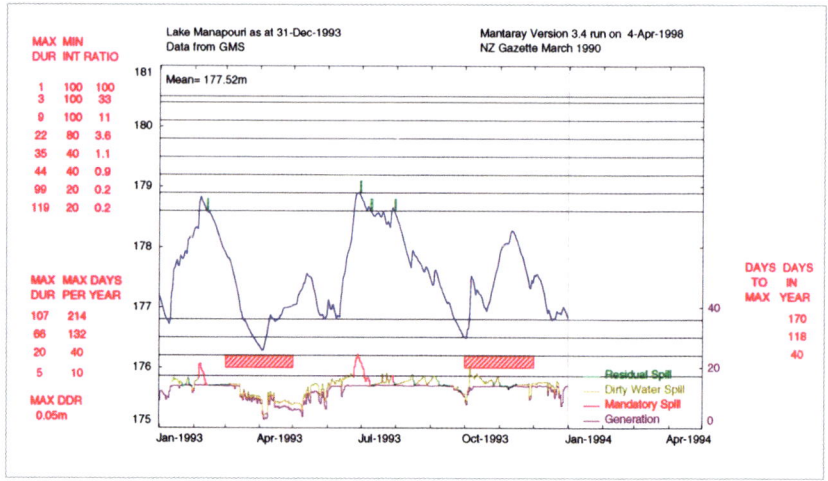

Manapouri lake-management guidelines and plotting of its levels using the MANTAray model, January 1993–January 1994.

a government decree that all resource consents issued in the form of empowering legislation would be reissued as consents by the relevant regional councils under the Resource Management Act 1991. In light of earlier problems experienced by ECNZ with water-right renewals for their Tongariro power scheme, and subsequently their upper Waitaki hydroelectric complex, the corporation extended an invitation to any concerned or interested stakeholders to join a working party. Clearly this would be a demanding exercise, and some 20 organisations became involved. Four guardians contributed to several 'task groups' set up by the working party, which included helping to identify the most appropriate researchers for each. The guardians were reassured by the working party's unanimous agreement that their role was an integral aspect of the resource consents. Both our lake-management guidelines and the lakeshore-monitoring programme were included in the consents.

In the original development act, there had been no provision for compensation flows down the lower Waiau River through the Manapouri control structure. This was to become a serious issue. Trial flows were recommended, as were the gate opening and closing procedures for both the Te Anau and Manapouri (Mararoa) control structures, to simulate natural patterns of the river flow more closely. Following these trial releases, there was general agreement for 16 cumecs over the five warmest months and 12 cumecs during the cooler five months, with the other two months being transitional.

It seemed remarkable to me that all interested parties were satisfied with the outcome of the Waiau River Working Party, whose activities included forming three trusts aimed at restoring the natural resources lost and providing financial compensation where lost values could not be restored. Apparently, all parties were satisfied, since the regional council received no formal objections to any of the consents sought in late 1996. This reflected not only the spirit of the exercise but also the important roles of the ECNZ facilitator, Mark France, and the working party chair, Jan Riddell. The working party would continue to function (as the Waiau Working Party) with a supervisory role, particularly to assess results of the comprehensive monitoring programme. The guardians retained membership and also their responsibility for overseeing lake-management guidelines in consultation with the power station owners.

The resource consents require lakeshore monitoring at five-yearly intervals, or at the discretion of the guardians and the regional council, whenever the guidelines have been exceeded. To date, the results of monitoring have generally been very satisfactory. Typical of the reports is one provided in 1996 by professor Bob Kirk. Referring to lakes Manapouri and Te Anau in 1989, he stated:

> The beaches ... are not 'forced' in any way by the Operating Range and the manner in which ECNZ staff handle it from day to day and year to year. In my view that is real management success because it's not simply an absence of adverse effects, it's the possibility to promote essentially natural behaviour ... I think the long record now available there is unique in both management and scientific terms. It shows some extremely interesting and important aspects of the environment, not least how beaches behave longer term and how they both respond to and recover from major 'traumas' like the earthquake and floods of 1988, meanwhile

being under continuous human management of water levels. In my view, the long record also serves to demonstrate to science and the community alike how folk and agencies can come together to make an 'environmental success story' such as the management of Lakes Manapouri and Te Anau has been.[85]

A SECOND TAIL-RACE TUNNEL FOR WEST ARM

From early on, the guardians were made aware that the tail-race tunnel suffered higher than expected head loss and that there was thus the prospect of a second, but it was not until April 1994 that we were formally presented with a proposal. The executive summary of this 'Manapouri Tailrace Investigation Project' declared that an additional 228 mW of power could be 'generated from the same amount of water, utilised within current guidelines'. Accepting that the 'original Power Station proposal and the nationwide opposition that followed is rightly recognised as the beginning of New Zealand's "green" consciousness', ECNZ endeavoured to undertake wide consultation 'to achieve a project which is environmentally aware':

> At present it is believed that the majority of impacts will be restricted to the construction phase and site. It should also be noted that the proposed new site will be restricted to the areas which have been affected by previous construction works. Potentially the greatest environmental impact will be the disposal of spoil from the second tailrace. It is proposed that, through appropriate planning, the spoil which will be deposited at Deep Cove on the existing disposal area can be rehabilitated and revegetated to a better standard than presently exists.[86]

The guardians offered their unanimous support for this project through to its completion. We had always supported maximising the efficiency of water use. This proposal involved increasing the power station's peak generation capacity by almost 30% from 585 to 760 mW and the annual generation by some 13%, without increasing the throughput of water or modifying the lake-management guidelines. A further 6% increase in annual generation (or about 710 gWh, a 19% increase over that possible

SAVE MANAPOURI – AND BEYOND

Interpretive sign of the Manapouri–Te Anau power scheme, which features at three locations in the area.

at the time) would be possible while complying with the guidelines. This would nevertheless require an additional resource consent to address the additional discharge of fresh water into the marine environment and ecosystems of Doubtful Sound and possible impacts on the lower Waiau River. The former remains the subject of continuing research.

The guardians were kept fully informed on progress with the second tail-race tunnel and the specially designed 10 m-diameter tunnel-boring machine that the engineers used. We were represented both at the 'start up' and at the official opening, a major celebration at Te Anau and Deep Cove in May 2002. At the celebratory dinner in Te Anau, I was ostentatiously placed at the top table with the prime minister and senior executives of Meridian Energy. Considerable credit for the excellent environmental standards and public relations maintained throughout this exercise must go to the project manager, Tom Martin, who was specially commissioned from the US. The second tunnel is apparently performing to specifications.

MANAPOURI SAVED

In 1998 our silver jubilee was celebrated with a special event at the Manapouri Lakeside Motor Inn, attended by about a hundred invited guests, including the Minister of Conservation, Nick Smith, the local MP Bill English and many other notables. The minister unveiled a special plaque, mounted on a large rock that had been transported from the heart of the second tail-race tunnel. The inscription reads:

MANAPOURI SAVED

The Manapouri Campaign (1959–72) was New Zealand's greatest environmental battle involving thousands of New Zealanders from all walks of life. The campaign saved Lakes Manapouri and Te Anau from being raised for the purpose of hydro-electric generation.

This monument is a tribute to the campaigners, their love and respect for natural beauty. Their fortitude and tenacity triumphed over political and official indifference.

A tribute is also paid to the Guardians of Lakes Manapouri and Te Anau whose dedicated and vigilant work since 1973 has preserved the natural beauty and ecological values of the lakes.

Save Manapouri was a catchcry of a generation. It echoes still.

'In wilderness is the preservation of the world': Henry David Thoreau

The year after was my final annual report. When rumours circulated that the minister had terminated my role as a guardian, it was reassuring to be approached by senior ECNZ staff as to whether I would be willing to do contract work for the corporation. Surprised but delighted, I commented that the NZED's past general manager, the late Bruce McKenzie, 'would probably turn in his grave if he knew such an offer had been made'. I appreciated being asked by Meridian, the new SOE owner/manager, to peer-review the next lakeshore-monitoring report of Manapouri and Te Anau, and by TrustPower, the report for Lake Monowai. I was also invited to attend future meetings of the guardians where I had the opportunity to witness the excellent leadership of

SAVE MANAPOURI – AND BEYOND

Dedication of the commemoration rock, Manapouri, left to right: Roger Sutton, myself, Minister of Conservation Nick Smith, and Southland Conservator Lou Sanson, 7 October 1998. Pat Mark.

the new chair, Mason Stretch, geography master at John McGlashan College in Dunedin and ex-Fiordland College pupil, who had been a guardian for several years. Winton hydrologist Dave Riddell succeeded Mason in 2008, followed by Chris Shaw of Te Anau in 2011 and Teri McClelland of Invercargill in 2012. I continue to receive their reports and follow their activities with interest.

I have been delighted to present the Manapouri–Te Anau case study at two international conferences, in 1993 and 1998. The first was in Stresa, Italy, at the Fifth International Conference on Lake Ecosystem Conservation and Management, where I presented a paper co-authored with Mark France of ECNZ and Glen Lauder of DOC, with financial support from ECNZ and the University of Otago. One of the few contributions from the Southern Hemisphere, this paper was a rare bright spot among the generally depressing reports from 35 countries, which mostly described the serious and continuing degradation of water quality and quantity, alongside declining biodiversity, throughout the world. Water depletion, siltation, toxic chemical contamination, acidification and particularly eutrophication were among the most frequent agents of ecological degradation described.

The second presentation was in Banff, Canada, in 1998, at the North American Lake Management Society's 18th International Symposium, Co-operative Lake and Watershed Management: Linking Communities, Industry and Government. Kieran Devine of ECNZ, Carol West of DOC and I co-authored an outsized poster, 'Integrating Nature Conservation with Hydroelectric Development: Conflict resolution with Lakes Manapouri and Te Anau, Fiordland National Park, New Zealand'. The case study fitted perfectly with the symposium's theme, and the society invited us to submit a full paper to their journal *Lake and Reservoir Management*. This appeared in the March 2001 issue, with an impressive cover photograph of Lake Manapouri supplied by Fiordland Travel Ltd. While the article had the same title as the poster, Keith Turner, CEO of Meridian Energy (owner of the Manapouri power station since April 1999) replaced Kieran Devine.

In 2009 the guardians called on me to make a joint submission on Meridian's application to increase maximum flows and modify management of lake levels, within their formal guidelines, as a component of the Manapouri Tailrace Amended Discharge Project (MTAD). This followed the successful operation of the completed second tail-race tunnel. Concerningly, Meridian proposed to hold the lakes for shorter periods in both their high and low operating ranges by extending the periods in their main ranges. I emphasised the legal requirement to protect the existing patterns and ecological stability of the lakes' vulnerable shorelines. In order to meet this legal requirement, it was important for the lakes to span their full natural ranges periodically. While this was generally accepted, the commissioners decided that future monitoring would determine the matter and, if necessary, there would be future negotiations between the guardians and Meridian. The guardians did not appeal the decision, and I have not had further discussions on the issue.

In 2012 I was also persuaded by David Kember, secretary of the Wellington-based national Save Manapouri Campaign Committee, to make a joint submission to the Parliamentary Finance and Expenditure Select Committee on the Mixed Ownership Model Bill. In our submission we expressed our view that, with the dilution of government control inherent in the bill, Meridian would be either incentivised or pressured to manage the lake levels in a way that could stress their vulnerable natural shoreline features. We noted the current 'safety margin' adopted in recognition of this vulnerability. Our submission asserted that this would probably not continue once management was required to consider both private and government interests. Predictably, the submission was obviously ignored when the committee later reported.

On reflection, there were times during the Save Manapouri Campaign when I wondered whether my career as a scientist would be wrecked by political ill-will or the manipulation of officialdom. In his history of the campaign, *Manapouri Saved*, Neville Peat quotes me as saying, 'as a young scientist, I felt vulnerable – at times out on a limb on an issue that was highly political. Many government scientists, unable or unwilling in terms of job security to speak out themselves, urged me to take a stand.'[87] To that I should add that one very senior government scientist, Sir Charles Fleming FRS, geologist and senior palaeontologist with the DSIR Geological Survey, was an outspoken critic of the lake-raising proposal. Fleming was undoubtedly my most important peer and mentor on this issue.

Despite such anxiety, my long involvement with the Manapouri–Te Anau issue has been satisfying on several fronts. I have had the opportunity to use the knowledge acquired to promote important ecological aspects of lake management;[88] the numerous islands in Manapouri are of particular scientific interest[89] and along the way, I wrote a number of papers,[90] eventually co-publishing details of the final and successful outcome with Meridian's CEO in an international journal.[91] My greatest satisfaction, however, has been being able to convey to the wider public the value of natural areas and the significance of integrating ecological principles to achieve the sustainable use of our natural resources.

6

QUANGOS I HAVE KNOWN

Over many years, I have been involved with a wide selection of environmental societies, boards and organisations – both Quasi-Autonomous Non-Governmental Organisations (quangos) and Environmental Non-Governmental Organisations (ENGOs). Much less common now than they used to be, quangos were once a popular means by which government departments sought input from the wider community (the Guardians of Lakes Manapouri and Te Anau, discussed in Chapter 5, is one notable example). ENGOs, by contrast, have no direct government involvement. On both a regional and national level, the dynamics of such organisations uniquely influence environmental outcomes in this country and are thus commonly politically charged.

The quangos I have known have fulfilled many different tasks. After Manapouri, the Environmental Council's Working Party on the Environmental Movement in New Zealand, for instance, assessed, among other issues, the availability of government information on matters environmental. Its main recommendation was that, with limited exceptions, government information should be readily available whenever in the public interest. This was certainly a general feeling following the Manapouri controversy. Despite amendments, the Official Information Act 1982 today remains an important tool in dealing with many current environmental issues. Another quango, MAF Qual's Advisory Panel on the Biological Control of Gorse, assessed the proposed introduction of the European gorse mite amid widespread concern that it would result in the demise of gorse and impact on the honey industry. After much consultation the panel approved strict conditions for initial trials. Since then, kills of up to 20% of individual bushes have been reported, but total removal seems unlikely.

From the time of their inception in the 1960s, quangos have materially shaped the character and extent of New Zealand's conservation lands. As well as recommending protected status for tracts of land with high conservation value, they have also played a role in managing prospective development – forestry and hydroelectricity, for instance – to limit adverse effects on the natural environment but with varying success. Quangos are thus an important historical lens through which to understand the contemporary New Zealand landscape. I have endeavoured here to relate the workings of various bodies with which I have been involved, illustrating that numerous now-celebrated parks and reserves have their origins not in the enlightened attitudes of politicians and bureaucrats but in isolated acts of strong advocacy by the interested public.

TECHNICAL ADVISORY COMMITTEE ON RESERVES AND SCENIC AMENITIES, DUNEDIN REGIONAL PLANNING AUTHORITY, 1968–78

This municipal quango was formed to advise the Regional Planning Authority on reserves and other scenic amenities within the Dunedin City area.[92] During my time on it, the committee managed to raise the profile and status of several local reserves. The boundaries of Mount Cargill Scenic Reserve were extended and defined, and the upper slopes and skyline of Flagstaff were transferred from a tree-planting reserve into Flagstaff Scenic Reserve.

Chaired by geography professor Ron Lister, the committee also zoned the Dunedin Town Belt, distinguishing the predominantly exotic section in the south from the largely indigenous section to the north. We emphasised the importance of controlling weeds, particularly sycamore, in the native section. Voluntary groups were organised to assist with this problem before the council staff assumed responsibility.

In 1973 we completed a report, 'Otago Harbour as a Regional Recreational Resource',[93] which paid particular attention to Aramoana, at the harbour's entrance. Despite the industrial zoning of much of the flat land there, we recommended that the intertidal portion be formally reserved to protect its high ecological values. We were, of course, unaware of the two highly controversial aluminium-smelter proposals that were soon to follow, the second of which eventually resulted in an even larger area being formally protected. My separate involvement in the Save Aramoana Campaign is discussed in Chapter 7.

SCIENTIFIC CO-ORDINATING COMMITTEE ON BEECH RESEARCH, NEW ZEALAND FOREST SERVICE, 1973–83

The Scientific Co-ordinating Committee on Beech Research contained representatives from all relevant government departments[94] – the Botany Division and Soil Bureau of the DSIR, the Wildlife Service, MAF and the Forest Service – alongside two nominees from the Royal Society of New Zealand. Established in the early 1970s, the committee grew out of general public concern at the Forest Service's proposed South Island Beech Utilisation Scheme. It was chaired by Colin Bassett, director of the Forest Service's Forestry Research Institute, with senior ecologist John Nicholls as technical advisor.

The South Island Beech Utilisation Scheme sought to establish some 400,000 ha. of exotic and mixed exotic–native forests in North Westland and western Southland, with smaller areas in the Nelson and Catlins regions. The committee was created specifically to address scientific aspects of this proposal. We soon recognised the need for a representative system of reserves for baseline research and biodiversity/ecosystem conservation – referred to as 'ecological areas' – within these regions. The committee assessed serious local erosion following clearance of indigenous forest in parts of North Westland and associated comprehensive catchment studies of nutrient and soil losses under different logging regimes at the Mai Mai Research Area near Reefton.

A major responsibility of the committee was determining the need,

QUANGOS I HAVE KNOWN

New Zealand Forest Service's Scientific Co-ordinating Committee for Beech Research, left to right, back: Harry Bunn, Colin Bassett, John Nichols, Morgan Williams, a conservancy forester, Colin Ogle, Geoff Baylis; front, Eric Godley and Mike Leamy.

extent and design of these forest reserves. Considerable discussion centred around the guidelines for selection. These were distilled into seven principles:

1. It should represent the full range of land-forms, soil sequences, animal communities and unmodified vegetation of the ecological district. The inclusion of some modified vegetation may sometimes add to the value of an ecological area;
2. It should be large with, say, a minimum of 1000 ha; a single large reserve is preferable to two or more smaller reserves of the same total area. This is particularly true for preserving the greatest diversity of bird populations;
3. It is considered legitimate to create small reserves to preserve unique features of special value, although these could present special problems in protection;
4. It should include at least one complete undisturbed catchment of a permanent waterway;

5. It should have a compact shape, with the minimum perimeter for the area involved;
6. Wherever possible, its boundaries should be clearly defined by natural features;
7. It should be unroaded, at least within the main catchment.[95]

The committee also developed a biogeographic framework of ecological regions and districts within which to assess adequate representation. The North Westland Beech Project Area exercise – where 11 ecological districts were identified, with some 20 areas recommended for protection – did much to redress the historical imbalance in altitudinal distribution of formally protected lowland and upland forest.[96]

The outcome was so well received by the public that the minister of forests requested that the committee complete a similar exercise for all state indigenous forests. Rapid progress was made: by July 1983 some 55 ecological areas embracing about 100,000 ha. had been gazetted, while the minister had approved in principle a further 58 areas covering 144,000 ha. The committee had also recommended an additional 28 ecological areas totalling 59,000 ha. I am unsure about the final outcome, the committee being disbanded soon afterwards, to be replaced by the Protected Areas Scientific Advisory Committee (PASAC). I was not a member of this, a joint committee between the Forest Service and the Department of Lands and Survey, as I had 'muddied the waters' with this department over the Nardoo debate (see Chapter 4), but it played a similar role spanning both departments.

Not all recommendations of the Scientific Co-ordinating Committee were formally gazetted. Despite a major catch-up exercise by DOC soon after its establishment in 1987, some remain only as proposals. The Burmeister Ecological Area, for instance, recommended by the committee largely on my advice, covers much of the coastal plain between Hindley Creek and the Arawhata River in South Westland. This area contains the country's southernmost pakihi, as well as important ecological sequence representing transitions from pakihi wetland to shrubland–woodland and mixed beech–podocarp–broadleaved forest.

I supervised a project with several students on these sequences in the mid-1970s.[97] This mixed forest covers extensive areas on the flood plain as well as an impressive series of adjacent slacks and dune ridges arranged parallel to the coast and associated with recent aggradation of the coastline, which was studied later.[98]

In 1977 Peter Wardle, Bill Lee and I were asked to advise on conservation needs for George Wilkinson and Keith Garrett's Land Use Study of South Westland,[99] a joint exercise between the Department of Lands and Survey and the Forest Service. Peter recommended reservation of much of the Ohinemaka forest block west of the state highway between the Mahitahi and Paringa rivers, while I recommended the Burmeister area and Bill his area of research interest, the Red Hills to the south. All three areas have since been protected as part of the South West New Zealand World Heritage Area (Te Wāhipounamu),[100] the Red Hills being incorporated into Mount Aspiring National Park.

As well as the Scientific Co-ordinating Committee on Beech Research, I was also involved with another Forest Service committee, the Protection Forestry Research Advisory Committee, from 1973 to 1978.[101] The Protection Forestry Division had been created on the advice of Jack Holloway, who initially led the division, later to be succeeded by John Morris. This research committee sought ways of stabilising steep (protection) land: forests, shrublands and alpine vegetation of the mountainous regions outside of both the national parks and the South Island pastoral high country. The main research area was the Craigieburn Range of mid-Canterbury. However, planting trials, mostly of lodgepole pine, were widespread and subsequently mostly invasive.

NEW ZEALAND NATIONAL PARKS AND RESERVES AUTHORITY, 1981–90

As the Royal Forest and Bird Protection Society's nominee, I was a member of the National Parks and Reserves Authority for its full term. Replacing the National Parks Authority, it was in turn replaced by the Conservation Authority. Chaired throughout by David Thom, a civil engineer from Auckland, the authority had responsibilities under

Members of the National Parks and Reserves Authority walking the proposed Kepler Track, November 1985.

the National Parks Act 1980 and the Reserves Act 1977. It had many notable achievements, due in no small part to the commitment and patience of its chair and the enthusiasm of all members to achieve what was possible in conservation – with one interesting exception, involving a grazing concession in Westland. The authority functioned in co-operation with the Department of Lands and Survey, particularly Director General Bing Lucas, who was renowned for his commitment to conservation in New Zealand and abroad.

One of our first major exercises was to assess a proposal to add Waikukupa and South Okarito state forests to Westland National Park. In 1982 the government proposed including these two extensive, contiguous areas of mixed podocarp rainforest, which lie on the fluvio-glacial lowlands between the Waiho (Franz Josef) and Fox rivers, to the national park. In doing so, it was taking account of the overwhelming majority of some 3500 submissions received on the future of these forest areas. While the authority was unanimous in its support, some members had doubts about southern Waikukupa. Here the Cook River had several years earlier flooded many hectares of kahikatea forest. With the trees starting to collapse, the area looked much less impressive than the rest of the forest. Soil scientist Les Molloy, the Federated Mountain Clubs (FMC) nominee, and I were keen to include the flood-devastated area as a valuable example of the natural dynamic processes on the outwash plains of Westland. As the discussion went past midnight, Bing Lucas told us that the Minister of Lands, also Minister of Forests, Jonathan Elworthy, had indicated that if the authority couldn't reach a decision, the whole proposal was off; the government was losing enthusiasm. However, Les and I persisted and finally won acceptance of our ecological message, with the authority resolving to recommend full representation.

Although the entire area was eventually declared a national park, Westland commissioner Julian Rodda undermined it by allowing a grazing concession on the flooded area soon afterwards. Unsurprisingly, later ecological surveys revealed serious weed invasion and degradation associated with this grazing, a problem that probably continues to this day. You win some, you lose some, despite best efforts.

Among the most notable of the authority's achievements was the establishment of two new national parks, Paparoa and Whanganui. Paparoa National Park (30,327 ha.) was opened in November 1987 after protracted discussion and debate with West Coast local authorities, communities and the Forest Service, which had previously administered the area. By contrast, local authorities and communities strongly supported the creation of Whanganui National Park (74,231 ha.), so that this proposal had a much shorter gestation. This park was opened in December 1986. The only major delay here was connected with Māori claims of ownership of the Whanganui River. As a result, the river was excluded from the proposal and still remains outside of the park.

The authority also had protracted discussions with the mining fraternity over adding the Red Hills mineral belt to Mount Aspiring National Park. This issue was finally resolved when the authority undertook to review the situation if and when a commercially viable enterprise could

The National Parks and Reserves Authority inspecting the proposed Whanganui National Park, May 1987.

be demonstrated for minerals in the area. While inclusion of the Haast Range in the park was less controversial, there was some concern with its lower elevation limit being set at 600 ft (183 m), this being just above the toe of the slope. The lower elevation limit would exclude all of the coastal plain, with its potentially merchantable forest, and open river flats adjacent to the lower Arawhata and Waiatoto rivers.

The proposal to add Waitutu State Forest to Fiordland National Park also involved stiff negotiations. Most contentious was the question of access to the Māori-owned (Waitutu Inc.) lands of the lower terraces, which might be required for future logging operations. The state forest area was finally added to the park, with conditions to address any future access needs. In the North Island, the impressive podocarp forests of Whirinaki were added to Te Urewera National Park. In Canterbury–Westland, the authority also negotiated small extensions to Arthur's Pass National Park.

Other than national parks, the authority's most significant achievement was establishing the Protected Natural Areas Programme. This resulted from the Minister of Lands, Koro Wetere, vesting responsibility for major sections of the Reserves Act in the authority. Launched in 1983, the programme followed the DSIR's Biological Resources Centre developing appropriate survey methods and criteria as well as a biogeographic framework of ecological regions and districts on which to base the surveys. Over the 1983–84 summer, field surveys were undertaken in four widely separate areas: Rodney Ecological District near Auckland, involving mostly privately owned land; East Cape Ecological District, involving largely Māori land; and the Mackenzie Ecological Region and Old Man Ecological District in the South Island, both of which were mostly high-country pastoral leasehold land.

A nationwide Register of Protected Natural Areas in 1984 confirmed that reserves were virtually absent from the South Island high country. In future years the authority concentrated much effort on improving this situation. Special teams, including university students employed by the Department of Lands and Survey, conducted the fieldwork, with supervision provided by DSIR, the Forest Service and university staff. The authority maintained some oversight of the programme and offered enthusiastic support throughout.

LAND SETTLEMENT BOARD, 1984–86

Becoming a member of the Land Settlement Board in its last three years was entirely unexpected, given my earlier dealings with it over the Nardoo catchment (see Chapter 4). Created by the Land Act 1948, the board consisted of 12 members. The minister of lands was the chair, the director general of lands its deputy (and usual) chair. The other members were the deputy director general, the department's field director (overseeing land development), nominees of the secretary of the treasury, the director general of agriculture, the valuer general, the general manager of the Rural Bank and Finance Corporation, and four non-government members appointed by the minister. Of these four non-government members, two were appointed after consultation with Federated Farmers. The other two were to represent the general public interest. Nevertheless, at the time, both of these other non-government positions were occupied by men who had held senior positions with Federated Farmers (John Kneebone was an ex-dominion president and Arthur Scaife an ex-chairman of their South Island high-country section).

Being aware that the ombudsman had criticised the board's composition with regard to its responsibilities for conservation and recreation – criticism made in the course of the Nardoo conflict – the opposition Labour Party responded. Following lobbying by Gerry McSweeney, Conservation Director of Forest & Bird, the party adopted as part of its policy for the 1984 General Election the desirability of wider representation on the board. After Labour won the election, Gerry contacted the new Minister of Lands, Koro Wetere, complimenting the government on this aspect of their policy. Gerry also noted that the terms of the two non-specified, non-government board members had expired and offered to supply the minister with names of three possible candidates. I reluctantly agreed to my name being included for one of these positions, given my recent clash with the board, but did so in the knowledge that the minister would likely make the appointment.

Subsequently, Allan Evans and I were invited by the minister to serve on the board; Allan was then president of FMC. We were to represent recreation, conservation and scientific interests. However, we had no voting rights since the two former members in these positions, curiously or fortuitiously, had just been re-appointed. We were warmly welcomed by the Deputy Chairman, Bing Lucas, and other board members to our first meeting but also reminded that our role was non-statutory and therefore without voting rights. There were many important issues and we were unconstrained in commenting on them (including the Nardoo issue: see Chapter 4). Within a year, I was offered a full voting position on the board, when Arthur Scaife retired.

Of particular interest to me was the board's deliberations on its proposed Mavora Lakes Pastoral Park in northern Southland, part of the original Burwood Station, which Lands and Survey had acquired for

Land Settlement Board, 1985, with the two new members: Allan Evans and me (front row, third and second from right), and the chair George McMillan (front centre).

land development. The Mavora area in the upper Mararoa catchment contains the North and South Mavora lakes, and comprises 35,000 ha. of mixed beech forest, shrubland, red- (copper) and snow-tussock grasslands and alpine-plant communities, including an ultramafic belt, at the more remote northern end of the station. The road entrance to the Mavora area is through impressive mixed mountain–red–silver beech forest and past the two lakes, where the valley opens out into tussock grassland over much of the broad valley floor and mountain slopes.

The board, having decided that the Mavora Lakes area would not be intensively developed, released a draft plan in April 1984 for a 'Mavora Lakes Pastoral Park', with the stated intention of combining conservation and recreation with some continued pastoral farming. Justification for continued extensive grazing was that 'the presence of cattle in this otherwise stark mountain landscape provides an additional scenic dimension ... and a realisation of pastoral productivity to support the economic infrastructure of Southland and New Zealand.' Moreover, cattle grazing within the park was seen 'as being an important part of the overall park concept, only to the extent that it is compatible with other recreational and conservational values, as a management tool for the consolidation of native pastures and to reduce the incidence and severity of fire'. According to the authors of the draft plan, 'retention of limited cattle grazing will help retain the purebred beef herd of New Zealand ...'[102]

Some 133 submissions were received, and 36 submitters spoke to their submissions. The department's subsequent 'declaration' stated: 'A wide variety and diverse range of opinions were expressed in the submissions and during the hearings. All submissions have been given full consideration.' In considering the plan prior to approval, the Land Settlement Board had available a summary of submissions received on the draft plan. Indeed, all submissions were seen by the board members, and a clear majority of submitters had recommended that the park be transferred from the Land Settlement Board to the department's Reserves Section as a formal reserve without grazing by stock. Submitters expressed widespread concern for the impact of cattle on the stability of the stream and riverbanks, together with the water quality. Even the Southland Catchment Board made a strong plea for formal reservation. Forerunner of the MfE, the Commission for the Environment, in its submission, recommended that the exercise be repeated, with the public being given a range of options for future use of the area rather than only the department and board's preference for grazing. Following wide-ranging discussions, the board resolved to proceed with the management plan virtually unchanged from the draft. It did, however, omit the word 'Pastoral', formalising the title as Mavora Lakes Park.

The 1985 management plan reveals the farming and agricultural bias of the majority of the board. The bias was further confirmed in the board's decision to retain the Mavora Lakes within its jurisdiction, despite this important recreational and conservation area being bounded by a national park along its northwest margin and Snowden State Forest to the southwest. According to the plan, 'the concept' behind the park included, among other things, that grazing would be carried out by the Department of Lands and Survey. This was for three reasons: to add a pastoral dimension to the park, for fire control and to assist in developing Hikuraki Farm Settlement.

The plan described the area's 'landscape' as follows:

> The original tussock and beech vegetation of the area has been largely modified by burning, browsing wild animals and the early introduction of extensive grazing. While limited extensive cattle grazing continues as a land use today and provides an additional scenic dimension, the landscape of the valley system still remains essentially natural in character due to the low occurrence of man-made structures and elements, and the dominance of native vegetation cover.

As to 'Area evaluation', the plan stated:

> The grazing of cattle on a limited basis within the Park is seen as being an additional component of the overall park concept to the extent that it is compatible with other recreational and conservational values, and may reduce the incidence and severity of fire and provide members of the public with an additional scenic dimension. The grazing of the Mavora Lakes area supports the development of the farm settlement in the lower reaches of the Mararoa River Valley.

In respect of the prized Mavora fishery: 'Although the park area has been subject to extensive grazing by sheep and cattle since 1859 at significantly higher rates than present, the trout fishery is still in a healthy state.' Indeed:

> The park area has been recognised as being of national and regional significance because of its scenic and recreational attributes. The area is essentially in a natural state containing conservation and protection values (ie. landscape, historical, flora and fauna, fishery, wetlands, water and soil) and can be maintained or enhanced with suitable multiple land use management.

To control fire, the open tussock grassland would 'be grazed annually to encourage fresh green growth during spring and summer so that the vegetation does not become a fire hazard'. The grazing of cattle should be retained 'at a level sustainable by the native vegetation and water and soil values of the area':

It is considered that cattle grazing in this area will reduce the potential fire risk, assist easy foot access through the park, provide an additional scenic dimension, support the development of the lower farm settlement programme and the economic infrastructure of Southland, and ease the decline in New Zealand's pure bred beef herd numbers.[103]

Mavora Lakes Park was transferred to DOC when it was established in 1987. Later, it was incorporated as an eastern outlier of the South-West New Zealand World Heritage Area. Disconcertingly, grazing and other interests associated with the management plan persisted even after the park was transferred. A questionable deal was struck between Landcorp and DOC: Landcorp (which inherited the Land Settlement Board's role) would conduct monitoring of the impacts of its cattle on conservation land as payment for the department allowing it to graze its cattle. Unsurprisingly, the monitoring claimed to show negligible impact. This finding was disputed by DOC, which sought independent monitoring by Landcare ecologists to contest Landcorp's claims.

Curiously, the revised management plan permitted continued limited grazing by cattle, but during summer rather than winter. This meant grazing in the area would no longer provide relief against pasture damage on the Landcorp farms during winter, a factor claimed to be the original basis for authorising grazing on the Mavora tussocklands. Subsequently, the area was identified in the Southland Conservation Management Strategy for designation as a conservation park. While this has yet to occur, happily the provision for cattle grazing appears to have lapsed.

During my three-year term on the Land Settlement Board, I visited many other farming development areas around the country. It became obvious to me that the Lands and Survey Department's standard of servicing for this quango was much higher than for its only other, the National Parks and Reserves Authority. As I was the sole person to serve on both, this would not have been obvious to any other member. Such differential treatment was consistent with the two organisations' relative strengths, the pro-development bias in internal decision-making, and the prospects for career advancement within the department. Conservation and recreational organisations identified all these aspects when they prevailed on the government, following the 1984 General Election, to reorganise Lands and Survey, together with the Forest Service, so that conservation and development responsibilities could be clearly separated.

TASK FORCE ON WETLANDS, NEW ZEALAND ENVIRONMENTAL COUNCIL, 1982–83

The Environmental Council established this committee at the request of the minister for the environment, following growing concern for the depleted status of the country's wetlands. The minister's brief to the council was to 'consider and report to him on the environmental implications of wetland use and management with appropriate recommendations'. Convened by council member and Deputy President of Federated Farmers, Gordon Stephenson, the panel consisted of Bernard Card of the Department of Lands and Survey, Roger McLean of Massey University, Keith Thompson of Waikato University, and me, with Bob Priest from the Waikato Valley Authority appointed to assist in servicing the committee.

The committee travelled widely throughout New Zealand, discussing wetland issues with major players and inviting submissions. Some 49 were received, including six from government departments and another six from local authorities. The situation was clearly serious. Our report, 'Wetlands: A diminishing resource',[104] concluded that the extent of wetlands in New Zealand was less than 10% of what had occurred naturally, and that the decline in both quality and size was continuing. Despite many definitions for what constituted a 'wetland', we provided our own:

> Wetlands is a collective term for permanently or temporarily wet areas, shallow water and land–water margins. Wetlands may be fresh, brackish or saline, and are characterised in their natural state by plants and animals that are adapted to living in wet conditions.

The committee comprehensively classified New Zealand's wetlands using maps of both terrestrial and coastal wetland–estuarine systems.[105] We found that not only is there not much wetland left in New Zealand, little of it remains in pristine condition, with some types of wetland now very scarce. Rarely seen as providing impressive scenery, wetlands are often difficult to access and therefore rarely visited. Their wildlife is usually secretive, their plants sometimes unimpressive and their many values often only appreciated after they are destroyed. Once developed, wetlands can rarely, if ever, be returned to their original state. Although poorly appreciated by the general public, they have a range of scenic, biological (including palaeoecological) and recreational values, and play an important role in regulating water retention and release, providing flood control, influencing water quality and nurturing fisheries.

The committee advocated that further modification of wetlands be deferred until after a comprehensive inventory had ranked New Zealand wetlands according to their national and international importance. This inventory of all remaining wetlands should be conducted on a regional basis to provide a full national coverage. Furthermore, the committee asserted that the government should develop a wide-ranging wetland policy for general application. At that time, most organisations and departments with responsibilities for wetlands had no satisfactory policy, and co-ordination between them was generally poor. We advocated that high priority should be given to reserving an adequately representative sample of the main wetland types; that those not reserved should still be managed sustainably; and that the government should promote covenanting of privately owned wetlands.

An extensive pictorial section in our report emphasised the wide range of values associated with wetlands and also the equally wide range of threats. The wetlands included in this section were:

- Lake Heron (Canterbury; largest of the Ashburton lakes)
- Farewell Spit (Northwest Nelson; with Ramsar designation)
- Kopuatai Dome and Whangamarino Swamp (Waikato; both since given Ramsar designation)

- Miranda wetland (Thames Estuary, Waikato; since given Ramsar designation)
- Lake Ellesmere (Canterbury coast)
- Lake Waipori–Lake Waihola (Eastern Otago; since protected)
- Aramoana saltmarsh (Dunedin; now protected)
- Lake Wairarapa (Wairarapa)
- Great Moss Swamp (Southeastern Otago, Lammermoor Range; since inundated for irrigation water storage)
- Kepler Mire (Southland, Manapouri–Te Anau basin)

The report described Kepler Mire (*ca.* 800 ha.) as destined for reservation but not yet gazetted. This remains the case today, although it was later included in the South West New Zealand World Heritage Area.

At the time the committee visited Kepler Mire, the western boundary fence cut across the stream and associated sedge-dominated wetland on the margin of the mire and fitted poorly with the visual and ecological requirements of a well-planned wetland reserve. Our visit resulted in a prolonged discussion with Lands and Survey staff as to the values of the shallow streams and swampy ground on the bog margin, an integral part of the wetland complex. Referred to technically by the Swedish term 'lagg', the bog margin should be included together with the central raised peat dome, we emphasised, to retain the integrity of the mire system. The value of having an experienced, highly reputable and influential farmer as convenor of our committee was evident when Lands and Survey decided to relocate the boundary fence along the line recommended by the committee, thereby including the lagg section within the wetland complex.

At the time of our assessment, only two New Zealand wetlands had been recognised as internationally significant in terms of the Ramsar International Wetland Convention: Waituna wetland near Invercargill and Farewell Spit in Golden Bay. Since this time, three others have been added – Whangamarino and Kopuatai in the Waikato and Miranda on the Thames Estuary – and several others are currently proposed.

NEW ZEALAND MOUNTAIN LANDS INSTITUTE, 1989–92

The New Zealand Mountain Lands Institute was a national organisation established to advise the government on comprehensive and consistent policies for mountain-land resource use. Operating through a Mountain Lands Committee, a subcommittee of Lincoln College Council, it replaced the redundant Tussock Grasslands and Mountain Lands Institute. Funded through Vote: Environment, the diversely constituted committee was to provide 'experience and expertise rather than representatives of any particular user group'.[106] The institute's staff of Chris Kerr and Brian Robertson serviced the committee, and Brian also edited its journal, *Review*.

The goals of the institute and its committee were to:

- examine and review any aspect of mountain-land resources or their uses
- identify issues and options for the management of mountain-land resources
- act as a forum for public debate seeking consensus on issues related to the use of mountain-land resources
- advise national and local governments on comprehensive policies for the use of mountain-land resources
- make information publicly available.

Through 'debate and consultation', the committee would attempt to resolve conflicts arising from the use of mountain lands. It would also offer independent advice to the minister(s), and advise central, regional and local governments on comprehensive and consistent policies for mountain-land use. Interest groups could also bring issues to the committee for investigation. The committee was to report annually to the minister of lands through the Lincoln College Council.

One of the first tasks of the committee was to assess proposed amendments to the Land Act 1948. Our submission accorded with the government's desire to achieve rationalisation of land tenure in the high country while ensuring that its contractual obligations to lessees

QUANGOS I HAVE KNOWN

Two nationally significant wetlands. TOP: *Teviot Swamp, ca. 1000 m, among snow-tussock grassland within Beaumont Station (currently undergoing tenure review) on the Lammerlaw Range, eastern Otago uplands.* ABOVE: *Kepler Mire, a patterned wetland with numerous small islands, and part of Southwest New Zealand World Heritage Area, ca. 200 m, Manapouri Basin, western Southland, with Lake Manapouri in the background.*

were protected. The committee sought to amend the act to provide it with statutory flexibility so that its objectives might be achieved in the interests of high-country lessees, the Crown and the public. As well as recognising the Treaty of Waitangi, the revised Land Act was intended to provide for sustainability, equity, efficiency and accountability.

At the minister's recommendation, the institute established a programme of investigation to address the serious issue of hawkweed, appointing a core group to investigate the problem,[107] and in October 1990 hosting a forum at Lincoln University. This was attended by over 60 people representing property holders, crown and regional management agencies, and scientific disciplines, including university scientists. The forum addressed the extent and seriousness of the problem, research needs, remedial measures, land-management options and costs. The ensuing report stated that:

> [T]he effects of post-burn grazing by sheep and rabbits include weakened tussock grasses and grasslands, loss of palatable inter-tussock vegetation and increased bare ground. Such effects allowed the spread of less desirable species along with the adventive grasses of pastoral value. Recent research [shows] ... that hawkweed infestation is symptomatic of depleted or deteriorated grasslands rather than the primary cause of their degradation. This important conclusion needs research over a wide range of sites with long-term measurements and research into the ecological processes involved.

According to our report, hawkweeds affected some 42% of the South Island land area, an area considerably in excess of the total area of pastoral runs. In terms of a way forward, the Hawkweeds Core Group saw its immediate task as developing research strategies for both the short and long term:

> ... the fine wool industry in the mountains and the conservation estate are both at grave risk if we do nothing. Pastoral futures and nature conservation futures as they have been conceived are both so threatened by this grassland degradation that within 10 years we may expect
> to have only a skeleton fine wool industry in the mountains and few representative tussock grasslands in the conservation estate.[108]

Following receipt of the report, the Minister for the Environment, Simon Upton, invited the ministers of conservation, science, lands, agriculture and forestry to join him in assembling a co-ordinated response to the problem.

After a consultative process, the institute also addressed in detail guidelines for the burning of tussock grassland. Its recommendations were 'indicative' guidelines only, to be applied to 'specific local conditions'. The overall conclusion, however, was that, on the available evidence:

> burning of tussock grasslands is inherently unsustainable ... [Burning] depletes both the soil and the vegetation resource ... [There is a] need for further information on the effects of fire ... In particular, information on the loss of nutrients, organic matter in soils and micro-organisms by fire is considered essential to a fuller understanding of the consequences of fire in this environment.[109]

Advising against issuing consents to burn any fescue–tussock grassland, the institute stated that such burning was unnecessary, and that burning of snow-tussock grassland to enhance pastoral use should be severely restricted. The sole exception 'may be in the instances where burning is the only practical means of controlling unwanted woody shrubs'. Any burning of snow-tussock or red-tussock grassland should be restricted to land below 1000 m (excluding land protected by snow cover), occur at not less than 20-year intervals, and be during spring only. There should be a post-burn spelling period of at least one full year before any grazing. If consents *were* ever granted to burn snow- or red-tussock grassland, they should be subject to these conditions. The whole of the area burned would need to be oversown and top-dressed to ensure that no loss of nutrients or ground cover occurred. This condition should not, however, apply to conservation land.[110]

Subsequent attempts by me and others to have the Otago Regional Council adopt these guidelines met with little success. The council stated that it preferred to interpret the guidelines as being specific for particular areas and not generally applicable.

After government funding was withdrawn, the institute closed down in 1992. While it functioned, members of its committee had engaged in discussions on a wide range of issues, including rabbits, wilding trees, landscape, tourism and chinchilla.[111] At one stage the committee visited the central North Island to inspect problems there associated with heather, wild horses, wilding pines and public access. As to wilding trees, the institute recommended that a specific policy should be regional in scope but be subject to an overall national policy statement. Celebrating the 'extremely valuable' role of the institute, chairman George McMillan commented that 'there continues to be a need for discussion, debate and identification of issues by the main stakeholders and interest groups and for consensus-seeking comprehensive and consistent advice to governments, both regional and national.'[112] While Lincoln University responded by stating its intention of 'exploring ways of maintaining its interest in, and work for, the sustainable use of mountain land resources', no replacement has yet been established.

OTAGO CONSERVATION BOARD, 1990–2001

For each of DOC's 13 conservancies at this time, the minister appointed conservation boards of 9–11 members to represent the wider community's interest in regional conservation management. A board's main role is to shape planning and policy as these affect public conservation areas within each conservancy. Predictably, my 11 years on the Otago board, seven as its chair, had both rewards and frustrations.

The greatest reward was the department's commitment to reserving a representative network of tussock grasslands and associated mountain lands. This was achieved through both direct purchase and – from the late 1990s, when it became operative – tenure review of high-country pastoral leasehold land. The two outcomes most satisfying to me were the Kopuwai Conservation Area and Te Papanui Conservation Park. Kopuwai Conservation Area embraces many of my early research sites on the upper slopes and crest of the Old Man Range, and was achieved largely through tenure review of Earnscleugh Station. Te Papanui Conservation

QUANGOS I HAVE KNOWN

Otago Conservation Board at Lake Alta, The Remarkables, December 1999, left to right: John Beattie, Rob Mitchell, Robin Jepson, area manager Chris Eden, board secretary Mark Clark, Otago conservator Jeff Connell, Gilbert van Reenen, me, Neil Simpson and Les Cleveland.

Park incorporated the Nardoo Scientific Reserve (see Chapter 4) and the high water-yielding areas of upland snow-tussock grassland and wetland on Rocklands and Halwyn stations. Also noteworthy was the department's acquisition, at the board's initiative, of 813 ha. of drylands at Flat Top Hill, adjacent to the highway on the southern outskirts of Alexandra.

Among my greatest frustrations was the outcome of the Little Valley conservation issue. This followed the minister of conservation's decision in 1993 to place a 'designation' (under the RMA) on some 1970 ha. of copper-tussock grassland to protect it from burning (and subsequent grazing). The designation was served on the Central Otago District Council (and the lessee) on the same day as the Otago Regional Council issued a permit to burn the area. Having been identified as an area 'recommended for protection' by my former student Brent Fagan in his Manorburn Protected Natural Areas survey,[113] I felt obliged to respond to the district council's call for submissions. Mine was one of 117

TOP: *Te Papanui 'Waterlands' Conservation Park, dominated by narrow-leaved snow-tussock grassland.* Gilbert van Reenen. ABOVE: *Minister of Conservation Chris Carter and me at the park's official opening – in fog – 29 March 2003.* Gerry McSweeny.

supporting the designation, well outnumbered by the 212 in opposition. During the five-day hearing, I was pleased to be able to defend the quality of Brent's M.Sc. project as well as promote the area's significant inherent values. As a baseline reference area, it also had importance and economic value for the farming community as a means to assess the generally degraded state of this grassland type throughout much of the Manorburn Ecological District.

Among the wide range of submissions received on the issue, Lincoln University agricultural economist Alastair McArthur's was particularly provocative. Referring to tussock grassland research generally, he claimed that most scientists associated with it were so 'green' as to be incapable of making judgments without bias. They were therefore open to suspicion some scientists could 'fudge' data and make 'extravagant claims'.[114] Descending to this level of criticism was galling. It reflected defensive reactions to the ecosystem degradation that had become clearly apparent to many scientists over the relatively short period of their working lives.[115]

Unsurprisingly, the district council recommended that the minister of conservation lift the Little Valley designation. Instead, however, protracted negotiation resulted in only 300 ha. of the 1970 ha. originally proposed being covenanted. A condition on such conservation covenants gives the occupier discretion as to who could access the area, and I was the only member excluded when the board subsequently visited on one of its field trips. Lessee Lyndon Sanders later told me his decision was a response to my suggestion to the minister that the Little Valley case be appealed to the Planning Tribunal.

There were other disappointments too. One of these was being denied a role in the prolonged debate over logging Māori land in the Catlins (indeed, the department requested that the board did not become involved with, or even publicly comment on, this issue). Another disappointment was that, as a board, we made little progress with increasing public concern over vehicle access to the Otago high country. Following a Cromwell public meeting convened by the board in May 1997, it became obvious that the issue was not likely to be resolved until tenure review had been completed.

The board's most significant exercise during my term was collaborating with the department to produce the first conservation management strategy (CMS) for the Otago Conservancy. This almost 700-page document had a ten-year gestation but the final product was something of which all contributors could feel justifiably proud. It contained not only an outline of management planning needs and opportunities on conservation land for the next decade, but also the most comprehensive description of the province's nature conservation values compiled to that time.[116]

The 77 submitters on the draft CMS focussed mostly on the Clutha River's Rongahere Gorge, including Birch Island, which was then under threat of flooding from a proposed high dam below Beaumont. Initially proposed by ECNZ, this plan was inherited by Contact Energy. A statement from the company – fortuitously just before completion of the CMS – that it would take no action with its proposed dam for 15 years prompted the board to recommend a further 'special place', the Rongahere Gorge, to the 40 already recognised in the strategy. Though the company in turn expressed its concern to the board, the department, the Conservation Authority and the minister, the board's recommendation was upheld and Birch Island was later formally protected. This should ensure a more level playing field if the dam proposal ever resurfaces.

There remained only one difference of opinion between the board and the department when the draft CMS was ready to be submitted to the Conservation Authority for formal approval. The board was keen to designate a Catlins Coastal Rainforest Park. Unimpressed, the department resisted the suggestion on the basis that 'rainforest' was not in the department's 'Doctionary'. The board, however, felt the term was appropriate and also had promotional value for the area, and the department finally agreed; so the Catlins now has the distinction of containing the country's first and only rainforest park. When Prime Minister Jenny Shipley, addressing a National Party conference in Dunedin in April 1999, commented that 'there is no reason why the Catlins can't be a national park', I responded in the press that '[a] national park in the Catlins would take much more to achieve than a wave of the Prime Minister's magic wand.'[117] Though my comment was intended in a lighter

TOP: *Lake Wilkie from the boardwalk, Catlins region, southeast Otago, February 2008.* ABOVE: *Professor Ulf Molau, a visitor from Sweden, and the DOC sign at Maclennan to note the Coastal Rainforest Park in the Catlins, November 2008.*

vein, I was reprimanded by the conservator on the grounds that this was not a comment a board chairperson should make in public. Despite the board's efforts to progress the idea, we could not get traction and so it was put in the 'too hard' basket.

Soon after the Otago CMS was finalised, it was put to the test when, during the drought of February 1999, the board was asked to support the department's proposal to provide emergency grazing of tussock grassland for the farmer adjoining the Rock and Pillar Scenic Reserve. Despite the board's claim that the now legally binding CMS did not provide for such grazing, the department subsequently gave its approval. In the *Otago Daily Times*, local MP Gavan Herlihy described the board's opposition as 'nothing short of an outrage'. Similarly, Gerry Eckhoff, Roxburgh high-country farmer and ACT list MP, said the board 'had shown a callous indifference to the plight of their fellow men'.[118]

About this time, two serious fires elsewhere in the region prompted the Minister of Conservation, Nick Smith, to seek free emergency grazing on DOC land for the affected farmers. Board members Les Cleveland, Jill Hamel and I met briefly with Smith, Herlihy and conservator Jeff Connell at Dunedin Airport to confirm the board's position that the CMS could not legally provide for even emergency grazing. We also rejected proposals from the department to allow grazing on the Rock and Pillar Reserve as well as the Bain Conservation Area and Flat Top Hill Conservation Area. We were somewhat less concerned with grazing proposed for the recently acquired copper-tussock grassland reserves in the Manorburn district. Free grazing was soon offered on one of these latter blocks. However, as a condition of sale, any grazing rights apparently had to be offered to the previous owner, who accepted even though he hadn't suffered a fire, so no emergency grazing ensued on conservation tussockland.

On behalf of the board, I formally complained to the Conservation Authority that the integrity of the Otago CMS had been seriously undermined. My complaint was upheld and the minister informed accordingly. I understand that the department could not establish a legal basis for the minister's decision to provide emergency grazing on conservation land. The debate surrounding this issue certainly raised the profile of tussock grassland conservation and also the more complex issue of a conservation document 'fettering' a minister (restraining a minister's discretionary ability). This issue is still debated in the context of CMSs and conservation management plans generally.

When then-minister Nick Smith made it known in 1999 that Conservation Board members should not serve for more than two three-year terms, I decided not to reapply. The department thereupon arranged several farewell functions. At these, conservator Jeff Connell announced the gift of a Grahame Sydney lithograph in appreciation of my efforts. Amidst these celebrations, staff under the new minister, Sandra Lee, contacted me requesting that I let my name be forwarded for reappointment. Sworn to secrecy, I was somewhat embarrassed to continue receiving farewell accolades from the department, and the more so when the appointments were announced. Jeff Connell, without further comment, rang to say he would like to deliver my Grahame Sydney artwork personally. This was followed within an hour by the board's secretary, Mark Clark, asking me to confirm that I was actually an applicant for the board. He said I had been given another three-year term. When Jeff delivered the lithograph with his wife Sandra, I could only joke that his wife's namesake 'had done the dirty on him', and that I would relinquish the chair as some solace to the department in acknowledgment of its several gestures. So after seven years, Les Cleveland again resumed the chair. Before completing this final term on the board, however, I had to resign when Forest & Bird nominated me in 2001 for the society's statutory position on the New Zealand Conservation Authority.

FIORDLAND MARINE GUARDIANS, 2001–13

In 1995 an active local group of Fiordland fishers and charter-boat operators, with local rūnanga, strove to develop an integrated management strategy for the fiords. Ultimately, this led to the establishment of the Guardians of Fiordland Fisheries and Marine Environment, chaired

Entrance to Hall Arm, Doubtful Sound, adjacent to Entrance Island Marine Reserve.

by John Steffens of Te Anau.[119] The guardians obtained funding from the MfE to retain marine fisheries biologist Laurel Tierney as their principal advisor, and sought advice from that ministry, the Ministry of Fisheries, Environment Southland, NIWA and DOC. At DOC's recommendation, University of Otago marine biologist Steve Wing was appointed as a further advisor, and another scientist, Ken Grange of NIWA, was also approached for advice. The guardians published *A Characterisation of Fiordland's Fisheries* in 1999,[120] a comprehensive bibliography in 2000,[121] and held their first public meeting in Te Anau in early 2002. Following this, there were further discussions with the Minister of Fisheries, Pete Hodgson, who recommended that I be appointed to represent environmental NGOs, as required by the terms of their grant.

An ex-Guardian of Lakes Manapouri and Te Anau, but no expert on marine issues, I joined the group in time for the launch of their Draft Integrated Management Strategy for Fiordland's Fisheries and Marine Environment in October 2002. Submissions were invited and some 436 received, analysed and used to modify the plan before it was officially launched by the fisheries and environment ministers in Te Anau in September 2003. The guiding vision of the Fiordland Marine Guardians – 'That the quality of Fiordland's marine environment and fisheries, including the wider fishery experience, be maintained or improved for future generations to use and enjoy' – is appropriate to Fiordland's grandeur and international significance. The initiative shown by the group – its philosophy of 'gifts and gains', whereby each stakeholder makes a concession for the greater good – is also highly commendable. At the official launch, the ministers formally committed to implementing the strategy with minimal delay, which they did in April 2005, when the Fiordland (Te Moana o Atawhenua) Marine Managment Act was promulgated with support of all political parties.[122]

In late 2004 an Implementation Committee led by the Ministry for the Environment guided the process to completion.[123] While the outcome was not likely to match Forest & Bird's original aspirations, this was also true for other stakeholders since compromise was the name of the game. However, the very effective ministry facilitator, Paul Irving, presented the eight 'representative areas' in the strategy as appropriate marine reserves. Special legislation provided an overarching conservation strategy, which included comprehensive monitoring, surveillance and management oversight of the fiords. This responsibility was to be shared among government, regional authorities and the guardians. Passed in 2005 as the Fiordland (Te Moana o Atawhenua) Marine Management Act – to be comprehensively reviewed after five years – the strategy certainly represented a major first step towards sustainable management of the fiords.

Hailed as a model for the country, the process of implementing the strategy was described in *North and South* as a 'blueprint for dealing with divisiveness over the key issues of our times'. The article's author, Peta Carey, termed the Fiordland Marine Guardians 'guardian angels'.[124] The Fiordland Marine Area now encompasses some 928,000 ha. It extends out to the 12-mile Territorial Sea Limit, from the eastern bank of the

Waiau River northwards to Awarua Point. Eight new marine reserves, totalling 9430 ha., and several smaller 'china shops', allow for more effective management of 'marine areas of special significance'.

Although parliament unanimously endorsed the legislation, my old adversary, Gerry Eckhoff – at this time an ACT List MP – managed to slip in some personal abuse. Eckhoff questioned my involvement with the Fiordland Marine Guardians, 'Quite frankly, Alan Mark is a bad appointment to have made to that group.'[125] Nevertheless, I was one of seven Fiordland Marine Guardians subsequently appointed by the minister for the environment.[126] Laurel Tierney, who had been facilitator for the earlier guardians group, was elected chair. With the full support of DOC, MfE, Ministry of Fisheries and Environment Southland, progress was immediate and significant. Section 3 specifies the Marine Management Act's purpose:

> In recognition of the Fiordland (Te Moana o Atawhenua) Marine Area's local, national, and international importance, unique marine environment, distinctive biological diversity, and outstanding landscape and cultural heritage, this Act—
> (a) establishes the Fiordland (Te Moana o Atawhenua) Marine Area and 8 marine reserves in that area;
> (b) implements measures to assist in the preservation, protection, and sustainable management of the marine environment and biological diversity of the Fiordland (Te Moana o Atawhenua) Marine Area;
> (c) establishes the Fiordland Marine Guardians to provide advice on fisheries management, biosecurity, sustainable management, and marine preservation and protection;
> (d) facilitates and promotes co-operation between the Guardians and management agencies, to assist in achieving the integrated management of the Fiordland (Te Moana o Atawhenua) Marine Area;
> (e) acknowledges the importance of kaitiakitanga.

Keen to have comprehensive monitoring undertaken, particularly in light of the five-year review, I concentrated my efforts on this task. I was delighted with the baseline monitoring of marine communities (first

Fiordland Marine Guardians at parliament, 17 March 2011, left to right: me, Jerry Excell, Mark Peychers, Alan Key, Anne McDermott, Ken Grange, Stewart Bull and Malcolm Lawson (chair). Alison O'Sullivan

year) and assessment of indicator species (second year) carried out under Steve Wing and consultant Kay Booth. The guardians also rescued the government's recently abandoned programme for containing the exotic invasive kelp *Undaria pinnatifida* in the fiords, imploring the minister to continue the programme when presenting him with their first annual report in 2006. The second annual report highlighted continued progress on this front, as did the strong support of the associated agencies. Statements by these agencies, appended to the annual reports, testify to the overall success of this initiative to sustainably manage the magnificent fiords of Fiordland.[127]

I mistakenly supposed my involvement with the guardians might be useful in keeping the fishing fraternity committed to their stated objectives, but this hasn't been an issue. The overall progress during my eight-year membership (I resigned in 2013) far exceeded my wildest dreams and augers well for the future. Four new members appointed in my time, to replace others who had resigned, were CRA8 Management Committee Chief Executive Malcolm Lawson (who replaced Laurel Tierney as chair), Invercargill recreational fisher Anne McDermott, and Te Anau commercial fishers Mark Peychers and Jerry Excell. Major achievements have been the publication in 2008 of a comprehensive *Users Guide to the Fiordland Marine Area*[128] and agreement to have the fiords considered for World Heritage status in the review of the Southland Conservancy's CMS in 2013. The outcome is awaited with interest.

NEW ZEALAND CONSERVATION AUTHORITY, 2001–

Having been re-elected to the national executive of Forest & Bird in 2001 – and as a result of Laura Dawson of Taupo deciding to relinquish her position as the society's nominee on the Conservation Authority – I was prevailed on to fulfil this very important role. As the society's nominee on the authority's forerunner, the National Parks and Reserves Authority, I felt somewhat reluctant to become involved again over a decade later. My successor in the Botany Department, Kath Dickinson,

With Kath Dickinson, my successor in the Botany Department, among the snow-tussock grassland on Flagstaff, Dunedin 2010. Dana Doodle

Members of the New Zealand Conservation Authority on Secretary Island, Fiordland, 2003, left to right, back: David Chandler, Peter Geddes, Marion van der Goes, Linda Conning, Wendy Nelson, Kath Dickinson, Bryan Hutchins, DOC support staff, Kerry Marshall (chair), me; front: Loraine Stephenson and John Nankervis.

was already an authority member as the Royal Society's nominee. With reasonable assurance that these two statutory appointees could come from the same small university department, I agreed to being nominated. Our appointment and re-appointment for three-year terms was later announced alongside two others from the Dunedin area, a record for the authority.

As specified in the act, the Conservation Authority has 13 members, mostly selected by the minister. The national equivalent of conservation boards, the authority's role is to approve CMSs and national park management plans – the main planning documents guiding DOC. The authority also gives advice to the minister on conservation issues of national importance. This is a demanding but generally satisfying exercise that brings one face-to-face with many names in conservation and, of course, many important national conservation issues.

The main issues being addressed during my two terms were pests, indigenous biodiversity, marine, fresh-water and tussock-grassland conservation, as well as visitor and recreation strategies. We also drafted general policies for both the National Parks and Conservation acts. With the first general policy for national parks having been completed during my time on the previous authority in 1983, I felt as though I had been reincarnated. But there was also a sense of real progress: non-forest conservation was now much more to the fore, with two tussockland conservation parks already gazetted and more in the pipeline. Molesworth Station in the southern Marlborough district, the country's largest high-country government property (186,000 ha.), was also destined for formal protection as a recreation park. This was finally achieved in 2005, after I had relinquished my place on the authority.

Membership was not, however, without its frustrations. A major one was the rising numbers of deer in remote areas of our national parks. From 2002 commercial hunting using helicopters virtually ceased as a result of increased regulations and fuel prices alongside decreasing overseas demand for New Zealand venison. Even getting the issue on the agenda was difficult: the authority seemed unwilling to consider conservation matters unless they were both nationally significant and likely to succeed. Fortunately, the commercial hunting industry began to pick up in 2006 as demand and prices both increased. However, the future remains unpredictable.

REVIEW PANEL ON FLORA, FAUNA AND LAND USE, MINISTRY OF RESEARCH, SCIENCE AND TECHNOLOGY, 1992–93

Chaired by Dr Margriet Theron, manager of the ministry's Science Review Division, this panel was the tenth in the ministry's science-review series.[129] Among its conclusions, the panel noted a poor ethnic and gender balance among science researchers, with the scientific workforce aging and low numbers of new graduates coming through in some areas, particularly in biosystematics. Notwithstanding the high level of commitment shown by all interviewees, individual researchers needed to upskill, both to broaden their skills base and gain specific expertise in areas such as electronic data-handling, modelling and the social sciences. We believed that science didn't promote itself well.

The panel also noted that information-transfer ought to meet specific stakeholder requirements at every stage, from research planning to communication of the results. Both a policy and technical advisory group were needed to cover databases of national significance, addressing such issues as funding, guardianship and access. In light of both the Treaty of Waitangi and the role of Māori as land-owning stakeholders – sometimes in areas most in need of sustainable land-use policies – urgent action was required to ensure their rightful place in the nation's science regime. As to Māori perspectives, the panel noted that, 'at the corporate level, Landcare Research appears to be making a real effort to respond to the aspirations of Tangata Whenua,' but that 'there were few Maori involved in research or research management'.[130] Social science research would not only facilitate information-transfer but also enable physical scientists to orient future research with regard to stakeholder needs.

According to its executive summary, our review covered 'all New Zealand's government-funded land use, flora and fauna research'. The report noted that there had been an overall reduction in funding these areas:

> In total there had been a net loss since 1987 of 55 scientific and technical staff from the immediate predecessor organisations to Landcare Research. Exacerbating this trend is the fact that biosystematics research capability had been drastically reduced prior to 1987.

We felt that a separate fund should be established, specifically to develop and maintain nationally significant collections and databases. The priority importance of high-quality, accessible databases was stressed. The panel also observed a lack of thought regarding priority-setting, with research programmes in many cases being the result of history rather than recent review and planning.

As to biosystematics collections, we saw ongoing funding as essential. Major collections lay with the government or museums, and their management and maintenance needed to be rationalised: 'Collecting for the sake of it should be discouraged in favour of strategic planning, and the proper description and cataloguing of existing material.' We also noted poor documentation of specimens, with a large number of inadequately described taxa consequently unidentifiable. The report advocated parataxonomic surveys (those using less-qualified assistants than the most-qualified taxonomists), with trained personnel conducting trial identifications of morphospecies (species or a species group based entirely on morphological features). The results of such surveys are of long-term value when planned in conjunction with specialists making use of well-curated permanent collections. At the other end of the spectrum, molecular biology, when applied to biosystematics, is a resource-intensive activity yielding valuable information and often identifying new species. Such work should be clearly focused (for example, on taxa at risk of extinction). I later confronted several of these issues first hand when revising and expanding my alpine plant book as a 'nature guide' in 2013.[131]

While uptake of many of these important issues has been painfully slow, significant progress has been made with staffing, national inventories and databases. However, competition-based, short-term funding policies continue to impede the growth of all sectors of science in New Zealand.

7

ROYAL FOREST AND BIRD PROTECTION SOCIETY OF NEW ZEALAND

As I grew more closely involved with Forest & Bird, the country's largest conservation ENGO, my dealings with the Native Forest Action Council on forestry issues became increasingly at 'arm's length'. Established in 1923, the society had grown steadily in membership and political influence,[132] and my decision to join it was largely pragmatic. The Nardoo tussock grassland controversy in the late 1970s (see Chapter 4) had taught me that scientists working on their own are often politically impotent when it comes to conservation issues. I considered that the society might benefit from scientifically credible inputs to its conservation proposals, as it had in the past (eminent botanist Dr Leonard Cockayne was the society's second president), including for ecosystems beyond its traditional focus.

An earlier contact with the society had, however, given me some cause for concern. In June 1972 I delivered the society's prestigious Sanderson Memorial Lecture at its annual meeting. Soon after being invited in July 1971 to deliver the following year's lecture, I was contacted by the Office of the Governor-General enquiring as to my topic since, as patron of the society, the Governor-General planned to attend. When I revealed some uncertainty on this, the Governor-General's secretary asked me specifically whether it would involve Manapouri. Stating that it almost certainly would, I was then asked whether I would be critical of the government on this issue; the Governor-General, I was informed, would not wish to attend in such a situation. Unable to offer any assurance, I replied that, hopefully, nearer the time, I could be complimentary of government, and that I should have a clearer idea by the following April. The secretary undertook to contact me at that time. Unfortunately, the situation had not improved by then so I indicated that I would indeed probably be critical in my address. Not wishing to constrain me nor risk political embarrassment, the Governor-General tendered an apology for the meeting.

While this experience clearly reflected the delicacy of the balance between respectability and activism, it was the events surrounding publication of my lecture that made me most question the society's professional standards. Entitled 'Conservation Issues at Home and Abroad', my talk had addressed the current status of the Manapouri controversy with which the society was also deeply involved. I concluded with a somewhat critical comment on the society's name and image – the Royal Forest and Bird Protection Society of New Zealand – in relation to its apparently much wider environmental concerns. In the ensuing publication, I was intrigued to see these comments on the society had been deleted without any consultation. On enquiry, I learned that the society's secretary had felt my comments would 'serve no useful purpose'. Similarly, he said any prior consultation with me 'would also have served no useful purpose'. I later realised that many members so cherished the royal charter that the society was unwilling to risk losing it by being forced to reapply for royal endorsement following a name change.

Despite this issue, I decided to join Forest & Bird in the late 1970s because of the possibilities for conservation achievements it offered. My election to the national executive in 1979 was part of an NFAC 'takeover' of the society, following failure to co-ordinate a collective approach to some major forest conservation campaigns at that time, particularly on the West Coast. I continued on the executive until 1997, and was elected president for five years in 1986, when the previous president, Alan Edmonds, moved from Waikato University to become manager of the QEII National Trust.

ROYAL FOREST AND BIRD PROTECTION SOCIETY OF NEW ZEALAND

There was stiff competition for the 10 executive positions during the late 1970s, with 22 nominations at the 1979 AGM prompting President Tony Ellis to warn against the 'disadvantages of a wholly new executive'[133]. Other scientists joining the executive during this period included John Morton, Professor of Zoology at Auckland University; Alan Edmonds, a plant ecologist from Waikato University; and Charles (later Sir Charles) Fleming, senior palaeontologist with DSIR's Geological Survey. Such credentials served to give a strong scientific basis to the executive's deliberations. This proved even more so when Gerry McSweeney, a recent Lincoln graduate with expertise in the South Island tussock grasslands, was appointed conservation officer in 1980 and elevated to the senior position of conservation director three years later.

DIVERSIFICATION OF SOCIETY ACTIVITIES

The society promoted national-park status for both the Paparoa and Okarito–Waikukupa regions in Westland. It continued to focus on indigenous forests and avifaunal conservation, particularly in the central North Island and West Coast, but there was also a concerted effort to diversify its activities into a range of non-forest indigenous ecosystems, particularly wetlands, shrublands and tussock grasslands.

This diversification showed in articles published in the society's journal. There were several on Central Otago's upland tussock grasslands and the South Island high country, including mine on 'A Disappearing Heritage: Tussock grasslands of the South Island rain-shadow region', pleading for more public support for tussockland conservation and emphasising that, in terms of our natural heritage, 'tussock grasslands are no less important than the battle to save our lowland rainforests that has now gained great momentum'.[134] Gerry McSweeney as conservation manager and I also promoted the tussock grasslands of the South Island as a 'forgotten habitat'.[135] There were several articles on the conservation importance of invertebrates and the largely treeless ultramafic (serpentine) areas of South Westland, promoting it for the highest conservation status,[136] which it later achieved as an extension to the Mount Aspiring National Park.

From the mid-1980s, Forest & Bird became involved in several conservation coalitions. Foremost among these was the Joint Campaign on Native Forests, which banded together Forest & Bird, NFAC and FMC to address major forest-conservation issues across the country. The campaign targeted logging in State-owned indigenous forests such as at Whirinaki Forest in the North Island, and Okarito, Waikukupa and Paparoa forests on the West Coast of the South Island. Similarly, the High Country Public Lands Coalition initially joined together FMC, acclimatisation societies and Forest & Bird, with Public Access New Zealand (PANZ), the New Zealand Federation of Freshwater Anglers and the Council of Outdoor Recreation Associations of New Zealand (CORANZ) later adding to the mix. A coalition of FMC and Environment and Conservation Organisations of New Zealand (ECO) ran a successful 'Vote for the Environment' general-election campaign, which shed light on major environmental issues, its proponents actively seeking out responses from the political parties and their local representatives. Forest & Bird branches also organised public candidate meetings before elections.

In 1983 the society turned its attention to the South Island high country. In that year, councillors for the first time conducted the society's council field trip into the Canterbury high country, at which Kevin O'Connor and others gave rousing talks. This was followed in November 1984 with a *Forest & Bird* journal issue largely devoted to the high country. In a joint article, Gerry McSweeney and Les Molloy described the very extensive area and special heritage features of pastoral leasehold high-country land, alongside threats to its conservation values.[137] Six iconic high-country regions were also presented in this issue: Mavora Lakes by Les Hutchins; the Lammermoor–Lammerlaw ranges by Brian Patrick; The Remarkables–Old Man–Garvie area by me[138]; the Ahuriri Valley by Bruce Mason; the Kaikoura ranges by Barry Dunnett; and the Molesworth–Inland Marlborough area by Les Molloy. In my second Sanderson Lecture in 1985, I had a further opportunity to promote

Lincoln professor Kevin O'Connor delivering the sermon on the mount on South Island high-country issues to Forest & Bird councillors, Porters Pass, November 1983.

conservation of what I called the 'Forgotten habitats – tussock grasslands, wetlands, shrublands and dunelands'.[139] A measure of the success of the tussock-grassland conservation campaign since this time is that substantial parts of these six regions are now formally protected and managed by DOC.

In 1987, on the centenary of New Zealand's first national park, Tongariro, the society issued The Tongariro Declaration in my name. This was a Charter for National Parks and Protected Natural Areas for the next 100 years. It read:

> The National Council of the Royal Forest and Bird Protection Society of New Zealand met at Whakapapa to mark the centennial of our National Parks system, which began there with the gift of the Peaks of the Tongariro volcanoes to the nation. While this is a timely celebration it is also a time of considerable concern for the future of our parks system. Radical changes in public land ownership, its administration and funding, and in our traditional social philosophy have meant that the present

and future of the system are not as secure as they should be after one hundred years. Therefore the Council of the Society recommends to the Government the following principles to ensure the adequate protection of these precious lands.

1. That the National Parks and Reserves system is a cultural benchmark of a nation.
2. The natural environment of New Zealand, its wildlife and plants, have innate values which place them beyond the exigencies of current economics.
3. This public estate is held in trust for future generations through the system of National Parks and Reserves.
4. Such a system requires absolute protection, excluding the possibility of pressure for exploitation by mining, development and other private interests.
5. The system requires national funding of a kind which places it beyond the pressures of economic changes and sectional interests, which seek an economic value and return.
6. The opportunity presently exists to identify the last remaining sectors of unprotected habitats to ensure that this generation will not allow the loss to the world, and all time, of places, creatures and experiences which distinguish New Zealand.[140]

Forest & Bird council meeting, Erewhon Station, October 1988.

Oteake Conservation Park, Hawkdun Range, north Otago.

In the same year, the society also took up the largely overlooked and virtually ignored issue of marine conservation. There was, and still is, a pressing need for an adequately protected system of marine reserves. Journal articles addressing these issues, by Bill Ballantine and others, appeared from the early 1980s to the present day.[141]

The South Island high country continued to feature in *Forest & Bird*, with particular editorial emphasis on the tenure-review process.[142] Tenure review has created major opportunities for conservation throughout the pastoral leasehold land of the high country. The first two tussockland conservation parks – Korowai/Torlesse Conservation Park in Canterbury and Te Papanui Conservation Park in Otago, both more than 20,000 ha. – were established in 2001 and 2003. Since then have come Eyre Mountains/Taka Rā Haka Conservation Park (65,160 ha.) in 2003; Ahuriri Conservation Park (46,655 ha.) in 2004; Hakatere Conservation Park (39,138 ha.) in 2006; Kaikoura/Clarence Conservation Park (88,066 ha.) in 2008; Ruataniwha Conservation Park (37,220 ha.) in 2008; Te Kahui Kaupeka Conservation Park (93,800 ha.) in 2009;

Hawea Conservation Park (105,260 ha.) in 2009 and Oteake Conservation Park (64,815 ha.) in 2010.

According to statements by politicians when it was introduced, tenure review would likely transfer about half of the 2.6 million ha. of South Island's 303 pastoral-leasehold properties for conservation. At the time of writing (31 January 2015), it remains somewhat short of that target, with 99 of the 303 properties reviewed plus five whole-property purchases and a 58.6:41.4% allocation to, respectively, conservation and freehold.[143] A new National government in 2008 had a policy of favouring private covenanting of high-value areas as an outcome of tenure review. Nevertheless, tenure review is continuing, and it seems that most lessees are willing to transfer considerable areas to conservation, if for no other reason than to obtain funding to purchase freehold title of their more productive lower country.

PROTECTION FOR WEST COAST INDIGENOUS FORESTS

In 1986 my first presidential duty was to become a signatory to the West Coast Forest Accord. This had been negotiated by the Secretary for the Environment, Dr Roger Blakely, between commercial forestry, West Coast local-authority interests, and conservation and recreational groups. Clearly the best that could be negotiated at the time, the accord was nevertheless signed with some trepidation. From the society's perspective, an unsatisfactory aspect was clauses extending the duration of logging in the Buller District. These were negotiated by West Coast and forestry interests without consulation with conservation or recreational groups. The accord did, however, create about 200,000 ha. of reserves, including Paparoa National Park. It was eventually revoked by legislation in 2001, which transferred indigenous forests then managed by the SOE Timberlands to DOC.[144]

The Tasman Forest Accord, also significant, was signed by the society, FMC, the Maruia Society (successor to NFAC), the minister of conservation and Tasman Forestry Ltd in June 1989. Safeguarding 52 significant areas of native forest throughout New Zealand, totalling 42,101 ha.,[145] the Tasman Forest Accord declared that 'Tasman Forestry shall adopt an environmental code of practice for its operations in New Zealand that will preclude the clearance of indigenous forest.'[146] Much of this accord has now been rendered obsolete by the international Forestry Stewardship Council, whose conditional endorsement is the current benchmark for forest products marketed with green labels.

Following the apparent success of the West Coast Forest Accord, the government soon afterwards established a similar committee to attempt to resolve how indigenous forests and other state-owned natural resources in South Westland, south of the Cook River, would be used in the future. The working party included representatives of the timber industry, citizens' groups, local and regional authorities, the Mahitahi Maori Committee, conservation groups, and government advisers from DOC, DSIR, the Ministry of Forestry and the Tourist and Publicity Department. State forests were to be allocated according to a spectrum from reservation to production, 'taking account of the impact and opportunities for the regional economy and other resources, including minerals, timber, agriculture, nature conservation, tourism and recreation, fishing, sphagnum moss gathering and community services and infrastructure'.[147]

Aware of the major conservation values at stake, the society decided to promote the case for a South West New Zealand World Heritage Area. The proposal was for a 2.2 million ha. region of lowland and upland forest, wetland, coastal areas and mountains, involving impressive landscapes together with several rare and endangered plants and animals. Published by the society, a book advancing the case, *Forests, Fiords and Glaciers: New Zealand's world heritage*,[148] was edited by Gerard Hutchings and Craig Potton and authored by leading conservationists.[149] As president, I had the privilege of writing the foreword. Magnificent coloured photographs added greatly to the appeal of this book, which not only sold well but, more importantly, provided a convincing argument.

The society's case was based largely on outstanding landscape and ecological values, together with many important cultural values.

However, it also outlined the significant economic advantages that could accrue in perpetuity through eco-tourism, provided that the region's indigenous biodiversity was kept intact. These long-term economic advantages were set against the potential of the 311,000 ha. of state forest to support an indigenous timber industry, given a best-case scenario of a sustainable forest-management system.

The South Westland Working Party conducted an elaborate consultative process involving a preliminary discussion paper, public meetings and a public discussion document, which received 3953 submissions from all over the country. Its 1988 report contained a package of recommendations covering management of the former state forests, minerals, agriculture, nature conservation, tourism and recreation, fishing, sphagnum-moss harvesting, community services and infrastructure.[150] All members agreed that 219,000 ha. of state forest land out of the 311,000 ha. available be recommended for conservation. However, a majority of the committee endorsed a proposal for 20,000 ha. of lowland forest to be evaluated for 'sustained ecosystem management': sustained yield of timber, putatively without significant detriment to the forest ecosystem. It was further recommended that the Cascade forest, part of the Red Hills, be allocated to DOC but with a caveat regarding future mining privileges.

Deeply concerned with the majority support for further logging in this area, the society arranged a deputation to the Minister for the Environment and Deputy Prime Minister, Geoffrey Palmer. This comprised myself as president, vice president Gordon Ell, Gerry McSweeney as conservation director, Sandra Lee as a representative of Ngāi Tahu and a Forest & Bird executive member and, fortuitously, David Bellamy, who happened to be in the country on another mission at this critical time. Following a brief discussion, Palmer invited Prime Minister David Lange to join the group. There was soon agreement that the entire area of government-owned land should be granted conservation status, with world-heritage status sought for the southwest region from Mount Cook in the north to Fiordland, including Waitutu, in the south.

ROYAL FOREST AND BIRD PROTECTION SOCIETY OF NEW ZEALAND

In 1989 the government formally nominated the region for World Heritage status, with official support from the Ngāi Tahu Māori Trust Board and Forest & Bird. The nomination was duly accepted by the World Conservation Union's World Heritage Committee and the region's new status was announced on New Year's Day 1991. The government funded a range of recreational facilities in the South Westland area, including a new visitor centre at Haast and several nature walks. Predictably, there were initially some outbursts of local concern about the initiative. However, as visitor numbers increased, these concerns were replaced by widespread public support for sustainable management and promotion of the region's ecological treasures.[151]

CREDIBLE CONSERVATION

My dual involvement with Forest & Bird and Comalco (the latter through the Fiordland Lakes Guardians) resulted in my suggestion to Comalco's General Manager, Kerry McDonald, that his company may gain more credibility from funding genuine conservation rather than running spurious television advertisements (as it was during the late 1980s). One particularly irritating to me was a Fiordland cascade being used in a Comalco advertisement with the message that Comalco was 'Managing Fiordland waters with care and respect'. Given the company's concerted efforts during the Manapouri Commission of Inquiry to have both Lake Manapouri and Lake Te Anau raised to the maximum possible extent, I discussed the issue with Kerry and suggested there may be more credible ways of obtaining publicity and support for his company.

Our discussion led to me pointing out that kākāpō in the southern region were desperately in need of additional conservation funding. I suggested he might discuss the possibilities of corporate support with Forest & Bird's Conservation Director, Kevin Smith. This proved fruitful and resulted in the formation of the Threatened Species Trust, involving DOC, Forest & Bird and Comalco, with a condition that Comalco's business promotion associated with this sponsorship be restricted to aluminium-can recycling. The outcome has been very successful, with kākāpō numbers increasing from 43 when the sponsorship was initiated to 126 in 2014. In recognition of this success, which involved leading-edge science, for example successful artificial insemination conducted by international specialists, the company (now Rio Tinto Alcan) was selected to receive DOC Southland's most prestigious conservation award in 2010. Kerry and I were both invited to speak at this celebration (I outlined the story) and I had the honour of presenting the award.

In 1989 Forest & Bird received the Royal Society of New Zealand's (RSNZ) inaugural Charles Fleming Environmental Award. In my role as president, I felt privileged to be able to accept the award at a special function in Dunedin.[152] Recognising Forest & Bird's efforts to protect the environment, the award also commemorated the achievements of distinguished scientist and conservationist Sir Charles Fleming, who had died in 1987. In the same year, Gerry McSweeney and I were invited to give a presentation on biotic impoverishment of New Zealand's forest ecosystems at The Ecosystems Center in Massachusetts, USA.[153]

During my last three years as president, I was fortunate and privileged to have politician and conservationist Sandra Lee serve on the executive. Our first Māori executive member, Sandra gave us an appreciation of the indigenous perspective on conservation and protection of our natural and cultural heritage. She was also invaluable as a member of our delegation to the Deputy Prime Minister, Geoffrey Palmer, in convincing the government to endorse our proposal for the South West New Zealand World Heritage Area. Sandra frequently referred to her time on the executive when minister of conservation under Prime Minister Helen Clark.

For her many contributions to conservation, the society bestowed a Distinguished Life Membership on Sandra in 2002. When we met subsequently, Sandra would remind me of the conservation mentoring role I had performed for her. In 2010 I was honoured to receive one of her pair of high-quality pounamu ear pendants at a function associated with the Pew Environmental Group's Te Papa Symposium on the Kermadec Islands. Based largely on my involvement with the Fiordland Marine Guardians, Sandra had invited me to Wellington to join a discussion panel for the symposium.

It has been a great honour to serve on the executive. As president, I felt humbled and proud to follow in the footsteps of New Zealand's most distinguished plant ecologist, Leonard Cockayne, its second president (1930–32), among many other dignitaries. In 1991 I was privileged to receive the society's Distinguished Life Membership. Terminating my executive membership in 1997, I returned unexpectedly in 2001 to support a significant change in the presidency when Gerry McSweeney offered to fill this important role. From 2002 to 2004, I was convenor of the executive's high-country task team as well as its nominee on the New Zealand Conservation Authority for two terms. More recently, in 2011 I was appointed one of three Forest & Bird ambassadors, along with Gerry McSweeney and Craig Potton. I have cherished this role in several subsequent conservation campaigns, including protecting Lake Sumner (successful) and the Denniston Plateau (unsuccessful).

Forest & Bird's three ambassadors, from left: Gerry McSweeney, Craig Potton and me, Hokitika regional meeting, September 2013. Marina Skinner

TIMBERLANDS: A POSTSCRIPT

A rewarding postscript to my activities on the Forest & Bird executive came unexpectedly in 2001. Some 132,000 ha. of indigenous forest, previously allocated to Timberlands as part of the West Coast Forest Accord, was transferred to DOC. Labour's decision was foreshadowed by its pre-election campaign of 1999 while in opposition, when its conservation policy had differed substantially from the government's. The latter had decided to proceed with indigenous logging by Timberlands following a management plan released for public submissions. I was involved in organising and drafting the 32-page submission by fellows of the Royal Society of New Zealand, including seven ecologists and two economists, and presented on behalf of the society's academy. Our submission expressed concern particularly for the lack of peer review of the science behind the management plan, and queried the legality of the beech scheme, the lack of economic information and the inadequate consultation process. There were also auditing and transparency issues.

Of the 36 'substantive submissions' (a government-retained consultant's decision) entered, including the Royal Society's, it soon became apparent that these were evenly divided between support and rejection of the scheme. A vast majority of the total 12,354 submissions, however, opposed the scheme. Surprise publication, in early August, of *Secrets and Lies*, by Nicky Hager and Bob Burton, Wellington and Tasmanian environmentalists, had politically charged the issue.[154] *Secrets and Lies* seriously undermined the credibility of Timberlands and its indigenous logging proposal. Based on a windfall of leaked documents on Timberlands West Coast (TWC) and its PR consultants Shandwick NZ Ltd, the book set the media alight with its wealth of politically sensitive revelations. It was mostly devoted to the tactics of the TWC public relations campaign to render impotent the efforts of several major environmental groups, senior politicians and many innocent but concerned bystanders, who threatened its aspiration to continue logging indigenous old-growth rainforest as a component of its West Coast operations.

No group was too big or small for Timberlands' attention. School children and teachers, university staff, clergy, a TV soap opera and even the Body Shop were all targeted. The detail was impressive and, moreover, never publicly challenged by either Timberlands or Shandwick. Amid calls from opposition political parties for a full inquiry into the many serious allegations the book raised – not least being misuse of taxpayer funds and whether Prime Minister Jenny Shipley had deliberately misled the House – the government attempted to defuse the issue. Just a week after publication, and probably earlier than planned, it formally announced its decision to proceed with logging.

A general election was only months away and the strength of public opposition was obvious, so Labour included in its manifesto a clear rejection of the beech scheme. The party won the election and, true to its word, terminated both the scheme and the West Coast Accord with special legislation. This legislation, transferring the 132,000 ha. of TWC indigenous forest to DOC, also made provision for some $120 million in compensation to West Coast local authorities.

My name was among many mentioned in *Secrets and Lies*, but I was the only one referred to as a 'smart bastard':

> When the respected Professor Alan Mark of Otago University wrote a careful letter to Timberlands explaining his concerns about the logging, the letter was referred to the PR company Shandwick for reply. One of the two main consultants contemptuously wrote in a memo to the other: 'Klaus, Take a look at this smart bastard – what a pity he wasn't born on the West Coast! R McG.' Shandwick was keen to make sure that copies of Timberlands' response to Alan Mark's letter were distributed to a number of ministers. In a memo to Timberlands, McGregor from Shandwick wrote. 'A F Mark Letter: Here's the latest letter with the new revisions included. Could you please check it and gain the necessary approvals for despatch. On second thoughts, I don't think we should send it off from here because the copies to the Ministers should have a Compliments Slip signed by Dave [Hilliard]. Do you agree? ... I'll e-mail it to you so you can print it out onto your own letterhead and despatch.'[155]

Intrigued by this treatment, I wrote to Mr Hilliard 'as a professional ecologist and fellow of the Royal Society of New Zealand, which has a Code of Professional Ethics for professional scientists that I attempt to uphold,' asking him to confirm or correct the statement relating to me.[156] Mr Hilliard duly replied, acknowledging that my letter was referred to their 'communications consultants' for reply, but could not remember

> ... the precise process followed ... I always give final approval before a letter is sent. I have not seen the internal memo between Shandwick staff so I cannot comment on the alleged statement referred to in your letter. I can say I do not condone such behaviour. My concern is to see the genuine requests for information are treated with professional courtesy at all times.[157]

I then wrote to Mr Sorensen, Chief Executive of Shandwick NZ Ltd, and received an interesting response, quoted here only in part:

> Your letter, referred to in the book, was passed on to me by a colleague. The reference to you as 'A Smart Bastard' may represent an illustration of the incredulity that consultants felt upon reading your letter. Alternatively, the term 'Smart bastard' is a colloquialism, which is not always uncomplimentary and can in some cases represent a degree of admiration. I do not recall which of those two options the reference represented. Should you have taken offence at the reference then please accept my apologies, but bear in mind this was an internal communication between two individuals and therefore privileged to the extent it was not intended for anyone else's sight.[158]

The Timberlands scandal also extended to the issue of what role science plays in debate about sustainable management of many natural environments. The issue likewise surfaced in the Manapouri–Te Anau debate. I fully endorsed the opinion expressed by Andy Pearce, Chief Executive of Landcare Research, when he discussed the issue in a *Press* opinion piece following the Labour government's decision to curtail the beech scheme:

ROYAL FOREST AND BIRD PROTECTION SOCIETY OF NEW ZEALAND

> ... sustainable harvesting of natural forests means some trade-offs must be made, for example between maintaining the 'natural character' of the forest and the amount of trees harvested. Defining which trade-offs are 'acceptable', if any, is a social and political problem. Science can assist people in forming views about acceptability and sustainability – it cannot make decisions for them. Scientists contesting the Government's decision, like [name withheld] seem to believe that decisions about sustainability are the preserve of science. Landcare Research does not hold that view.[159]

HURUNUI WATER PROJECT

For more than a decade, Lake Sumner and the Hurunui River in North Canterbury have been the target of plans to build large dams for the benefit of dairy farming on the Canterbury Plains. At the time of writing, the Waitohi Irrigation and Hydro Scheme (WIHS) proposes four dams on the Waitohi River, with intakes from both the Waitohi and the Hurunui rivers to supply the reservoirs. The scheme, which would also generate electricity, is set to cost approximately $100 million more than its immediate predecessor, a more destructive proposal to dam both the Hurunui South Branch and Lake Sumner, raising the lake level with a 2 m dam at the outlet to increase storage for irrigation downstream.

At the urging of South Island Forest & Bird co-ordinator Chris Todd, I visited the lake with a concerned local identity, Edward Snowdon, in April 2010. We spent a day circumnavigating the lake and the adjoining Loch Katrine, armed with a surveyor's level and staff. Boffa Miskell, the environmental planning consultant for the project, had already concluded that the effects of the dam would be 'minor or less than minor'.[160] We soon became suspicious of Boffa Miskell's measurements and conclusions, seeing the canopies of southern rātā and other tree species dipping into the lake on its northern fringe with the lake only half way up its natural range of 3.21 m. Indeed, we concluded that there must have been an error in their levels.

We measured the water level near the lake outlet and it was 0.619 m above the historical minimum. We also checked the levels of a surprising variety of native species: fringing trees of southern rātā on the steep rocky faces east of Pinafore Bay, and to the northwest of Breaksea Bay at least two adult kāmahi trees, neither of which were commonly known to be present and both clearly threatened by the proposed raising of the lake. My report was forwarded to Boffa Miskell and Environment Canterbury (ECan).[161] A flight cancellation prevented me from attending a hearing on the proposal until a second round, which was on the proposed Hurunui Waiau River Regional Plan and proposed Plan Change 3 to the Natural Resources Regional Plan of ECan.

I was asked to present my report to a formal hearing and, ahead of this, contribute to a caucus meeting (expert conferencing) of all those making submissions on the plan. When no proponents of lake-raising appeared for the caucus meeting, three opponents – Dr Colin Burrows (retired University of Canterbury plant ecologist), Nicholas Head (DOC) and I – compiled a two-page joint statement for ECan. In it we emphasised the national significance of the Hurunui catchment, in particular Lake Sumner, the only natural lake left in Canterbury.

Edward Snowden, Christchurch, assisting with the Lake Sumner shoreline study, Breaksea Bay, April 2010.

ROYAL FOREST AND BIRD PROTECTION SOCIETY OF NEW ZEALAND

I was later asked to present a submission at a formal hearing, similar to an Environment Court, with a former senior judge, Peter Salmon CNZM QC, as chair. Chris Todd and I presented this for the society at the Lincoln Centre on 15 October 2012. We learnt of the outcome of our efforts from an ECan press statement on 18 April 2013. We had succeeded! The proposed dam at the lake outlet, as well as an 85 m dam in the adjacent South Branch, were rejected, while the Waitohi catchment, a foothill tributary lower down the Hurunui, was suggested as a more suitable source of irrigation water. This is still under investigation.

SAVE THE DENNISTON PLATEAU, 2011–13

My first major involvement as a conservation ambassador was with the campaign to save the Denniston Plateau in North Westland from coal mining. A 1700-ha. area exhibiting remarkable biodiversity and an internationally unique ecosystem, the Denniston plateau was targeted by an Australian company, Bathurst Resources, for opencast mining over a six-year period, an operation which at the time of writing (March 2015) has very recently begun (February 2015: despite a collapse in international coal prices). Symbolically, in 2011 Prime Minister John Key opened the company's New Zealand office in Wellington while Bathurst was still seeking resource consents to mine the plateau. The most expensive campaign ever run by the society, Save the Denniston Plateau took place in the Environment Court, High Court, Court of Appeal and Supreme Court, in parliament and the media.

I had paid a casual visit to the area some years earlier but got to know the plateau much better during the Forest & Bird BioBlitz in March 2012. This involved 150 volunteer enthusiasts amassing relevant scientific information to inform an appeal to the Environment Court by the society. The mission of my group of 13 volunteers was to collect information on the range of tussock grassland–shrubland–wetland communities on the plateau. For this, we were blessed with very conducive weather for the critical two days. On the days either side of the BioBlitz, the conditions were typical Denniston 'pea-soup'. Rod Morris, Alf Webb and I – the Dunedin contingent – experienced such weather while gathering additional information (including a range of photographs) over three extra days.

My role in the court hearing was to advance the international conservation and biodiversity values of the plateau. For this I invoked both the World Heritage and Ramsar Wetland conventions (New Zealand being a signatory to each). After an informal workshop at the society's makeshift office in Christchurch, I submitted to a two-day preliminary caucus meeting, alongside two others: Willie Shaw and Kelvin Lloyd of Wildland Consultants. Despite the presence of eight opponents at the caucus, held in Wellington before a commissioner, I obtained agreement that some criteria of both international conventions were fulfilled by the plateau. Although the plateau was held to be too small to qualify on its own for World Heritage status, it was agreed that, if and when Kahurangi National Park was nominated, the plateau would significantly complement it. As for Ramsar criteria, there was no dispute that Denniston

Denniston Plateau escarpment below Mt Rochfort, March 2012.

Denniston Plateau bioblitz: my study group at the proposed mine site, March 2012.

would adequately satisfy one important criterion: that greater than 1% (indeed 4–5%) of the total known population of a threatened faunal species, the giant endemic land snail *Powelliphanta patrickensis*, occurred in the relevant wetland, here in the 120-ha. area proposed for mining.

I presented this and additional evidence in the Environment Court at Greymouth before Acting Principal Environment Judge Laurie Newhook and two commissioners, and was stringently cross-examined by the applicant's lawyer, Jo Appleyard. Forest & Bird General Counsel Peter Anderson was modestly confident when the hearings finally concluded just ahead of the Christmas recess. However, the initial judgment in late March 2013 was sobering. An interim decision indicated that mining was 'likely' to go ahead but only if Bathurst could come up with satisfactory offsets and compensation measures. The judge noted the case was 'finely balanced ... So finely balanced indeed that while our present inclination is to grant consent, much will ultimately depend on whether appropriate conditions can be worked out.'

Mining commences on the Denniston Plateau, February 2015.

Here the case rested for some time. Initially, we were confident that the threshold for 'appropriate conditions' could not be met, but eventually the society was forced to accept the court's finding in favour of Bathurst. The decision was partly based on the proposal's economic and employment potential. Also significant was that the conservation land was only classed as 'Stewardship Land'. It therefore had the lowest level of conservation protection and had languished with this status for the quarter-century during which DOC had been responsible for its management. Even the Minister of Conservation, Nick Smith, used this fact to justify permitting access over conservation land for mining purposes. When deciding not to appeal further, the society entered into a settlement agreement with Bathurst. In the words of campaign leader Debs Martin: 'Our grounds for appealing the decision would not have overturned the final outcome, and we decided to negotiate for a better outcome about protecting the reserve area.'[162]

ROYAL FOREST AND BIRD PROTECTION SOCIETY OF NEW ZEALAND

DUNEDIN BRANCH ACTIVITIES

Being a long-time member of the local branch has brought many rewards. I have been both chair and deputy chair of the Dunedin branch. I have periodically organised trips, talks and other events, contributed to submissions and been involved with tenure review on behalf of the branch (as well as on my own behalf). Branch-led ecological restoration exercises, many of which I have organised, have been both demanding and rewarding, particularly at Jacks Blowhole (Tunnel Rocks Scenic Reserve) in the Catlins, Te Rere Yellow-eyed Penguin Reserve on the eastern Southland coast and Caversham Valley in Dunedin City.

Among the most satisfying of such branch activities has been completion of two boardwalks to aid appreciation of outstanding indigenous ecosystems, at Lake Wilkie in the Catlins and at Aramoana saltmarsh, now an Ecological Area, at the entrance to Otago Harbour. These boardwalks were funded mainly through significant donations from the Marjorie Barclay Trust. On behalf of the branch, I offered to attend – fortuitously, as it turned out – the first meeting convened by the trustees, and was both surprised and delighted to receive a substantial cheque for the branch, the first of many. Having received this donation, I persuaded the branch committee to invest it in a boardwalk through the impressive forest–swamp vegetation sequence beside pristine Lake Wilkie in Tautuku Scenic Reserve. Being close to the education centre, the boardwalk provides a valuable ecological education opportunity for the many visitors to this area. The popular boardwalk onto the saltmarsh at Aramoana was similarly funded. Both projects were overseen by DOC.

As a branch (and executive) member, I also assisted with initiating the wilding tree control programme in the southern high country. Despite widespread concern for the increasing wilding tree problem, there was little being done to address the issue. Moreover, many stakeholders made it obvious that they saw the problem as not entirely of their making and well beyond their individual capacities. However, the Dunedin branch had a very encouraging response to a stakeholder meeting which I had it convene in December 1998. Some 25 organisations were represented, including regional and district councils, the commissioner of crown lands, high-country sections of Federated Farmers, Otago and Southland conservation boards and conservancies of DOC, recreation and conservation organisations and all five commercial forestry companies in the southern region.

A formal accord, based on the relevant clause in the 1995 'Principles for Commercial Plantation Forest Management in New Zealand',[163] was adapted to suit the Otago–Southland situation and offered for collective consideration. The text was as follows:

> Wilding trees in Otago and Southland have a variety of sources including commercial forestry, as well as plantings for soil conservation, landscape and shelter purposes. In order to eliminate or minimise the adverse effects of wilding trees on the ecological and landscape values of indigenous vegetation, particularly tussock grasslands, the undersigned major stakeholders (being commercial forestry companies, major landholders or land managers, local authorities, conservation boards and relevant committees of the high-country section of Federated Farmers, the Forest and Bird Protection Society and other conservation/recreation groups) undertake to support, encourage and assist with the containment or control and, where feasible, eradication of wilding trees.[164]

Almost all organisations present formally endorsed the accord. The commercial stakeholders indicated they were already committed by virtue of being members of the New Zealand Forest Owners Association. When it next reviewed its Plant Pest Strategy, the Otago Regional Council showed its commitment, at least in relation to the worst offender, lodgepole pine (*Pinus contorta*).

Ironically, in recent years legislation related to climate change has set the scene for wilding-tree-weed proliferation. The Emissions Trading Scheme, the Permanent Forests Sink Initiative (PFSI) and the Forests (Permanent Forest Sink) Regulations 2007, created by the Climate Change Response Act 2002 or subsequent amendment acts, all permit

TOP: *Jollies Spur, Mid Dome, photographed May 2013 after boom spraying the wilding stand of* Pinus contorta *in January 2013.* ABOVE: *Mid Dome Wilding Tree Trust, left to right: Michael Skerrett, Ali Timms, Geoff Kean, Allison Broad and myself, May 2012.* David Miller.

credits for carbon sequestration and have thereby encouraged exotic forestry. The new problem species is Douglas fir (*Pseudotsuga menziesii*), which is now being planted in several high-country areas for both timber and carbon credits. In some cases, the planting has been environmentally negligent, as for example Landcorp's 2012 planting of 180 ha. of Douglas fir near the upper limit of its Waipori property, adjacent to both Te Papanui Conservation Park (250 m downwind) and Stoney Creek Tussockland Scenic Reserve (200 m upwind) – this despite the SOE's forestry consultants stating that the threat of wilding spread was 'high'. Before the trees were planted, the previous tussock cover had been sprayed with a desiccant then burnt.

With the support of Environment Southland Chair Ali Timms and Larry Burrows of Landcare Research, I publicly challenged this planting, and was interviewed by Radio New Zealand. Answering a provocative question by reporter Ian Telfer, I indicated the possibility of removing them with voluntary support. This prompted an immediate response in the media from the Forest Owners Association spokesperson that I was a 'Knight of the Realm turned vigilante'.[165] I later engaged the ombudsman to obtain information on commercial aspects of this planting, which had been refused on the basis of 'commercial sensitivity'. At a site visit I requested with members of Landcorp's executive group in April 2014, it was resolved that Landcorp would produce a MOU with DOC on its responsibility for wilding control on adjacent conservation tussocklands, and that no further plantings would occur pending a search for a non-aggressive species.

Since 1998 efforts to control wilding pines across the southern South Island high country have certainly expanded and diversified, though not yet sufficiently to address the enormity of the problem. Wilding-tree control teams now operate out of Queenstown, organised initially by Eco-Action under Colin Day, and, more recently, the Wakatipu Wilding Tree Group in collaboration with the Queenstown Lakes District Council. In Dunedin, the branch initially engaged Dave McFarlane, then Rhys Millar, Matt Thomson and, most recently, Wiremu Bretton as its

ROYAL FOREST AND BIRD PROTECTION SOCIETY OF NEW ZEALAND

Dave McFarlane and myself with the Otago Regional Council's Environmental Award for Forest & Bird's wilding pine control efforts, February 2004. Katharine Dickinson

Wilding Tree Independent Contractor. Funding has come from various sources, and the branch's tally as of 2010 exceeded 200,000 wildings of all sizes and several species.

Importantly, there has been a general change in attitude towards wilding trees in the high country. DOC, Environment Southland, LINZ and MfE have all been active, particularly with the serious problem at Mid Dome in northern Southland. The Otago high-country section of Federated Farmers established a wilding-tree subcommittee, which functioned for several years. In 2006 I was invited to be a trustee of the Mid Dome Wilding Trees Charitable Trust to oversee eradication of *Pinus contorta* wildings from some 250 ha. of stands planted there in the 1950–70s for erosion control. The 12-year strategic plan the trust developed has been constrained by limited funding despite several significant grants. It has been reassuring to see much more effective control methods develop over my time with the trust – both boom and basal-bark spraying using a potent herbicide 'armageddon' brew. There has also been much stronger commitment, including from politicians, to control and even eradicate wilding trees elsewhere in the high country. Much remains to be done; as DOC's Keith Briden has stated, 'The cost of procrastination is enormous.'[166]

8

OTHER RESEARCH ACTIVITIES

While my main research has involved upland snow-tussock grasslands and, more recently (and fortuitously), lakeshore ecology, I've been fortunate to work on most other indigenous ecosystems of southern New Zealand. Such indulgence has been possible in part because, in the early stages of my career, there were relatively few practising plant ecologists working in the southern South Island. Historically, forest ecological studies were concentrated in the southern high-rainfall regions, particularly Fiordland and Mount Aspiring national parks, and I was lucky to be involved in much of the initial research. I describe here selected projects, though there are many others, past and on-going.

SECRETARY ISLAND: THE IMPACT OF DEER-BROWSING
In 1959 my mentor, Professor Geoff Baylis – a foundation member of the Fiordland National Park Board and keen to expand knowledge of the park's ecology – led a trip to Secretary Island on Fiordland's western fringe. The research team was made up of myself, fellow plant ecologist Peter Wardle, lichenologist Jas Murray and three student assistants (David Anderson, Lindsay Pearce and Jim Watt). We based ourselves at a tent site in Blanket Bay, at the 80 sq. km island's southeastern end.

The trip was originally intended to be a mere reconnaissance, but when it became apparent that the island was still deer-free, a detailed study of the vegetation accessible from our campsite seemed urgent. Following a second visit in February 1960 – this time with Ross McNab

Secretary Island subalpine silver beech forest at 880 m above Blanket Bay, showing total loss of the five-finger Pseudopanax colensoi var. fiordensis *subcanopy through selective browsing by red deer soon after their establishment on the island. December 1981.*

substituting for Jas Murray – several papers were published in the first volume of the *New Zealand Journal of Botany*. These included an overview of plant communities,[167] a more detailed description of the composition and regeneration features of the beech–podocarp forest on the lower slopes,[168] and a description of the low-alpine vegetation from treeline to the summit of the island's highest peak, Mount Grono (1196 m).[169] We also included a list of vascular (higher) plants recorded in the course of these two visits.[170]

Aware that deer may eventually reach the island, we were keen to extend our studies to other parts. From tent bases at Astelia Stream on the northeastern coast in February 1964 and Grono Bay on the southwestern side in 1967, we traversed much of the remainder of the island. These two later visits confirmed that the vegetation pattern for the more accessible parts of the island was similar to what we had previously described. However, during our 1967 visit, we were concerned to see obvious signs of deer presence, probably a lone animal, at Grono

OTHER RESEARCH ACTIVITIES

One of the last remaining deer to be culled by DOC's Secretary Island hunting team.
DOC press release, 3 September 2014.

Bay, with damage confined to bark stripped from three-finger (*Pseudopanax colensoi* var. *ternatum*) and five-finger (var. *fiordensis*) and accessible fronds taken from hen and chickens fern (*Asplenium bulbiferum*). Two additional papers were published from these visits.[171]

Attempts by the Forest Service to 'nail' this animal were unsuccessful, and by the time of our next visit in 1975, the signs of deer usage were both distinct and much more extensive, with some 63 animals having been shot on the island by Forest Service staff.[172] During our next five-day visit in 1981, we reassessed the impacts of deer on areas described during our previous visit. We also established some permanent plots to follow future trends more precisely since the more sensitive areas and plant species were now quite obvious.[173] At this time, few mature trees of three-finger and five-finger remained alive but most stems were still standing as skeletons of the previous sub-canopy layer, while hen and chickens ferns had virtually succumbed to persistent grazing on all accessible sites. Deer were now turning to some other ferns, particularly prickly shield fern (*Polystichum vestitum*) and whekī (*Dicksonia squarrosa*), while most other ferns appeared to be still unaffected. Both lancewood species – *Pseudopanax crassifolius* at lower altitudes and *P. lineare* above – had mostly broken stems that gave access to their palatable growing tips, yet plants of both species were showing a distinct ability to resprout close to the removed tips.[174]

Despite the 'special area' status for the island having been lifted, we continued to plead for more effective deer control. This status had been established because of the island's initial deer-free state – the condition of vegetation remained obviously superior to that of the surrounding mainland. However, the possibility of reinfestation by animals swimming the few kilometres from the nearest mainland was initially given as the reason why eradication was not being seriously attempted.[175] The later, successful eradication of rats from Breaksea Island allowed that island to substitute for Secretary as a 'special area', and both saddlebacks and mohua populations were established there in the 1990s. Now, the deer-eradication project on Secretary has been fully embraced, and the island has been reclassified as a 'restoration' island, with over 500 deer removed since 2008 (now down to the last few) and an expansive stoat eradication programme in action. There has been obvious recovery of the vegetation and several threatened bird species have been released.

VEGETATION SUCCESSION: CHANGES ALONG ENVIRONMENTAL GRADIENTS

In May 1962 I led a student expedition to study forest succession on landslides above Lake Thomson, west of Lake Te Anau's Middle Arm. We described plant communities on three landslides aged 14, 49 and 78 years old (dated from annual growth rings of mānuka), together with the adjacent mature silver-beech forest. Being of the same parent material, aspect and slope, the slides were ecologically so similar that we concluded the only significant differentiating factor was time.[176] When the study was repeated 24 years later, we were able to compare the temporal factor with spatial differences on the three slides. This

OTHER RESEARCH ACTIVITIES

ABOVE: *Lake Thompson landslide area, Fiordland National Park, December 1962. The most recent slide (centre right) is dominated by 14-year-old mānuka (indicating when this slide probably occurred); to its left is a 78-year-old stand dominated by mountain beech, southern rātā and kamahi, with mānuka persisting; then a 49-year-old stand dominated by mānuka and rātā; and on the far left is undisturbed (climax) forest dominated by silver beech.* ABOVE: *Upper Dart valley below Cascade Saddle showing major hillside collapse due to the receding glacier, March 2007. A study of the moraines associated with the recession indicated the plant succession involved (Sommerville et al., 1982).*

confirmed the overriding importance of time in characterising the stages of this classic example of a primary rainforest succession.[177]

Among many other examples of plant succession, those on the Dart Glacier's lateral moraines in Mount Aspiring National Park are particularly impressive. I assisted with an Honours project to study these in some detail.[178]

In another selection of studies, we compared altitudinal gradients in forest composition and structure in three Fiordland areas[179] – where beech species dominate and play a major role – with that on Mount Anglem on beech-free Stewart Island.[180] Elsewhere, at Fiordland's remote West Cape, a different sort of ecological gradient – from forest to shrubland to tussock grassland over gently rolling, non-glaciated terrain – was found to be more associated with subtle changes in topography, particularly as it affected drainage, than with changes in elevation.[181] Similar vegetation sequences were described on the undulating plateau in the highest parts of the Catlins region. Here, cushion bog with copper-tussock grassland graded through shrubland and woodland into coniferous–broadleaved forest dominated by mountain cedar or pāhautea (*Libocedrus bidwillii*).[182]

VEGETATION SURVEY AND MONITORING OF MOUNT ASPIRING NATIONAL PARK

At the request of the Otago National Parks and Reserves Board and Lands and Survey, I spent two summers (1968–70) completing a vegetation survey of Mount Aspiring National Park for use as a basis for both interpretation and management. The timing was fortuitous. Efficient transport into this large and mountainous area was provided by helicopters, their operators having just begun frequent forays into the most remote regions for commercial hunting of the huge red deer populations there. I covered the southern half in the first season, with Ranger Mervyn Burke of Glenorchy as field assistant. In the second season, Conway Powell – at that time a graduate student of Geoff Baylis's and fellow enthusiast for the area – assisted me with the northern half. While the shooters were gutting carcases from their dawn heli-hunt, the pilots delivered us from our valley floor campsite to an adjacent valley to offload our camping gear, then to the high tops, with just a snack, wet-weather and survey gear in our day packs (map, aerial photographs, binoculars, compass, altimeter, ice axe, hand lens and collecting bags).

We would descend to our camp before dark, on the western ranges dropping below the treeline before dense fogs accompanying the early afternoon sea breezes stole our view. En route, we sampled the plant cover so as to describe its general altitudinal pattern and composition. Boundaries between major plant communities were sketched on the aerial photographs as we moved down-slope. The descents were rarely as straightforward as our scans from air in the morning might have indicated. The tree canopy, in particular, could conceal quite difficult terrain but fortunately we had no serious mishaps. Despite the frequent helicopter rides, I managed to wear out two pairs of boots on this job.

As well as providing a vegetation map of the park, our survey created a real opportunity to assemble a comprehensive plant collection from areas that were generally poorly known botanically. Chief Ranger Ray Cleland was keen to have a representative collection for the park's Wanaka headquarters; I wanted a duplicate collection for the Otago Botany Department's herbarium. Invaluable for local transport and bringing in supplies, helicopters also provided us with a means of periodically transferring our plant collection back to civilisation to complete the drying process. We would sort and press the samples on most evenings. A total of 571 species of higher plants were collected and their general distribution described. It was demanding and painstaking to separate, annotate and press these in newspaper and corrugated cardboard, given our pup-tent accommodation.

While the occasional hut or bivvy proved a godsend for this exercise, our most traumatic and memorable event was at Williamson Flat in the Arawhata Valley, where we camped near an almost empty 9 x 9-foot tent of no obvious ownership. The tent contained two empty four-gallon food tins with tight-fitting lids. These were used to hold my burgeoning plant

Upper Arawhata Valley, showing degraded alpine snow-tussock grassland in the early stages of recovery from serious degradation caused by high numbers of red deer. March 2007.

press above a slow-burning primus. This worked so well that I decided to refill the primus before turning in for the night. I was woken by the deafening sound of an exploding tin, caused by the burning paper in the press after its nylon ties had melted and the press had collapsed onto the primus. The tent was aglow as I raced in. I managed to extinguish the inferno using the mass of damp plants, some of which suffered with scorched edges that still persist on a number of herbarium specimens.[183]

This vegetation survey[184] provided a chance to monitor the effects of huge deer numbers before they were drastically reduced with the continuation of commercial heli-hunting. Generally too remote for serious recreational hunting, the park has extensive non-forest areas so that commercial heli-hunting proved highly effective. The vegetation at the time of my survey was highly degraded because of very high deer

OTHER RESEARCH ACTIVITIES

densities, particularly in the more remote western regions. However, the prospects for recovery seemed good, given the dramatic reduction in deer. Some 25,000 red deer were reputedly shot in the Waiatoto Valley in one year, so there was a reasonable prospect that numbers would remain low enough for the vegetation to recover.

On completion of my survey, I recommended to the park board and Lands and Survey that they initiate a vegetation-monitoring programme. This was accepted despite some reservations from within the Forest Service that the exercise would have mere political value. Approval was given to establish up to 100 permanent photographic points at representative sites throughout the park. With assistance from the Forest Service, 68 points were installed in 1970 and a further 20 in 1973, distributed among the six major vegetation types as follows:

John Barkla and Geoff Rogers at the photo-point site in the upper Joe valley, Mt Aspiring National Park, for the 2007 resurvey of low-alpine curled snow-tussock grassland.

- forest (13)
- subalpine scrub (6)
- valley grassland (6)
- low-alpine snow-tussock grassland (55)
- high-alpine fellfield (6)
- open successional communities (2)

A set procedure for locating, photographing and recording was established, but formal written descriptions of the vegetation were limited by time and the financial constraints associated with requiring a helicopter for the exercise.[185]

Four resurveys at five-to-eight-year intervals were conducted up to 2007 to provide a 37-year record for those sites that have remained intact. All major plant communities have shown obvious improvement. In the case of subalpine shrublands and low-alpine snow-tussock grasslands, the recovery has been impressive both in the restoration of snow tussock dominance and the return of the more palatable associated species, often from seed sources on inaccessible bluffs.[186] By 1999 these two communities, at least, were assumed to be essentially similar to their condition in the pre-deer era.[187] A decline in commercial deer hunting, associated with tighter government regulations, use of 1080 as an alternative pest-control method and fluctuations in market value in the early 2000s, makes for an uncertain future.

Helicopters were essential for this monitoring exercise, given the size of the park, its changeable weather and the rugged terrain. Before the days of GPS, finding painted marker stakes from the air was not always easy and could certainly test the skills of a pilot. Some were willing to put down where others had previously landed, close to a monitoring site, but others refused and chose to wait at a preferred site some distance away, often out of sight. This could cost valuable time. My closest call, however, on our first resurvey in 1977, was not pilot-related but due to the forestry field assistant.

Taking off early in the morning from Burke Flat in the Haast Valley,

OTHER RESEARCH ACTIVITIES

in a Hiller (which seats three with the pilot in the centre), the assistant failed to adequately secure my frame pack on the outside rack. It became airborne as we were overflying the Gates of Haast bridge en route to the Wills Valley. Having very fortunately missed the tail rotor, the pack disappeared into the forest on the steep slopes above the bridge, whereupon we returned to Burke Flat with no choice but to abandon the exercise. Our day's search for my pack and its valuable contents (a near-new camera and tripod plus my inscribed aerial photographs and wet-weather gear) proved challenging among abundant stinging nettle and was fruitless. Efforts by a bus load of forestry cadets the following day were no more rewarding. The pack given up for lost, the Forest Service claimed on the helicopter company's insurance.

Some 15 years later, the Haast police rang the Botany Department, inquiring after a certain 'Alan Mark'. His name and address were still legible on a sheet of waterproof 'paper' in the remains of a frame pack picked up by a passing motorist on the roadside near the Gates of Haast bridge (the motorist was apparently relieved to be told the owner was still around). It was wrapped and returned to me but at this stage had no more than sentimental value. Other than the metal frame, waterproof base and identifying sheet of wet 'paper', the pack and contents were barely recognisable and worthless.

SOUTHLAND ECOLOGY AND CONSERVATION
In the mid-1970s I was invited by Wildlife Service to contribute a botanical perspective to takahē management in Fiordland's Murchison Mountains, and in the course of my studies of takahē ecology and conservation, deer issues again arose. These studies, made in collaboration with Jim Mills, who was then managing the programme, showed the preference of takahē during the snow-free period for certain species of snow tussock, apparently selected on the basis of their relatively high nutrient values. The midribbed snow tussock, *Chionochloa pallens*, was the preferred species, followed in decreasing order of preference by *C. flavescens* (later corrected to *C. rigida* subsp. *amara*), *C. crassiuscula*

Snow-tussock grassland pattern in the Chester Burn, Murchison Mountains, Fiordland National Park, in relation to landscape factors and preferred takahē habitat. Mid-ribbed snow tussock (Chionochloa pallens) *dominates the unstable debris (talus) slopes with shrubs (right) and, being nutrient-rich, is the preferred takahē habitat.*

and *C. teretifolia*, which was never touched. Interestingly – but of great concern – red deer showed generally the same preferences.[188]

Our winter visits revealed the apparent dependence of takahē on the underground stems or rhizomes of the summer-green, thousand-leaved fern *Hypolepis millefolium*, particularly where it was most abundant in the subalpine forest. We found that the rhizomes at this time of year have a high concentration of starch, which obviously attracted the takahē.[189] The important plant ecological inputs to the takahē conservation programme have since been assumed by my colleague Bill Lee.

Further south, the typical eastern Fiordland wetland of Borland Mire, adjacent to the eastern boundary of the national park at Monowai was studied and described as part of a University Extension Department's summer ecology course, which I often taught.[190] On our recommendation, Lands and Survey later acquired Borland Mire for its conservation value.

OTHER RESEARCH ACTIVITIES

Located within one kilometre of Borland Lodge, this lowland raised mire has since become a valuable educational asset for groups based at the lodge.

ECOLOGICAL STUDIES OF THE WAITUTU MARINE-TERRACE SEQUENCE
Given the growing debate over Southland's Waitutu Forest during the mid-1980s, I was aware that a deeper understanding of its ecological importance could be valuable. The Forest Service had designated the area a long-term wood resource, despite limited knowledge of its high ecological values associated with the distinctive sequence of marine terraces. A comprehensive ecological survey was organised by geologist Chris Ward and myself following our helicopter visit in September 1984, funded by Les Hutchins and accompanied by David Bellamy and others, including a television crew. The visit, revealing a sequence of at least 10 marine terraces to rival the world-famous Mendocino terraces, the 'ecological staircase' in California,[191] sent Bellamy into raptures. Apparently, the Mendocino terraces have been seriously modified by development whereas the Waitutu terraces looked pristine.

Reconnaisance group on Hump Ridge en route to scan the Waitutu terrace sequence (behind) ahead of the detailed study. Left to right: Chris Ward, David Bellamy, Les Hutchins and Tony Hughes, September 1984.

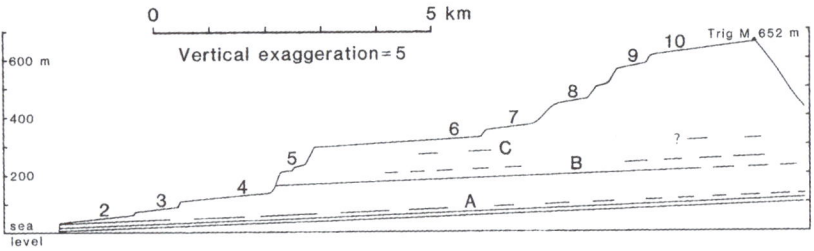

An aerial view (top) and profile diagram of the Waitutu marine terrace sequence, western Southland. The 10 marine terraces and three river terraces are shown.

Our survey in May 1985 involved a party of 12 and spanned 10 days. The results were published by the Royal Society in 1988 in a series of eight 'collected papers' describing the distinctive geology-geomorphology of the terraces, their unique vegetation, flora and fauna (birds, insects and snails all featured) and the associated soil patterns.[192] However, the survey did not confirm the postulated long-term, uninterrupted soil–vegetation chrono-sequence spanning the last 640,000 years (and thus extending back well into the glacial period). Although the terrace surfaces had not been directly affected by the glaciation, devegetation and surface ablation had apparently occurred under the severe peri-glacial climatic conditions that prevailed during the glacial period. Differential accumulation of wind-borne fines (loess) during and directly after the glacial period also complicated the picture somewhat.

If the survey could not confirm an uninterrupted soil–vegetation chrono-sequence, the vegetation pattern was still highly idiosyncratic, courtesy of a range of soil factors including gradients in soil wetness associated with increasing elevation, soil development and minor topographical differences on particular terraces. Being extensive and essentially unmodified, the terrace sequence contained a valuable soil–vegetation complex representative of marine terrace ecosystems that had formerly been more widespread around New Zealand but which, like those in California, were now largely lost to development. The full extent of the terrace sequence was considered to justify formal protection through reservation. This included the lower – and youngest – three terraces, which were in separate Māori holdings.

Although debate on the issue did not cease with our publications, the terrace sequence's unique values were generally accepted, even by those politicians who eventually negotiated a $12 million deal with the major landholder, the Waitutu Māori Trust Board, to secure management of the area by DOC. This approach was consistent with that taken for the adjoining ex-Forest Service area, later added to Fiordland National Park but with ownership of the Māori land retained by the trust board. The forest on one of the two smaller Māori land blocks was subsequently secured by the government.

ECOLOGICAL STUDIES IN SOUTH WESTLAND

I have been involved in several studies, both before and after the establishment of Te Wāhipounamu – South West New Zealand World Heritage Area. The intention behind these was to demonstrate the breadth of ecologically significant features in the South Westland region. Four of these studies are worth describing here: studies of hard beech (*Fuscospora (Nothofagus) truncata*) forest stands, epiphytic communities on rainforest trees, the Haast Okuru parallel dune/swale systems and Hapuka estuary.

In respect of the first, Bill Lee and I provided a detailed description of some of the hard beech stands that Selwyn June of Canterbury University had previously revealed as significant southern outliers – the only ones known south of the 'beech gap' in central Westland. These stands occupy glacial mounds on the flood plain between the Waiatoto and

Arawhata rivers, south of Haast, and show very precise restriction to the relatively warm and dry northwest-facing slopes. We described the two most extensive stands on Nissan Hill and MacFarlane Mound. On these relatively warm, well-drained slopes, the size–class distributions and diameter growth rates of hard beech stems indicated they are competing effectively with podocarp and broadleaved tree species, including the two other beeches present, silver (*Lophozonia (Nothofagus) menziesii*) and mountain (*Fuscospora (N.) cliffortioides*).[193]

While the distribution of these three beech species is somewhat erratic in South Westland, the greatest enigma is where hard beech might have survived during the glacial period, given the relatively warm sites this species currently occupies. Though these sites are the warmest in the region, moraine material on them indicates they were covered by glacial ice at some stage. Our speculation that survival might have been possible on seaward-facing slopes on the coastal hills south of the Arawhata River mouth, or perhaps beyond the present coastline when the sea level was lower, was later challenged by Peter Wardle, who suggested that hard beech may have been reconstituted through hybridisation of red and mountain beech during the post-glacial period. This suggestion was itself refuted by Canterbury University ecologist Peter Haase on the basis of DNA analyses, which indicated that the local hard beech stands have considerable antiquity. The question of survival of hard beech in this area during the glacial period remains unresolved.

I have long been impressed by the rich and lush communities of perching plants associated with some of the larger podocarp trees in the Haast region, particularly a large kahikatea near the mouth of Cole Creek some 14 km north of Haast. Colleague Katharine Dickinson and I made a study of this large kahikatea, using an extension ladder for access, recording 28 different climbing and perching plants on it. These included seven shrubs, five climbers, 10 ferns, five orchids and one nest epiphyte (grass-like plant), plus at least 18 lichens, five mosses and six liverworts. We claimed a possible world record for the number of higher plants on the tree but this could not be sustained.[194] (Sadly, this very

OTHER RESEARCH ACTIVITIES

Kahikatea (Dacrycarpus dacrydioides) *tree at Cole Creek near Haast, South Westland; some 28 species of vascular plants were found on it.*

impressive tree blew down in May 2003.) In fact, a 1938 record of 36 vascular species on a kauri tree in Northland put paid to this, as did one of 65 vascular plant species for a single tree in Costa Rica, published simultaneously in 1993.

A later study involving Katharine and Robert Hofstede – a colleague from Ecuador with previous experience of epiphytes in the tropical rainforest of Colombia – was made further north near Lake Moeraki. Here we studied three host trees – two kahikatea and one silver beech – growing close to the lower Moeraki River. We recorded a total of 61 vascular plant species and 94 non-vascular crytogams (mosses and liverworts) and lichens. We also sampled the biomass of epiphytes,

215

and values for all of these three features were similar to those of the richest tropical rainforests. The 49 vascular plant species recorded for one kahikatea tree is now the record in New Zealand – and perhaps for temperate rainforests generally – but is still well below the 65 species recorded for single trees in tropical rainforests in both Costa Rica and French Guyana.[195]

Katharine and I also made a detailed study of the striking pattern of parallel dune ridges and alternating wet hollows or 'swales' running parallel to the Haast coast. We laid out a 2.3 km thread-line across a typical sequence of six parallel ridges in Okuru forest from close to the road heading south from Haast. The main challenge here was crossing some of the wet depressions, which contain numerous ponds, some of considerable depth. The thread-line ('hip chain') that we ran inland to mark the line of the transect also prevented us from getting lost or disoriented in the relatively flat and featureless forest segments.

A mixed podocarp–beech–broadleaved rainforest up to 33 m tall dominates the dry beach ridges here, with shrub margins (mostly of

View south across the series of dune ridges and swales (hollows) between Haast and Okuru, South Westland, produced as the coastline has extended over the past several thousand years, aided by ca. *50 million tons of sediment deposited annually by the several large rivers in this region*

OTHER RESEARCH ACTIVITIES

One of the Haast dune ridge/swales (see opposite) as seen from the highway that crosses it between the Haast and Waita rivers.

manuka) separating the forested ridges from the herbaceous wetlands that occupy the swales. These wetlands show a striking transition – from sedges and umbrella fern on the younger western swales, where the peat depth is only 2–3 m, to much shorter plant cover with mosses and small sedges predominating on the older more eastern swales, where the peat depth exceeds 5 m.[196] The highway north of Haast crosses one of these swales and provides a fine view southwards along it.[197] This intriguing landscape pattern is best appreciated from the air.

Eleven kilometres south of Haast lies Hapuka estuary near the river mouth and we made a study of this small but impressive estuary where DOC has now created an interpretive boardwalk. We deemed the estuary essentially intact and an important representation of the range of ecological features, collectively worthy of conservation, in the World Heritage Area. Although only 11 ha. in extent, Hapuka estuary is unrivalled in the region in terms of its naturalness and vegetation patterns. These extend in a series of zones from subtidal sands, through saltmarsh, mānuka shrubland and podocarp woodland fringe, to a very impressive stand of tall podocarp–broadleaved rainforest located on the dune ridge alongside the marsh.[198] A track traversing the wetland and an observation platform in the forest allow a viewer to scan westward through a natural window, across the saltmarsh all the way out to the Bench islands, which lie a few kilometres offshore. The nearby motelier said this estuary walk is a 'goldmine' for his business.

NOKOMAI PATTERNED WETLANDS

In her 1989 Protected Natural Areas Survey, my colleague Katharine Dickinson outlined the international significance of the Nokomai wetlands on the southern Garvie Mountains in southern Central Otago.[199] Since that time, I have studied this complex in some detail with several colleagues. These extensive wetlands, located at 1300 m elevation among low-alpine snow-tussock grassland at the head of the Dome Burn and Roaring Lion Stream, are characterised by an extensive series of pools elongated at right angles to a very gentle slope. The pools are frequently studded with numerous small circular islands.

Referred to as 'patterned wetland with string pools and island tarns', these wetlands closely resemble patterned mires in Tierra del Fuego and the northern subarctic region. Initially, we set out to describe the patterns, including an intriguing underground pipe system draining one of the pools, and to indicate how the islands may form given the presumed very slow rate of water-level rise.[200] We also examined the area's vegetation history from pollen buried in the peat. This showed that the wetlands had developed only about 600 years ago, coinciding with repeated fires that destroyed both forest and tall scrub communities and are associated with early Māori occupation of the Otago hinterland.[201] Runholder Brian Hore greatly assisted us in our survey, transporting heavy peat-coring equipment to our site with his helicopter and enabling us to take revealing aerial photographs.

In the Northern Hemisphere, scientific opinion on patterned wetlands indicates their origin variously in physical and biological processes, including down-slope gravitational movement of material,

OTHER RESEARCH ACTIVITIES

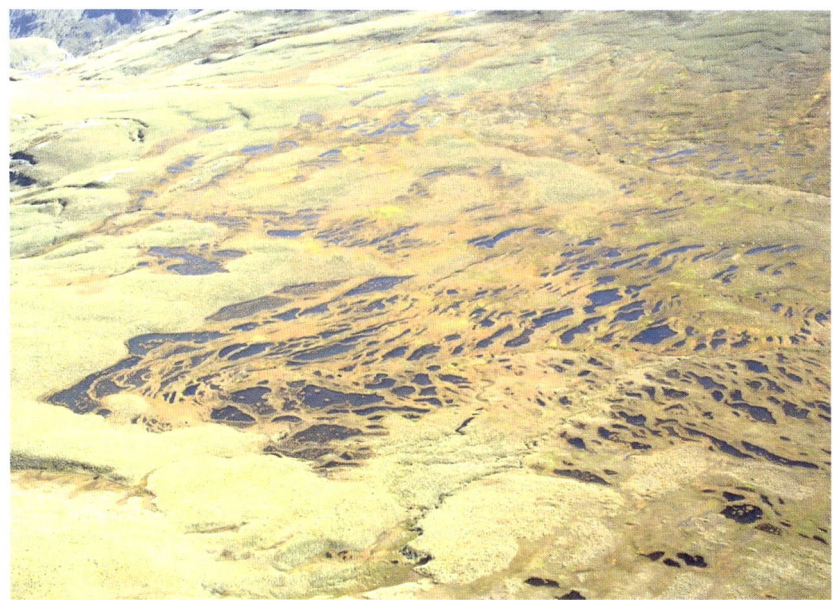

ABOVE: *Aerial view of the extensive Roaring Lion patterned mire on the southern Garvie Mountains, Central Otago. The numerous pools, elongated at right angles to the gentle slope and with numerous small islands, are distinctive features of this internationally significant wetland.* BELOW: *The islands are more obvious from the ground.*

seasonal freeze-thaw, and differential growth rates between plant species. We were able to dismiss the climatic explanation for New Zealand's patterned mires on the basis of their unexpected occurrence near sea level in the Okuru dune swales; however, the processes operating within them require detailed studies over several seasons: we have established some permanent monitoring sites. A study on the Dome Burn and Roaring Lion mires found little mixing of water within these wetlands. The surface water draining across them is derived from both rainfall and run-off from the surrounding slopes. The availability and chemistry of the water on the mire surface seems to determine variations in plant cover.[202] Despite its international significance, the Nokomai wetland complex presently has no formal protection, though the runholder Brian Hore is aware of their importance and has assured us they will not be damaged or endangered.

ECOLOGY OF MĀNUKA

Mānuka (*Leptospermum scoparium*), the most common indigenous shrub in the lowland wetlands of South Westland and Fiordland, also features on lakeshores in the region. It has been studied in some detail in relation to its extremely wide environmental range and tolerance. At the other environmental extreme, mānuka is common in open mixed shrubland on the drier fringes of woody vegetation in Central Otago, inland Canterbury and elsewhere. In forested regions, it usually dominates the early stages of a succession following disturbance of a site (usually by fire). However, being highly light-demanding, it cannot regenerate under a closed canopy and is eventually replaced by forest cover where the environment suits. We have found it may persist in the canopy for up to a century before taller forest trees overtop and eliminate it.[203]

Under my supervision, Chinese student Yin Ronghua from Wuhan studied the wider ecology of mānuka, his analysis revealing a link between variations in both leaf shape and the form (shape) of a shrub, and the simple factors of latitude, altitude and distance from the coast.[204]

OTHER RESEARCH ACTIVITIES

Northern lowland plants are quite erect and have long, narrow leaves, whereas those in the interior of the southern uplands are more squat and with leaves more-nearly circular. This variation in leaf shape may be associated with favourable heat balance in a plant's leaves. An earlier study of mānuka's tolerance of waterlogged conditions found tolerance to be associated with the development of specialised ventilating tissue in its bark at and below the water line, a feature much more strongly developed in plants from moist regions (e.g. the Catlins) than semi-arid (Central Otago).[205] In 2003, in collaboration with South African fire ecologist William Bond, Katharine and I examined geographic variation in the occurrence of persistent closed capsules (serotiny) in mānuka throughout the South Island and Stewart Island. This may shed light on regional differences in fire history since serotiny is usually associated with a long history of fire.[206]

Mānuka is widespread and is also easy to experiment with. In 1979 secondary school biology teachers asked me to scope out a manual for their senior classes to investigate a range of ecological features of this remarkable species as an alternative to what most teachers were using at the time: gorse.

NEW ZEALAND ALPINE VEGETATION IN A GLOBAL CONTEXT
Keen to put the general features of New Zealand alpine vegetation in a global context, in 2000 Robert Hofstede, Katharine and I studied the plant distribution, life forms and environment – both climatic and soil – between the treeline and permanent snowline on Mount Armstrong, on the Main Divide near Haast Pass. Our study emphasised the many distinctive features of New Zealand alpine vegetation, in particular the dominance of tall tussock grasses in the low-alpine zone. These have their global counterpart not in the continental temperate mountains of the Northern Hemisphere but on the tropical high mountains and subantarctic islands associated with a less extreme, oceanic type of climate.[207] The dwarfed nature of plants in the high-alpine zone is less anomalous, being a feature of all alpine regions of the world.

In a separate paper, American colleague Larry Bliss and I described the range of high-alpine plant communities on the interior South Island mountains of Central Otago[208] – including the productivity of extensive cushionfield and herbfield communities there – and placed this in a world context.[209] Under my supervision in the 1980s, Joy Talbot undertook a detailed study of high-alpine snowbank plant communities on the Rock and Pillar Range of Central Otago.[210] Patterning of the ground's surface in areas of high-alpine vegetation on the Otago plateau summits range from stone nets and stripes to soil hummocks and stripes, as well as solifluction terraces and lobes, and ploughing boulders, each with their counterparts abroad.[211] Only the last four features are usually well-vegetated.

While these patterns have been described by several researchers, debate on which if any are active was at least partly resolved with detailed studies of soil hummocks, stripes and solifluction terraces on the Old Man Range. A large terrace was shown to be moving actively down a gentle slope at about 3.5 cm a decade. And contrary to earlier

View south along the crest of the Old Man Range, Central Otago, showing some of the soil stripes developed on gentle southern slopes. Dwarfed cushion plants dominate the exposed crests while larger herbs and lichens occupy the more sheltered hollows.

OTHER RESEARCH ACTIVITIES

A large active solifluction terrace on a gentle southeasterly slope on the crest of the Old Man Range, Central Otago. Dwarfed cushionfield dominates the exposed slope above the terrace while taller snowbank and herbfield plants occupy the more sheltered leeward sites.

predictions, soil hummocks on flat terrain transitioning into stripes on gentle slopes were also shown to be active through differential freezing during winter. While the crests regularly freeze, the adjacent depressions remain unfrozen. Such differential freezing over winter facilitates moisture transfer from the unfrozen soil to the frozen area, which is probably sufficient to retain the distinctive microtopography.[212]

In contrast to mānuka, the high-alpine forget-me-not *Myosotis oreophila* – the subject of a prolonged demographic study – has perhaps the most restricted range among our native plants. It was first collected in 1891 by early botanist Donald Petrie from Mount Ida in northern Central Otago. Despite several searches by Petrie and others, it was not seen again until 1986, when Don Bruce, working with the PNA survey team, found it in a very small area (~0.5 ha) on the northern Dunstan Mountains. Our monitoring over 15 years revealed a 'boom and bust' situation over the first few years. Indeed, more plants were recruited and died over the first five years than in the rest of our 15-year study period.

Botanical artist Nancy Adams working on our co-authored book, New Zealand Alpine Plants, *on the Old Man Range, January 1971.*

This implied that the whole population could have turned over within this period.[213] Continued studies, however, have indicated much greater stability in the population than initially supposed. This we estimate has ranged from about 13,000 to 21,800 plants over the study period. Another much smaller population has since been found further south on the mountain, though it is still unclear just what is limiting the very local occurrence of this plant, but, given its location near the crest of the range, it could be one of the species most vulnerable to global warming.

In 1966, on my first study leave to Europe and Scandinavia, it became evident to me that New Zealand needed a well-illustrated, user-friendly book on alpine plants. My professor Geoff Baylis agreed and suggested I contact his friend, botanical artist Nancy Adams. Nancy was enthusiastic, and we collaborated over three summers in collecting most of the 600 alpine plants in flower for our book, *New Zealand Alpine Plants*.[214] In the course of collecting, and with a curiosity about similarities and differences in flowering patterns between New Zealand alpines and those abroad, I made a detailed study of 100 natives. This revealed both

OTHER RESEARCH ACTIVITIES

A day following the launch of Above the Treeline: A nature guide to alpine New Zealand *at the Te Anau Visitor Centre, with one of the field-trippers to Mt Burns catching up over lunch in the field. January, 2013.* Bridget Mark.

similarities (floral initiation in the preceding autumn) and some intriguing differences (synchronous but irregular, year-to-year flowering in several genera). There was also a striking similarity in the environmental controls of flowering between one of the commonest and early flowering New Zealand snowbank plants, *Caltha obtusa*, and that of an equally common European snowbank species, *Soldanella minima*.[215] With continued interest in and demand for a field guide to our unique alpine flora and many name revisions, based largely on recent advances in molecular phylogenetic methods, I had an opportunity for a further revision. This time it was a genuine field guide, based on photographic images and even including some lower plants (bryophytes and lichens), as well as the equally unique alpine fauna.[216]

9

ENGO AND LOCAL GOVERNMENT INVOLVEMENTS

Over five decades I have been a member, or otherwise connected with, several ENGOs (Environmental Non-Governmental Organisations), a selection of which I relate here. While the largest, Forest & Bird, has over 50,000 members and is nationwide, other ENGOs have been regional or community organisations. As a founding member of Ecology Action in Dunedin in the early 1970s, I was involved with environmental campaigns and 'clean-ups' as well as presenting Environmental Merit and Demerit Awards to various local companies and organisations. At other times I have been invited to speak publicly on development proposals in my capacity as an ecologist/environmentalist, by ENGOs with which I have had no formal connection.

At their best, ENGOs are the foot soldiers of environmentalism, and my experiences with them have been variously rewarding and frustrating on both human and conservation fronts. Typically, every active member has his or her private environmental agenda so that group tensions can arise. However, there is also camaraderie in the common interest uniting members, and I have made lasting friendships in the course of being involved with some groups. I have also learnt valuable, if at times difficult, lessons about the nature and accessibility – or inaccessibility – of power but have always dealt with principles, not personalities.

ENGO AND LOCAL GOVERNMENT INVOLVEMENTS

I include my time on the Otago Catchment Board in this chapter – even though the board was not in any sense an ENGO – because of a common thread of resource sustainability's inevitably political nature. As a Labour elected representative on the board for over a decade, I strove to use my position to achieve positive environmental outcomes. However, while there were certainly successes, the board often failed to exercise its jurisdiction adequately for want of unity, nerve or conviction. For all my efforts, major deteriorations continued before my eyes. Despite significant progress in recent decades, conservation and sustainable resource management continue to push against this prevailing wind of decline. It seems that nature conservation is mostly about reducing the rate of loss: there are very few real gains to be made.

NATIVE FOREST ACTION COUNCIL: THE MARUIA DECLARATION, 1975

The Native Forest Action Council (NFAC) and its predecessor, Beech Action Committee (BAC), were initiated in the early 1970s, largely in response to the Forest Service's South Island Beech Utilisation Scheme. This scheme planned to log substantial areas of indigenous forest and replace these largely with exotic or mixed exotic–indigenous ('enriched') stands in an attempt to match the North Island's investment in exotic forestry. Some 400,000 ha. of beech and mixed beech–podocarp forests were targeted, mostly in North Westland and western Southland, with lesser areas in Nelson and a limited area of about 11,000 ha. in the Catlins.

NFAC was organised mainly by Guy Salmon and Gwenny Davis in Nelson. I was invited to become part of an advisory group, alongside Charles Fleming in Wellington and John Child in Dunedin, to improve its status. NFAC managed to see the Beech Utilisation Scheme substantially modified and reduced. However, its most considerable and long-standing achievement was as its successor, the Maruia Declaration.

The 1975 Maruia Declaration petitioned the government to promote retention and sustainable management of our indigenous forests. Asserting that New Zealand's remaining native forests had greater

Station Creek Experimental Forest, Maruia valley, North Westland; a beech-management exercise in an attempt to satisfy the NFAC (later Maruia Society) demand for indigenous forest management as an alternative to the exotic forest conversion or enrichment, proposed in the 1970 South Island Beech Utilisation Scheme.

intrinsic value than any material gain to be derived from logging them, but that their exploitation and destruction was accelerating dramatically, the Maruia Declaration laid down six principles:

1. Native forests, wherever they remain, need recognition and protection in law.
2. The wholesale burning of indigenous forests and wildlife has no place in a civilised society.
3. The logging of virgin forests should be phased out by 1978.
4. Our remaining publicly owned native forests should be placed in the hands of an organisation that has a clear and undivided responsibility to protect them.
5. To reduce commercial pressures on native forests, the growing of fine quality exotic and native timbers on land not presently forested should be given encouragement.
6. It is prudent to be conservative in our consumption of these forest products, especially newsprint and packaging paper, which make heavy demands on our precious resources of land, energy and water.[217]

ENGO AND LOCAL GOVERNMENT INVOLVEMENTS

Some 350,000 signatures were obtained for the Maruia Declaration, enough to encourage the Forest Service to agree to a Management Policy for New Zealand Indigenous State Forests by 1977. Approved by the Minister of Forests, Venn Young, the policy recognised that indigenous forest had a range of desirable functions that needed to be defined in specific areas. Leaving options open for future management, it stated that indigenous forests would no longer be cleared 'unless the need is adequately demonstrated'. The policy had immediate effect, with the document describing management practices that had been changed in key areas. In the central North Island, clear-felling and conversion to exotic plantations was now 'giving way to various forms of felling aimed at retaining a forest structure or to complete reservation of selected stands of virgin forests'.[218]

According to the policy's preamble, the new object behind managing state indigenous forests was to 'perpetuate indigenous forests both as natural forests and as managed stands'. Indigenous forests would only be cleared if a study of the social, environmental and economic effects could demonstrate that national and regional welfare would be enhanced by doing so. The public would have the opportunity to examine any such proposal and, if necessary, lodge objections. It also addressed the market orientation of sawn native timbers: '... indigenous sawn timbers and veneers should be milled, processed and marketed in a way that ensures their intrinsic qualities are put to best use'. Use of native timber for purposes that could be met by a locally grown exotic wood was to be minimised. Conversely, the policy recommended maximising recovery of finishing and decorative grades or specialised products.

The policy also addressed recreational use of forests, protection measures and the reservation of forests for scientific purposes. As to the latter, indigenous forest reserves were seen as fulfilling a need to:

> ... understand and explain natural processes; maintain bench-marks for measuring change on initially comparable developed land; maintain genetic diversity of plants and animals; and preserve rare plants, native

fauna, archaeological or other historic sites, particularly topographical features and geological and soil sites.[219]

However much provisions like this may appear elementary to today's more enlightened populace, they represented highly significant advances at the time. As part of the overall response, the Forest Service's Scientific Co-ordinating Committee on Beech Research was established (see Chapter 6). Regarding Westland, the policy identified tension between concern for the regional economy on the one hand (and existing legal commitments) and, on the other, a desire to protect indigenous forests. As to North Island kauri forests, these were 'being managed in terms of the specific policy approved in 1973, and increased effort has been put into investigating the possibility of a small sustained yield of this species'. Legislative amendments would grant indigenous forests 'greater prominence', making specific provision for wilderness areas and liberalising access. Prescribed procedures would allow for 'wider public involvement in forest management'. Future generations will be able to judge the level of achievement.

The council continued to achieve while still part of the Joint Campaign of Native Forests (with Forest & Bird and FMC: see Chapter 8) but the campaign eventually dissolved when NFAC changed its name to the Maruia Society in 1988. The Maruia Society then became the Ecologic Foundation in 1999 with Guy Salmon (who had spearheaded both NFAC and the Maruia Society) as its director.

SAVE ARAMOANA CAMPAIGN, 1974–84

In the decade following 1974, two proposals surfaced to build the country's second aluminium smelter at Aramoana near the entrance to Otago Harbour (the first being at Tiwai). Attracting considerable controversy, both proposals eventually collapsed. At the time, the landowner, the Otago Harbour Board, had zoned the area in question 'industrial', despite the Department of Lands and Survey designating the salt marsh of national importance as part of a nationwide coastal survey. In 1974 Otago Metals Ltd, a local company acting for Swiss Aluminium

Ltd, first proposed to build a smelter on this 'industrial site'. When this failed, the consortium South Pacific Aluminium Ltd[220] received strong support from the National government, with Bill Birch's 1979 National Development Act being invoked to fast-track construction.

I played a relatively minor role in both campaigns. I was involved in public debates on the Otago Metals proposal, with other opponents pitted against engineer David Collingwood, who fronted this smelter proposal. In light of my Manapouri involvement, I was keen for others to front the campaign, and there was no shortage of strong candidates: Geoff Neill, Peter Bradshaw and Ralph Allen, among others, all played major roles. Inexplicably, Collingwood was later appointed by Forest & Bird as its conservation director. Since I was not a member at this time, I was not privy to the circumstances of his appointment, nor constrained by the society's directive that the smelter topic was 'off record' when he gave his first talk to the Otago branch. Collingwood was eventually

View south across the Aramoana saltmarsh to the shipping channel with Otago Peninsula beyond, showing the jointed rush Apodasmia *(Leptocarpus)* similis *on slightly higher ground (foreground) grading into the mixed shallow pools and dwarfed marsh, dominated by glasswort* Sarcocornia quinquifolia. *The popular boardwalk and viewing platform, built by DOC for Forest & Bird in 1999, accesses a representative cross section of the saltmarsh and also facilitates bird watching.* Janet Ledingham.

View north across the Aramoana saltmarsh, March 1970.

moved to the position of editor to make way for his newly recruited replacement, Gerry McSweeney.

The second South Pacific smelter proposal was clearly much more serious. Both Dunedin City and Otago University were deeply divided on the issue. The university was commissioned to undertake several research projects to provide background information for the massive environmental impact report for this second proposal in 1981, produced in collaboration with the Otago Harbour Board. The university's chemists were in favour while the biologists were strongly opposed to the smelter. In the Department of Economics, there was deep division between the two professors. The Head of Department, Michael Cooper, voiced his support, while aluminium specialist Paul van Moeseke maintained that the smelter would prove uneconomic. Highly disillusioned by the issue, Paul was unaccustomed to the abuse he suffered from several quarters, including from some cabinet ministers, particularly Bill Birch. Despite being vindicated when the proposal was eventually abandoned largely on economic grounds, Paul chose to move from the University of Otago to a similar position at Massey.

ENGO AND LOCAL GOVERNMENT INVOLVEMENTS

Assisted by the Save Aramoana Campaign, the local community was novel in drawing public attention to its cause and expanding this into a national campaign. Aramoana residents declared an 'Independent State of Aramoana' and had border guards posted at the narrow road cutting at Te Ngaru approaching the industrial zone. The movement also issued special commemorative stamps, based on a painting by Don Binney (*Puketotara, Twice Shy*), for both publicity and fund-raising.

Fletcher Challenge, which fronted this second smelter proposal for the consortium South Pacific Aluminium Ltd, arranged serious discussions with many interested parties. Through these discussions, we persuaded it to recognise the saltmarsh's important ecological values, particularly its diverse wader avifauna. Hugh Fletcher, company director, took a keen interest and even reminded listeners of the saltmarsh's significance on a local talk-back radio show with deputy mayor Jean McLean. McLean's on-air support showed tunnel vision. Emphasising the smelter's economic value to the city, she enthusiastically anticipated demolition of Aramoana's 'tin shacks' and looked forward to seeing the 'mudflats' developed. At this suggestion, Fletcher responded that the company was siting the smelter 'to protect the unique biological values of the saltmarsh'!

We had obviously got our message across. The consortium further revealed this in its 1981 environmental impact report, proposing that the saltmarsh be designated a 'wildlife refuge'. It would be separated from the actual smelter site on adjacent non-tidal land by a waterproofed bund wall. With the Harbour Board formally involved in the proposal, this report was later to prove significant in determining the future of the saltmarsh.

The smelter proposal finally died when the Labour government refused to guarantee supply of its electricity needs. Following the proposal's demise, opponents challenged at several stages the Harbour Board's efforts to have the site redesignated as industrial in the district plan. They were eventually successful, with the Planning Tribunal – the forerunner of today's Environment Court – confirming the saltmarsh's

Conservation Minister Denis Marshall opening the Aramoana Ecological Area.

designation as a formally protected wildlife refuge. Later, as a result of local government re-organisation, the government determined that all areas of foreshore and seabed then vested in harbour boards and other local authorities be returned to Crown ownership. Because of its outstanding ecological values, the saltmarsh and adjacent area were transferred to DOC and later appropriately designated an ecological area.

The Aramoana Ecological Area was officially opened by the Minister of Conservation, Denis Marshall, in November 1994. A small plaque was placed on the roadside in the adjacent sandhills to commemorate the efforts of the Save Aramoana Campaign. With the support of the local community, Forest & Bird subsequently funded (with a grant from the Marjorie Barclay Trust) a boardwalk to give public access to the vulnerable saltmarsh. This was officially opened by Mayor Sukhi Turner in August 1999.

ENGO AND LOCAL GOVERNMENT INVOLVEMENTS

OTAGO CATCHMENT BOARD, 1974–86

Impressed by the Kirk Labour government's enlightened attitude towards sustainable resource management, in 1974 I was persuaded to run as the Labour candidate for the Otago Catchment Board (and Regional Water Board) in Dunedin City's local body elections. My four three-year terms on the board, while time-consuming, allowed me to address many issues of concern and interest. Most notably, these were management of the Otago high country, and allocation of the region's water resources for abstraction, discharges, conservation, recreation and hydroelectric development. The board was an interesting mix of representation and personalities, with three Dunedin City members, five country members and four appointed members from government departments.[221]

During the 12 years I spent on the board, I saw only marginal improvements in the success with which we managed to prosecute land-users for unauthorised burning of tussock grassland or pollution of waterways. This was particularly the case with the lower Taieri River and Kaikorai Stream. As one-time chair of the Water Resources Committee, I engaged the Mosgiel Borough Council in serious debate about its ongoing failure to meet water-quality standards imposed by the board for the lower Silverstream and lower Taieri waterways. Despite this failure, the borough continued to promote industrial and population expansion.

In 1975 I persuaded the board to place an injunction on the contractor who was building a road to the Obelisk rock tor outcrop on the crest of Central Otago's Old Man Range. The road was for a TV translator tower and, on the upper high-alpine slopes above 1500 m, greatly exceeded the original specifications, destroying a strip of cushionfield 20 m wide on both sides for much of the last kilometre. The board transplanted some 800 narrow-leaved snow tussocks from 1250 m to a 400 sq. m roadside patch to reduce wind erosion of the bared soil, extracting a fine of $10,000 to cover costs. We also established 10 monitoring transects to assess recovery relative to the adjacent undisturbed cushionfield. Subsequent monitoring has revealed very slow restoration of the plant

High-alpine cushionfield and impressive shaft tors of chlorite schist on the crest of the Old Man Range at ca. 1650 m, January 2009.

cover. After 11 years, it was weakly dominated by blue tussock and still far short of the plant cover and composition of the undisturbed cushionfield.[222] Even after a quarter of a century, the recovery remains far from complete.

On further enquiry, we discovered that the television tower itself was to be built virtually over the Obelisk, an impressive shaft tor of schist rock on the highest point of the range. Local DSIR geologist Ian McKellar and I lodged a formal complaint with the Nature Conservation Council, which had apparently approved the plan with only one proviso: that the tower be painted green! Stafford McDonald, the council's field officer, agreed to take me to the Broadcasting Council's Wellington office to discuss the tower's siting. The council agreed to move the tower but only a very limited distance away from the Obelisk since it needed clear lines of sight to Kuriwao Peak near Clinton, Coronet Peak and Mount Cargill. The proposed site was apparently perfect for this: I was told, 'God made this site just for us.' Of course, the tower was never painted, given the extreme exposure of the site.

ENGO AND LOCAL GOVERNMENT INVOLVEMENTS

The single most notable and contentious issue addressed by the Otago Catchment Board during my time on it was the Clyde dam. As with every other relevant statutory organisation, the board had approved the two low-dam proposals for the Cromwell Gorge (Scheme H) while maintaining majority opposition to the Clyde high-dam proposal (Scheme F). The new government had announced this 'bombshell' decision for upper Clutha hydroelectric development in mid-December 1976. The low-dam scheme had been approved by the previous Labour government; moreover, advisory bodies set up by both the previous and current governments had also recommended Scheme H. The National government justified its belated choice on the grounds that Scheme F would produce more (2%) electricity at an earlier date and significantly lower cost than Scheme H. It also claimed that Scheme F had application for irrigation and recreation as well as electricity generation. No comprehensive documentation was supplied to support these claims, despite provisions in the Water and Soil Conservation Act 1967 that covered water rights.

Following this unexpected, highly contentious decision, the board called a special meeting in January 1977 to discuss the issue. At that

Paul Powell, author of Who Killed the Clutha?, *stands in the Cromwell Gorge ahead of its inundation in the early 1990s.*

meeting, we resolved – with one dissenting vote – to advise the government of our continuing opposition to Scheme F in view of the board's statutory responsibility for water and soil conservation. In a statement accompanying our resolution, we highlighted the critical shortage of high-fertility land in the upper Clutha suitable for intensive and diversified farming. In respect of this, the board 'had been wholly consistent in its opposition to the destruction of such land for any reason'. The only foreseeable long-term development prospects for the Upper Clutha lay in 'exploiting its limited soil resources, its climate and its unique scenery'. The board emphasised the Cromwell Gorge's unique combination of high-fertility soils, comparatively frost-free climate and high heat units in justifying its strong opposition to the proposed inundation:

> The Board is of the opinion that the loss of the Gorge orchards, small in area as they are, could have serious long-term effects on the future development of the region. As the body charged with the duty of ensuring the best long-term use of land and water resources, the Otago Catchment Board respectfully asks the Government to reconsider the decision adopting Scheme F in the light of the facts contained herein.[223]

While this stand was widely applauded throughout Otago, it received some unfavourable political reaction. Prime Minister Muldoon was reported as saying that the board members could resign if they did not approve of the government's decision, while local MP Warren Cooper accused members of creating a climate of mistrust in Otago and suggested the board should divest itself of members 'pushing their political barrows'.[224]

The Clyde dam being a government development, the National Water and Soil Conservation Authority issued the formal consents. However, the Otago Regional Water Board was required to provide a 'report and recommendation' to the authority for consideration when making its decision. In June 1977 the minister of electricity applied to the authority for the five water rights needed to operate the high (64 m) dam just above Clyde. As requested by the authority, the board received public submissions and conducted hearings on the issue before presenting its report.

It received 223 submissions – 14 on behalf of the minister and 209 others, of which 57 were from organisations and 152 from individuals. Those opposing the high dam numbered 181, three submitters supported the high dam (two conditionally), and the remaining 25 were concerned with protection of property or existing rights. Some 86 submissions came from beyond Otago – from Auckland to Invercargill.

The submissions addressed many relevant issues: the extra 2% of electricity purportedly generated by a single high dam, Scheme F's economics, the Cromwell Gorge's unique combination of high-class soils and climate, and serious social disruption, among others. Submitters also addressed the fact that the proposal was contrary to a wide range of official opinion. And the absence of an environmental impact report was of concern. The board considered all these aspects, informed both by submissions and its own information. However, public statements from two cabinet ministers prior to the hearings suggested to many that the government had already decided to implement Scheme F, despite proceeding with the normal democratic process, rather than declaring the Upper Clutha a water of national importance as provided for in the legislation.[225]

Our task was further frustrated by there being no multi-purpose plan for water rights applications, despite the legislation clearly requiring one. The board was required to consider the 'local and regional implications of the decision while also respecting the national needs'.[226] To that end, it made its decision on the basis of its statutory responsibility:

> to consider the productive value of the land which would be destroyed if the application to build the high dam was granted, as an all-embracing value judgement in relation to the electrical energy lost, when compared with alternative hydro-electric opportunities; the loss of an irreplaceable and highly valuable land and climatic resource that is unique in the region; the precedent already established by previous relevant decisions of the Town and Country Planning Appeal Board; and the lack of any positive

statement defining multiple-objective or any other tangible benefits to the district or region which would compensate for such losses.[227]

We recommended that:

1. The National Authority decline the application by the Minister of Electricity to dam the Clutha River 1.5 km upstream of Clyde bridge to a height of 64 m;
2. The Authority grant an application to dam the Clutha River at the same site ... to limit the level ... so as to retain as much as practicable of the horticultural soils of the Cromwell Gorge.[228]

Interestingly, these two recommendations were passed by only a relatively slim majority. In voting against the recommendations, the government members on the board followed head office directives, I was later (unofficially) informed.

Contrary to the board's interpretation of the relevant law, the authority considered it could not approve a level for the proposed lake lower than that required by Scheme F. It laid down conditions that climate, water quality and water-weed growth be monitored, with any consequent erosion to be corrected. The authority allocated up to nine cumecs for future irrigation, rural water supplies, frost fighting and other purposes. Thus it overrode the board, resolving in December 1977 to grant the minister of electricity water rights for the high dam. While accepting that the Cromwell Gorge's combination of soils, climate and relative absence of harmful frosts was unique in the area, the authority averred that there were other areas where stone-fruit growing was possible, provided that frost-fighting is practised. It did not accept that this unique combination outweighed the benefits of Scheme F over Scheme H.

Following a two-day visit to the catchment with board members, the authority considered the board's case alongside a 64-page Ministry of Works and Development (MWD) report.[229] Adopting this report, the authority approved water rights for the high dam without modification, claiming its decision was in line with the spirit and objects of the

The controversial 64 m-high Clyde High Dam, which backs water up well beyond the Cromwell Gorge.

Water and Soil Conservation Act. Specifically, the high dam would serve 'National and Regional interests in terms of the most beneficial uses of the water of the Clutha River, the promotion of soil conservation, the effects of the proposal on existing water users and the promotion of multiple uses of the water'. Finding that there was 'ample opportunity' for expanded orchards elsewhere in the region to replace those lost, the authority concluded that 'the advantage of power production outweighs to a significant extent the detriment of lost production from the land'.[230] Mostly to satisfy my conscience, I presented a personal submission to the select committee considering the Clyde Dam Empowering Bill, commenting specifically on the board's role and deliberations. Predictably, this was to no avail. The highly controversial act was passed essentially as drafted but with two National MPs admitting that 'it runs against principle'.[231]

The empowering legislation also contained provisions to compensate those organisations and individuals who had challenged Scheme F in the courts. Since that time, a number of serious landslides have occurred, threatening land stability in several areas of the Cromwell Gorge. These landslides have fallen under the jurisdiction of the Otago Regional Council, which replaced the Otago Catchment Board in 1990. Critics of the dam have associated huge cost overruns with inadequate initial investigations and other aspects of building the Clyde dam. Also controversial was subsequent sale of the dam at a highly subsidised price to Contact Energy, then an SOE but later privatised and now a mostly foreign-owned company. The saga of Contact's applications for resource consents, consent renewals and four options for additional development has been well publicised elsewhere.

SAVE CENTRAL, 2005–13

From 2005 to 2013, four controversial Otago energy projects featured in the headlines and letter pages, not only of the *Otago Daily Times* but also national newspapers: Project Hayes, Mahinerangi Wind Farm, and proposed dams on the Nevis and Clutha rivers. After privatisation in 1999, generator-retailer companies like Meridian (an SOE), Contact and TrustPower became major players on the New Zealand electricity market; more local, Pioneer Generation came later. In light of forecast growth in electricity consumption and the prospect of low lakes from late summer through early winter, a race developed to supply new renewable electricity and reduce reliance on non-renewable coal and gas generation located in the North Island.

Of the four projects, Project Hayes – Meridian's plan to build 176 wind turbines on the crest of the Lammermoor Range in eastern Central Otago, generating 630 mW of renewable electricity with the sacrifice of an expansive and remote, tussock-clad landscape – was the most ambitious and probably the most controversial. Project Hayes attracted vocal opposition from a number of well-known personalities, including two ex-All Black captains (Anton Oliver and David Kirk), a decorated ex-soldier (Graye Shattky) and artists and writers (Grahame Sydney, Brian Turner, Marilynn Webb, Gilbert van Reenen and Richard Reeve). As an environmental issue, Hayes was also linked with TrustPower's

ENGO AND LOCAL GOVERNMENT INVOLVEMENTS

Aerial view of the crest of the Lammermoor Range, site of Meridian Energy's proposed wind farm of 176 towers; the proposal failed to receive a resource consent based on predicted landscape impacts. The Old Dunstan heritage road is on the right.

Mahinerangi Wind Farm on the nearby Lammerlaw Range, the two wind farms being 17 km apart on an open tussockland peneplain landscape.

The dams were also bitterly opposed. Contact's plans for a third dam somewhere on the Clutha revived memories of the Clyde dam fiasco, while critics of Pioneer's 16-year plan for the Nevis described it as the death knell of a great wild river and a remote, spectacular tussock-grassland landscape.

After Project Hayes was given consent by the Central Otago District and Otago Regional councils, this consent was appealed to the Environment Court by a selection of parties, including Save Central, an unincorporated movement operating through the Central Otago Environmental Society. Two other appellants, the Upland Landscape Protection Society and the Maniototo Environmental Society, were also active in opposing the wind farms, but these faced an uncertain future in the midst of proceedings. The Upland Landscape Protection Society, which also faced TrustPower in the Environment Court, was eventually wound up after failed judicial review proceedings in the High Court. The Maniototo Environmental Society, mostly representing local landowners embittered by Meridian's plans, faced huge legal bills with what, at the time, seemed like little likelihood of victory.

Not legally in existence as an incorporated society at the time of the council hearings, the Central Otago Environmental Society was given leave to join other appellants on the basis of its objects and standing. Forest & Bird had decided not to become involved to avoid compromising Judge Jon Jackson's impartiality. Judge Jackson had earlier had to recuse himself from the Environment Court hearing for TrustPower's Wairau hydro proposal in Marlborough, in which Forest & Bird was an appellant. According to TrustPower's counsel, his Honour, having had long-standing connections with Forest & Bird, showed the potential for a conflict of interest.

In Judge Jackson's court, I gave evidence for the Central Otago Environmental Society in my capacity as a professional plant ecologist. My opposition to Project Hayes stemmed from the impact of infrastructure on the upland tussock-grassland landscape and its close proximity to an important historic feature, the Old Dunstan Road. I was particularly concerned with the proposal to 'direct-transfer' tussock grassland onto extensive areas affected by earthworks. Meridian planned some 150 km of new or upgraded roading, of which an estimated 60 km required widening to up to 12 m (later to be reduced to 5 m width for maintenance purposes). On to this displaced earth, it was planned to direct-transfer tussock-grassland communities. This method, previously attempted at its White Hill wind farm in Southland, had proved quite unsatisfactory. On that basis I recommended, if consent were to be granted, that Meridian be required to use an alternative, narrow-tracked, 4 m-wide Canadian crane, such as had been used by TrustPower for its Tararua Wind Farm, in place of the proposed giant crawler crane.

The court declined the application in a notable decision. Meridian had attempted to downplay the grandeur of the expansive upland tussock-grassland landscape, claiming it was not 'outstanding' relative to other locations in Otago, and that Project Hayes would not in any case be located in a formally designated Outstanding Natural Landscape. It further suggested that, if the landscape was outstanding, the wind farm and its infrastructure would not have a significant adverse impact on its qualities. The court rejected this proposition, finding on the evidence that Project Hayes would be located in an outstanding landscape, irrespective of the district plan classification, and that a giant wind farm would be inappropriately intrusive on these values. In a pyrrhic victory, Meridian successfully appealed the decision in the High Court on a technicality, which however referred it back to the same Environment Court and judge. After a six-year battle, Meridian withdrew its application.

Ironically, the origins of the Nevis issue arose in 1997 in the context of a Water Conservation Order placed on the Kawarau and Nevis rivers. A central stipulation in Schedule 2 of the order ('Waters To Be Protected') was:

> no damming allowed unless a rule in a plan or condition in any water permit granted makes provision for river flows to be provided at sufficient levels to enable kayaking to be undertaken in the gorge at times stated in the plan or permit, and the extent of any impounded water is not beyond S143:836485.[232]

Pioneer Generation – part of the Otago Central Electric Power Board before privatisation – subsequently purchased the leases of two high-country stations on either side of the river, Ben Nevis and Craigroy runs, both of which were also undergoing tenure review. In reply, Fish and Game New Zealand in 2006 applied to amend the 1997 conservation order so that damming was prohibited.

A special tribunal, convened by MfE to hear the matter, voted in support of the amendment on account of a rare native galaxiid of biogeographical significance, *Galaxias gollumoides*. However, parties from all sides appealed the decision. The judge assigned to hear the matter was once again Judge Jackson, sitting with two commissioners. Fish and Game, disconcerted that the tribunal's decision rested on the welfare of a single native fish species, argued the decision had given insufficient weight to either the river's value as a recreational fishery or its landscape values. Whitewater New Zealand sought recognition of the attractions to kayakers. Pioneer, the Central Otago District and Otago Regional councils all opposed the amendment.

In the Environment Court, I again appeared as an expert witness for the Central Otago Environmental Society, which contested the restrictive two-tier landscape classification proposed by the Central Otago District Council. The council had designated most of the valley 'Outstanding Natural Landscape'. Curiously and rather blatantly, however, it had assigned a lower class, 'Significant Amenity Landscape', to the area proposed by Pioneer for a hydro-storage lake in the lower valley, presumably to facilitate approval for inundation. Unsurprisingly, this designation was formally supported by Pioneer. In early August 2012, a witness caucusing session with an Environment Court commissioner proved clearly favourable to the three appellants, and just one day before the court hearing in Queenstown, agreement was reached as to the 'Outstanding Natural Landscape' of the entire Nevis Valley. This, we presumed, would spare the river from damming. However, a formal Environment Court hearing was convened, with Judge Jon Jackson as chair, to hear the case for a Water Conservation Order for the Nevis River, by Fish and Game and Whitewater New Zealand. Judge Jackson disagreed with his two commissioners on this issue, holding that a small dam above the Nevis Crossing should remain permissible despite the agreement. Nevertheless, by convention, the majority view was referred to the Minister for the Environment, Amy Adams, and in October 2013 she formally accepted the amendment.

In the wake of the storm created by Project Hayes, Contact's suggestion of a new dam or dams on the Clutha first took the form of a would-be 'conversation' with the public. Initiated by Contact's regional project manager and local-government politician Neil Gillespie (currently Central Otago deputy mayor), this was also a discussion on Contact's website in which the public submitted queries and thoughts on the proposed four options. Naming no specific preference as to whether a new dam would be at Tuapeka Mouth, Beaumont, Luggate or Queens-

ENGO AND LOCAL GOVERNMENT INVOLVEMENTS

TOP: *The lower Nevis valley, looking south up the valley, with the Hector Mountains on the right.* ABOVE: *Banner for New Zealand Wild Rivers Day (held by Pat Mark (left) and Janet Ledingham), celebrated by more than 200 supporters in the Nevis Valley, 29 November 2009.*

berry, Contact sought public feedback in an effort to avoid the stigma of being another corporate juggernaut, as Meridian had been depicted by opponents of Project Hayes. The company's efforts were not entirely successful, and a small but determined movement promoting 'Option 5' – no dams – surfaced, featuring a number of the same personalities who had been active in the Nevis and wind-farm conflicts.

Despite Contact's ultimately choosing not to proceed with any of its four options, the long-standing threat revived by this consultative 'conversation' resulted in a number of public meetings, which I attended. One outcome of these meetings was a shared sense that the pressure to exploit Otago's natural resources was symptomatic of a wider global ecological/environmental and economic collapse. This was occasioned in particular by widespread over-consumption and the flawed concept of unlimited economic growth. Out of Save Central, Option 5 and also organised opposition to Solid Energy's plans to build a lignite briquetting pilot plant near Mataura (a project that progressed no further when Solid Energy declared gross indebtedness and substantially trimmed its operations in May 2013) arose Wise Response – an appeal to parliament to conduct an urgent risk assessment for New Zealand in light of our deteriorating world.

WISE RESPONSE, 2011–
The origins of Wise Response date to early October 2011, when Wanaka kayaking operator Louis Verduyn-Cassels organised a public meeting in Alexandra on 'Adapting to Our Rapidly Changing World'. The meeting sought to discuss 'profound challenges [and provide] an opportunity to positively transform the way we live in the context of our supporting environment'. It focused on five themes – economic security, energy and climate security, business continuity, ecological/environmental security and genuine well-being – and aimed to emphasise the urgency of a national risk assessment with a holistic approach.

The Alexandra meeting had a number of consequences. We decided to elaborate on Option 5 for the Clutha River to Contact's Neil Gillespie.

ENGO AND LOCAL GOVERNMENT INVOLVEMENTS

The Generation Zero (GenZero) group presents its case at the Wise Response launch at the Otago Museum Reserve, 8 March 2013. Mark Jackson

I had also accepted responsibility for organising a similar public meeting at Otago University later in the month. The several broad-ranging presentations, together with the large and supportive audiences at this meeting, gave us further encouragement. As a result, a small, involved and concerned group met irregularly in the Botany Department seminar room. The regular attendees were myself, Dugald MacTavish, Professor of Physics Bob Lloyd, Emeritus Professor of English Jocelyn Harris, engineer John Cocks (Jocelyn and John both of Sustainable Dunedin City), Green Party representative Pat Scott and Mark Jackson of the Otago Polytech. Corresponding by email, several others took an interest in our activities from further afield.

So began a succession of such meetings in which we sought speakers from different disciplines and perspectives to discuss their views on our forecast global environmental and economic future, and New Zealand's place in it. The success of our first Alexandra and Dunedin meetings encouraged us to plan in a more serious vein. Others joined our periodic university meetings, and we decided to have a formal launch of the campaign.

We chose 8 March 2013 for an afternoon launch in the Museum Reserve, to be followed by an evening session at the university, and canvassed all political parties for support and a delegate. However, only three delegates came: local Labour MP Dr David Clark, Green Party Climate Change Spokesman Kennedy Graham, and New Zealand First's Conservation, Energy and Environment Spokesman Andrew Williams. The Māori and United Future Parties sent apologies together with positive responses, while the National Party showed little interest. When I telephoned local National list MP Michael Woodhouse, he reiterated a prior commitment. He also commented that we probably planned to 'set us [National] up to knock us down', to which I responded that this was not the purpose of our meeting.

I chaired the afternoon launch in the Museum Reserve. Among the speakers at the event, we had five from out of town and five locals.[233] Recent Otago graduate Louis Chambers from the environmental youth movement Generation Zero stole the show, aided by a flank of vocal supporters. An Otago law and economics graduate, Louis was soon to depart as a Rhodes Scholar. The three politicians present, when challenged to respond actively to the pressing issues raised, expressed concurrence with attendees but warned that cross-party collaboration was virtually non-existent in present-day politics. Despite this dampener, we ranked the meeting a success, and gathered signatures on a 10 m calico cloth as part of a petition to parliament. Fortunately, the rain held off. Our evening meeting followed a similar format but, of the politicians, only Kennedy Graham was present.

A think tank among speakers following the launch agreed we should take the issue to as many centres as possible, using the model of the Save Manapouri Campaign and Ron McLean's success in initiating some 19 campaign committees around the country. We also decided to approach the Parliamentary Commissioner for the Environment, Dr Jan Wright, to discuss an independent 'risk assessment'. I was subsequently interviewed by Jim Mora on Radio New Zealand, whose discussion panel for that day included right-wing politician and lawyer Stephen Franks and

ENGO AND LOCAL GOVERNMENT INVOLVEMENTS

Christchurch commentator Ali Jones. Discussion on our appeal for a risk assessment was split between a skeptical Franks and a generally supportive Jones. Later, there were more constructive interviews on Radio New Zealand with Kathryn Ryan's *Nine to Noon* and Chris Laidlaw's *Sunday* programmes.

The formal text of our appeal sought 'initiation and implementation of achievable plans to provide the following five key forms of national security':

- *Economic security:* A contingency plan in case of a sudden, deepening, or prolonged financial crisis, so that people's capacity to provide for their essential needs is enabled; including the ability of communities to be more self-reliant, with access to local resources, shorter supply chains, and resilient infrastructure.
- *Energy and climate security:* A plan to progressively restrict the extraction and use of fossil fuels, to promote a switch to genuine renewables, public transportation, superinsulation, and smarter use of existing energy systems, resulting in greatly reduced energy dependence, and lower greenhouse gas emissions.
- *Business continuity:* A plan to incentivise each business to actively explore economic and job opportunities in anticipation of an energy future that dramatically increases use of renewables and reduces greenhouse gas emissions and other forms of pollution.
- *Ecological/Environmental security:* A plan to ensure the adequate protection of ecosystems and their services associated with natural processes, essential for human welfare, as well as the maintenance of indigenous biodiversity.
- *Genuine well-being:* A plan for the transition from a debt-based economy, preoccupied with maximising economic turnover and GDP, to one founded on visionary long-term community sustainability, well-being, greater sharing of wealth and opportunities, resource security, and a constitutional assurance of genuine environmental resilience, that will, above all, enable future generations to function on an ecologically intact planet.

Endorsing the Universal Declaration of Human Rights, signatories to our appeal – more than 100 prominent New Zealanders from all walks of life – declared: 'it is our human responsibility to maintain the integrity of life support systems and the natural processes which sustain them, as well as the capacities and conditions for their renewal.' They also stated their belief 'that human-influenced climate change and pending oil constraints threaten our ability to meet the aforementioned obligations at all levels of society.'

In November 2013, when TVNZ flew me to Wellington to interview me for a documentary on Manapouri, Dugald and I met with the parliamentary commissioner to discuss Wise Response. The TVNZ interview went well, much better than our meeting with the commissioner. Dr Wright assured us she was well aware of the national and global constraints we outlined. She agreed with the limitations of using GDP as a measure of progress. Because we have the fossil capacity to fry the planet, she felt the only critical question was capacity of the atmosphere to assimilate carbon.

Dr Wright decided not to get involved with our movement. She wished to be 'solution'- rather than 'problem'-focused, and considered risk assessment fell into the latter category. If we could relate risk assessment to the economy, it was more likely to be seen as relevant. In framing any assessment, we needed to consider carefully 'Where does it leave you?' and 'What can one do with the results?' She was clear she would not undertake the assessment even if resources were made available. She had a small team, could not take on another project of this nature, and preferred to avoid the word 'risk', which was too easily dismissed by people: 'You take a risk each day you get out of bed.' She also considered the National government would not sanction or provide funds, additional resources or staff for such an assessment under any circumstances. As to alternatives, the commissioner speculated on a committee of informed persons undertaking our proposed risk assessment, rather like a futures commission. Agreeing it was desirable to have a 'hook', she was not convinced that a specific topic such as food security would work for New Zealand, and suggested instead the risk of 'agricultural monoculture'.

ENGO AND LOCAL GOVERNMENT INVOLVEMENTS

My wife Pat and me with the options wheel provided by Generation Zero for the Wise Response Society's presentation to parliament of their petition on 9 April 2014. There was great support for the GenZero representative, who secured the 'Miracle' option with her first spin of the wheel. I suggested we keep her on. Paul McGahan.

Despite our setback, we maintained our website – www.wiseresponse.org.nz – and continued with regular meetings, deciding to take the message to other centres. However, we realised that Wise Reponse, enormous though its issues were, would have to compete with several other regional and national campaigns. Focusing on increasing numerical support, we proceeded with the following petition:

To the House of Representatives:
We the undersigned, request that the House:
(1) urge Government to undertake a National Risk Assessment of: Economic Security, Energy and Climate Security, Business Continuity, Ecological/Environmental Security and Genuine Well-being, and
(2) from that Risk Assessment, develop and implement cross-party policies to avert any confirmed threats to future generations of New Zealanders.

I took our message and this petition to public meetings in 2013–14 at 12 centres, from Auckland to Invercargill, greatly assisted by the group Engineers for Social Responsibility.

We have now become an incorporated society and are delighted to count among our early supporters former prime minister Sir Geoffrey Palmer (now the society's patron) and theologian Sir Lloyd Geering, as well as many other prominent citizens. Several such people were present when we took the petition to parliament with 4600 signatures on 9 April 2014. Presentation of this petition was supported by messages from former British politician and ex-vice chancellor of Waikato University Dr Bryan Gould, engineer Gerry Coates, energy physicist Professor Bob Lloyd, economist Dr Geoff Bertram and Generation Zero. We presented it formally to representatives of the Labour, Green and New Zealand First parties; and the Labour spokesperson on climate change, Moana Mackey, presented it to the speaker of the House at this time. Within an hour of its presentation to the speaker, Kennedy Graham (for the Greens) complimented Wise Response to the House in a short speech, in which he stated that the petition was perhaps the most important one ever to come before the House. The petition was referred to the Finance and Expenditure Select Committee, which made an initial response (1 April 2015) that we requested to discuss further with them at the earliest opportunity. We now await the petition's deliberation by the Finance and Expenditure Select Committee, to which it has been referred.

FUTURE PROSPECTS

The growing support for our Wise Response campaign, and the increasing public awareness and concern for many aspects of our current lifestyle and political leadership, are cause for hope that we in New Zealand – and even the world at large – will soon realise that a sustainable environment is critical for sustaining the human race and the many functioning ecosystems, both natural and man-modified, that we humans depend on for our future welfare. The powers that be surely have a responsibility to ensure this.

ENGO AND LOCAL GOVERNMENT INVOLVEMENTS

Wise Response member Peter Barrett of Wellington and I, both Fellows of the Royal Society of New Zealand, presented a resolution to the Fellows Forum AGM on 29 October 2014:

> Request that the RSNZ Academy Council convene a group of experts to review and assess the risks associated with recent and projected trends in greenhouse gas emissions, the likely consequences for New Zealand in future decades and centuries, and consider options for both mitigation and adaptation, taking into account environmental, social and economic considerations.

This was passed unanimously, and the council organised a workshop in mid-February 2015, attended by 21 invited participants, which concluded that the RSNZ should consider a programme including three strands of work:

1. A succinct summary of existing information on New Zealand around the risks associated with recent and projected trends in greenhouse-gas emissions, and the likely consequences for New Zealand in future decades and centuries (to be completed as soon as possible)
2. An in-depth look into mitigation options for New Zealand, with long-term views, including risks, co-benefits, spill over impact, opportunities and barriers at local and national levels (taking 9–12 months)
3. An in-depth look into adaptation options for New Zealand (to be considered at a later date).

At the council meeting that followed, it was agreed that the RSNZ undertake the first two of these work streams, with the third to be considered by the council at a later date.

The convenors will be asked to suggest membership of the panels and then prepare a work plan that: includes ways to engage those the RSNZ is trying to influence from the beginning of the work; involves young people; considers effective communication to the key audiences; and involves a wide range of organisations and individuals in the preparation of the advice. The panel membership proposed by each convenor will be submitted to the council on 21 April for approval.

The outcome of these exercises will be awaited with both interest and concern, with the approach of the important COP 21 Conference to be held in Paris in late 2015 – a sequel to the earlier, mostly inconclusive international climate conferences at Lima in 2014, Warsaw in 2013, Durban in 2011, Cancun in 2010, Copenhagen in 2009, and Geneva in 2009, 1990 and 1979, which have all failed to deliver a satisfactory resolution. The Minister of Climate Change Issues, Hon. Tim Groser, has indicated that New Zealand intends to take a leading role at the Paris conference and has called for public submissions on what New Zealand's input should be. This could be a crucial conference in determining how the world is going to address the rapidly increasing problem of global warming and associated issues. But, as our Patron Sir Geoffrey Palmer stated in a recent speech to 350.org:

> The way the 2015 negotiations in Paris are shaping up it seems that the goal of legally binding targets upon nations for their carbon emissions will not be achieved, although that was the aim when the preparatory meetings started.

He also pointed out:

> ... deficiencies in the Resource Management Act (2004 Amendment) in its failure to deal with the effects of greenhouse gas (GHG) emissions on climate change when making rules to control discharges into air (S. 70A) and when considering an application for a discharge permit (s 104E) ... So New Zealand's key environmental statute is disabled from considering what is a critical issue relating to climate change [and moreover] ... changes to be made to the Resource Management Act proposed by the Government [have] no mention of climate change.[234]

It is further disturbing that Environment Minister Hon. Nick Smith, who is responsible for this important item of legislation and has indicated that some major changes are in the pipeline, has refused to give any indication as to the extent or implications of the planned amendments, and these are unlikely to be revealed before it is introduced to parliament. For this act – which was designed to provide protection for our New Zealand environment since it was promulgated in 1991, when it was subject to much preliminary discussion and debate – it is inexplicable and unacceptable not to have the proposed amendments (which are rumoured to be fundamental but in the guise of addressing a major housing problem in our largest city) openly discussed and debated prior to its introduction to the house. This legislation has always been complex and will undoubtedly continue to be, since it attempts to protect the environment while advancing economic goals. However, there are clear indications that any fundamental amendments to the act's founding principles will meet strong public resistance and, moreover, be likely to receive only the slimmest majority if and when it is presented to parliament. More recently, the government's loss of the Northland by-election has major implications for its plans for amendments to this act.

As Sir Geoffrey concluded in his presentation to 350.org: 'We must not despair. We must hope and we must act. We must stop being threatened and rise to the challenge. Big changes to climate change policies everywhere are as necessary as they are inevitable.'

Wise Response has accepted this challenge: we made a 31-page submission (along with more than 15,000 others) on the 'New Zealand Climate Change Target' discussion paper. It will be most interesting and also revealing to see the New Zealand government's input to the Paris Climate Conference in December. We must continue to do everything within our power, particularly on behalf of future generations, since, as has been said many times by many responsible people: 'We have not inherited this earth from our parents to do with it what we will. We have borrowed it from our children and we must be careful to use it in their interests as well as our own' or, put more succinctly by many notables including Ralph Waldo Emerson, Wendell Berry, Chief Seattle, Lester Brown, David R. Brower and others: 'We do not inherit the earth from our ancestors; we borrow it from our children.'

Let that be my and my generation's commitment!

EPILOGUE:
REWARDS AND RECOGNITIONS

Despite risking involvement in political aspects associated with my two main research fields – snow-tussock grassland and lakeshore ecology – there have been highly satisfying rewards and recognitions. These have come at the cost of having to respond to an intermittant barrage of criticism and concerted attempts at undermining one's scientific credibility.[235]

Retention of scientific credibility is essential to the debate of political issues, and also for one's prospects with any future political involvements. Even though ecopolitics is now a recognised field of endeavour, to which I have contributed conference papers on both of my major research fields (Mark 1988a; b), major involvement with muliple environmental issues is more likely to tarnish one's reputation (as a perpetual 'stirrer') as well as the image of the particular campaign. A scientist needs to be aware that if their credibility is seriously and successfully undermined, their scientific career can be threatened, perhaps permanently ruined. Fortunately, I did not suffer this humiliation but did witness it with a university colleague in the 1980s, in the trenchant debate on indigenous forest conservation and exploitation.

Continued family support is also critical when one is being subjected to (usually) public criticism from particular quarters in relation to support for a campaign based on objective assessments of research information. I am pleased to record the unwavering support of my own family members throughout all of my ecopolitical activities, though

EPILOGUE: REWARDS AND RECOGNITIONS

Our family at my 80th birthday party at the Orokonui Ecosanctuary, June 2012, left to right: Stephen (Christchurch, urologist), me, Alastair (Nelson, anaesthetist) Jenifer (Dunedin, university administrator), Pat, Bridget (Dunedin, pharmacist). Jean Fleming.

some have commented on the price in terms of discretionary time able to be spent with the family. Maintenance of close family ties and the independent successes of one's family members are also important aspects of personal rewards. In this regard I confirm my deep satisfaction derived from the personal successes of each of our four children, Jenifer, Stephen, Alastair and Bridget, both in their chosen professions and their family life (my current nine grandchildren should ensure continuation of the lineage), as well as my wife Patricia. She has both supported me and followed separate professional and conservation endeavours which have brought their own rewards and recognitions.

APPENDIX

WISE RESPONSE INC. ORAL SUBMISSION TO FINANCE AND EXPENDITURE SELECT COMMITTEE, 1 JULY 2015

Presented by:

Prof. Alan Mark, chairperson of Wise Response Inc. and Emeritus Professor in Plant Ecology, University of Otago; with

Dr Janet Stephenson, Director of the University of Otago's Centre for Sustainability;

Dr Susan Krumdieck, systems engineer and Professor of Mechanical Engineering, University of Canterbury; co-founder, Global Association for Transition Engineering; and

Paul Young, co-founder and executive member of Generation Zero.

On behalf of Wise Response, we appreciate the opportunity to present a submission to this Select Committee, and elaborate on the petition and submission made to the House of Representatives on 9 April 2014, with 4660 signatures (now 5036). In our nine-page written submission to the committee we renew a formal request of The House, based on our belief that New Zealand is facing an increasingly difficult future, with increasing risks to its economic, environmental and social well-being, many of which arise from resource use that is starting to exceed the carrying capacity, and the sustainability of many of the resources that we depend on for our welfare, and particularly the perceived needs of future generations.

APPENDIX

We share these problems with much of the world and in five major interrelated areas. As a group of well-informed New Zealanders, we formally request that The House: (a) initiates a parliamentary (i.e. cross-party) agreement to undertake a National Risk Assessment of Economic Security, Energy and Climate Security, Business Continuity, Ecological/Environmental Security and Genuine Wellbeing, as outlined in our petition, with an integrated, holistic approach; and (b) from this Risk Assessment, develops and implements cross-party policies to avert any confirmed threats to present and particularly future generations of New Zealanders.

DR JANET STEPHENSON:
We are concerned that New Zealand is underprepared for a future that will be startlingly different from the past; a future in which social and economic wellbeing are facing increasing risks, many of which originate internationally.

Recent reports by three well-respected global agencies – the World Economic Forum, the United Nations, and the global insurance market Lloyd's – provide different, but equally concerning, perspectives on these risks.

The World Economic Forum produces an annual *Global Risks Report*, defining risk as 'an uncertain event or condition that, if it occurs, can cause significant negative impact for several countries or industries within the next 10 years'. In its 2015 report the four highest-likelihood and highest-impact global risks are water crises, interstate conflict, failure of climate change adaptation and fiscal crises. In the statement we circulated to the Select Committee previously we included a diagram that showed these and other economic, environmental, geopolitical, societal and technological risks. The largest *increases* in risk likelihood and/or impact between 2014 and 2015 are interstate conflict, state collapse or crisis, spread of infectious diseases and energy price shocks: www.weforum.org/reports/global-risks-report-2015

The United Nations *Global Assessment Report* 2015 on disaster risk reduction focuses solely on risks relating to the natural environment: earthquakes, cyclones, floods, tsunami, volcanic ash, drought and climate change. It includes country-specific analyses of the likely costs of these events. For New Zealand, the UN estimates that by far the greatest risk is from storm surges and flooding, with probable annual average losses estimated at $US323 million and $US399 respectively. The report also states that global climate change is already modifying hazard levels and exacerbating disaster risks through changing temperatures, precipitation and sea levels, among other factors: www.preventionweb.net/english/hyogo/gar/2015/en/home/data.php?iso=NZL

Lloyd's is a major player in the global specialist insurance market. It regularly produces reports on emerging risks and their implications for insurance. Recent reports on risks from the natural environment note the dynamic changes already evident such as increasing occurrence of hurricanes and flooding. Lloyd's has also produced other reports on risks to society and security such as the impacts of global food system shocks, and the risks of business failing to adapt to a low-carbon economy: www.lloyds.com/news-and-insight/risk-insight

Almost all the risks identified in these reports have the potential to impact on New Zealand, either physically (storm surges, flooding, droughts) or through the economy (oil price shocks, interstate conflict, fiscal crises) or society (e.g. disease outbreaks).

In failing to identify, understand and prepare for these risks, New Zealand puts itself in a very vulnerable position. The livelihoods of current and future generations are threatened if governance focuses just on the short term, and assumes that the patterns of the past are a decent predictor of the future. But, clearly, we do not have the luxury of continuing business as usual.

This changing risk landscape means that risk is exacerbated when the short-term economic cost of taking action is emphasised over the long-term economic and social costs of *not* acting. The World Bank makes this point in a recent report that provides policy advice on transitioning to a zero-carbon future.

The solutions exist and are affordable, the report says, if governments take action *today*. It warns, however, that costs will rise the longer action is delayed. To keep global temperatures within the 2°C limit, waiting just 15 more years and taking no action until 2030 would increase costs of transitioning by an average of 50 per cent through to 2050.

The need for a long-term perspective on risk is one of the reasons we are asking for a cross-party agreement to undertake the risk assessment and to act on the findings – the issues are long term and are relevant for much longer timeframes than a term in parliament. As the World Bank says with respect to climate change: 'Getting to zero net emissions and stabilizing climate change starts with planning for the long-term future and not stopping at short-term goals.': www.worldbank.org/en/news/feature/2015/05/11/decarbonizing-development-zero-carbon-future

SUSAN KRUMDIECK:
There are plenty of examples internationally of countries that have undertaken their own national-level comprehensive risk assessments.

One example is the Strategic National Risk Assessment undertaken by the Department of Homeland Security in the US. The purpose there is to support national preparedness for threats that pose the greatest risk to the US, including terrorism, cyber attacks, pandemics, and catastrophic natural disasters. The assessment process has been used to support the development of collaborative thinking across all levels of government about prevention, protection, mitigation, response and recovery: www.dhs.gov/strategic-national-risk-assessment-snra

Ireland is another example, closer in scale to New Zealand. The foreword of their draft National Risk Assessment explains: 'One of the priorities of our country and our people as we move towards economic recovery is to ensure we learn from the mistakes of the past. One of those mistakes was complacency at a time of prosperity, so that serious questions were avoided. Never again should threats to our nation's future be ignored. Never again should dissenting voices be silenced when warning of risks up ahead.' The assessment sets out the risks (financial and non-financial) that Ireland faces, including in the longer term: www.taoiseach.gov.ie/.../Draft_National_Risk_Assessment_2015.html

The OECD is also encouraging nations to undertake all-hazards national risk assessments. Its recent *Recommendation on the Governance of Critical Risks* has been developed in recognition of the escalating damages due to extreme events. It warns that recent events are a stark warning for economic systems that are dependent on global supply chains. The *Recommendation* proposes actions that governments can take, in collaboration with the private sector, to better assess, prevent, respond to and recover from the effects of extreme events, as well as take measures to build resilience to rebound from unanticipated events: www.oecd.org/gov/risk/recommendation-on-governance-of-critical-risks.htm

Once a risk assessment has been undertaken, the next mission is to develop a risk management approach – formulating responses that build resilience and support strategic decision making: How are you going to react, and do you have the management systems in place that enable you to make the correct decisions whatever comes along, in time to make a difference?

The whole purpose of risk management is to enable the right people to make the right decisions at the right time. You have to have scientific measurement, monitoring and reporting, and you have to have trusted, independent experts interpreting the data. Your risk management engineers and experts create scenarios – then they stay on the job, adjusting their approach based on real-time observations, and working with local institutions and authorities.

One way of doing this is using the managed adaptive approach – 'planning in' from forward scenarios and using ongoing observations of problems as they arise. These scenarios must include compounding of coincident events and problems: 'perfect storm scenarios'.

APPENDIX

We need to get a good handle on the worst that could happen, we have to use scenarios to deal with the uncertainties, we need to 'practise' responses and decisions, and we need to observe and learn as we go along and things change. Engineering for the 'worst case' may provide measures needed in an environment of 'extreme' being the new norm.

PAUL YOUNG:
I'm here to represent younger generations of New Zealanders, who have more skin in the game when it comes to the longer-term risks we are discussing.

The serious flooding in Wellington, Dunedin, Hokitika and Manawatu–Whanganui over the past couple of months has given New Zealand a sense of the new risk environment that may result from the more frequent and severe weather events likely to be induced by climate change. We don't yet know the full impacts but Horizons Regional Council, for example, has put an initial figure of $120 million on the cost of flood recovery in the Manawatu–Whanganui region. Together with the Wellington, Dunedin and Hokitika events, this may not be far off the estimate in the UN *Global Assessment Report* 2015 mentioned earlier.

A risk assessment for New Zealand needs to assess the impacts of single-issue risks such as more frequent flooding, droughts and storm surges on the economy and society. But even more crucial is to understand the implications for New Zealand of combinations of risks playing out at the same time. Here are three brief scenarios based on realistic risks identified by the global reports referred to previously:

Scenario 1: Increasing numbers of climate refugees on boats attempt to enter New Zealand as a result of sea-level rise affecting their low-lying nations. At the same time there is a significant outbreak of highly infectious disease. How should New Zealand respond?

Scenario 2: Inter-state conflict with oil-producing nations leads to an oil price shock. At the same time, New Zealand's long-running favourable exchange rate drops significantly. The cost of petrol and diesel would skyrocket under this scenario. What options are there to reduce the significant impact on New Zealand's economic activity?

Scenario 3: The increasing costs of more extreme weather events significantly impact upon regional and national economies. At the same time low-lying infrastructure such as roads, sewerage and stormwater systems need investment to future proof them against sea-level rise and extreme weather events. Where is the money to come from?

The last example in particular highlights the intergenerational dimensions at play. Being unprepared for risks, and failing to take appropriate near-term actions to mitigate these, could see future generations in charge overwhelmed and unable to muster an effective response as multiple risks converge. As in medicine, prevention will invariably be better than cure. And as with the government's approach to social welfare, early intervention delivers the greatest value to society.

My experience is that a great many of my peers are deeply concerned, fearful even, about the future we will inherit in the face of escalating risks such as climate change. Many are losing faith in our political institutions to deal with these threats.

We need to see our leaders working together to effectively address the risks facing our society. Heeding Wise Response's request for a National Risk Assessment would be an instrumental first step in the right direction.

ALAN MARK:
In conclusion, we trust we have convinced the Select Committee of the urgent need for such a risk assessment and we request that the committee initiate its own specific enquiry into the subject matter of the petition, perhaps assisted by the Auditor General and/or the PCE, and/or the Prime Minister's Science Adviser, Sir Peter Gluckman; or the committee may refer the petition to The House with a recommendation for appropriate action.

ACKNOWLEDGEMENTS

Conservation achievements are rarely made with solo involvement; indeed, it would be rather naive to attempt a campaign alone. In my case, there have been people with a great diversity of backgrounds along the way. Firstly, I express sincere thanks to my family, who have greatly assisted with, or in some cases tolerated, particular campaigns, which have sometimes required frequent diversions from family life; there have also been the many successes that we have celebrated together.

I owe much to my teachers, particularly at tertiary level, and here Geoff Baylis at Otago and Dwight Billings at Duke were outstanding, as were many of my university colleagues, including research students, most notably Katharine Dickinson, Larry Bliss, Stephan Halloy, Bill Lee, Peter Johnson, Ralph Allen and Colin Meurk.

Among the farming community, the Reid brothers – Archie, Ken and Ron – as well as Bill Kofoed of Maungatua, gave freely of their knowledge, interest and involvement. In later years John McCambridge, Doug Matheson, Don Harley, Alastair Campbell, Pat Garden and John Beattie were all supportive and interested, as were those involved with the Hellaby Trust, particularly Lily and Arthur of the Hellaby family, as well as Eric Godley, Geoff Baylis, Reinhart Langer, Sir Malcolm Burns, Bill Truman, Bill Rolfe and Bill Lee.

The Manapouri and Te Anau controversy broadened my horizons and associates, from my initial ecological colleagues Geoff Baylis and Peter Johnson to many of the campaigners, some of whom were later Guardian associates. Most notable was my mentor and campaigner Sir Charles

Fleming, together with Ian Prior and Guardians Ron McLean, Les Hutchins, John Moore, Jim McFarlane, Wilson Campbell, Bill Bell, John Donaldson, Chris Henderson, Norman Jones, Mason Stretch and Dave Riddell, and fellow scientists Bob Kirk, Dick Pickrill and Larry Burrows, together with others with various roles: Kerry McDonald (Comalco), Colin Bambury, Mark France, Kieran Devine, Keith Turnar and Hector Jones (NZED). Among the senior politicians I tried to persuade and shared thoughts with were Norman Kirk, Helen Clark, Joe Walding, Russell Marshall, Ian Shearer, Hugh Templeton, Venn Young, Duncan McIntyre, Jim Bolger, Geoffrey Palmer, Simon Upton and Rob Muldoon.

David Thom and Les Molloy were close allies on the National Parks and Reserves Authority, Allan Evans on the Land Settlement Board, Gordon Stephenson on the Wetlands Task Force, Les Cleveland on the Otago Conservation Board, and Marion van der Goes, Wendy Nelson and Katharine Dickinson on the Conservation Authority. Colleagues in Forest & Bird are too numerous to name more than a few – Tony Ellis, Allan Edmonds, Gerry McSweeney, Gordon Ell, Kevin Smith, John Morton, Sandra Lee and Craig Potton.

Progress with the Wise Response Society has been due largely to local members Dugald MacTavish, Mark Jackson, Bob Lloyd, Jean Fleming, Jocelyn Harris, Pat Scott and Philip Temple, and, further afield, our patron, Sir Geoffrey Palmer, together with John la Roche of Auckland, Jonathan Boston of Wellington and John Peat of Christchurch.

Production of this book has been ably assisted by Richard Reeve of Dunedin, who spent countless unpaid hours helping me shape the manuscript; and Jane Connor of Nelson, who also managed my recent alpine field guide. Rachel Scott, publisher of Otago University Press, made the call for this publication. I also thank Sir Geoffrey Palmer for accepting my request to produce a foreword for the book.

NOTES

1. Lough et al. 1987; Mark and Wilson 2005.
2. I was considerably assisted in my findings by Geoff Baylis. See Mark 1955; Wardle and Mark 1956.
3. Billings and Mark 1957; Mark 1958; Mark 1959.
4. These data were obtained with improvised, frost-tolerant evaporimeters. See Mark and Smith 1962.
5. Mark 1965a.
6. The vegetation pattern created by the snow fence was first described in 1991 – see Smith et al. 1995 – and studied again in 2002, 2003 and 2011. See Mark, Korsten, Guevara et al. 2015.
7. The recording on the Old Man Range was continued in collaboration with the Catchment Board until March 1963, providing a four-year record (see Mark 1974a), with three of the sites on the central transect of the range being used for the snow tussock study. The two Maungatua and three Coronet Peak sites were also run over the same three years (April 1960–March 1963).
8. Mark 1965b; Mark 1965c; Mark 1965d; Mark 1965e; Mark 1965f; Mark 1968; Mark 1969; Mark 1974b.
9. The high-altitude slim snow tussock, which replaces narrow-leaved snow tussock above approximately 1250 m, only became formalised in 1970.
10. This was achieved by quartering 20 tussocks carefully with a spade at each site, planting one quarter at its home site, two at the other two sites and the last quarter at the Botany Department garden near sea level in Dunedin.
11. Such fire-stimulated germination occurred on the Old Man Range in 1961. See Mark 1965e.
12. Payton, Lee, Dolby et al. 1986; Mark 1993b; Mark 1994a.
13. *Ibid*.
14. Payton and Mark 1979.
15. Moore 1955; Mark 1980a; Mark 1993a; Mark and Lee 2003.
16. See Mark 2005.
17. Mark and Rowley 1976
18. Holdsworth and Mark 1990.
19. Mark, Rowley and Holdsworth 1980.
20. McSavaney and Whitehouse, 1988.
21. Press release, 18 August 1988, released by John Miller, author's personal archive.
22. Pers. comm.

23. *Otago Daily Times*, 26 August 1988.
24. Submission by John Williamson, John Allen and Rodney Patterson to Otago Regional Council public hearing on Burning Permit Applications, Alexandra, May 1992.
25. Pers. comm.
26. Fahey et al. 1996.
27. This value was considered minimal for water gains to a unit area of snow-tussock grassland from intercepted fog since the rain gauge could accommodate only a relatively small simulated tussock – a plant with 40 tillers rather than the more usual 400 for a mature snow tussock (Mark 1988c). Moreover, the rain gauge was placed in the grassland community without removal of another tussock; interception gains by a single tussock are known to decrease in relation to increased density of tussocks (Mark, Rowley and Holdsworth 1980).
28. Ingraham and Mark 2000.
29. *Ibid.*
30. *New Zealand Ecological Society Newsletter* 97, March 2001: 11–12.
31. *North and South*, April 2003.
32. Ingraham and Mark 2000.
33. Ingraham et al. 2008.
34. Mark 1998c.
35. Mark and Dickinson 2008.
36. Kepner et al. 2012.
37. As part of my M.Sc. study, I had determined by counting growth rings that the oldest of these shrubs pre-dated European settlement.
38. Dickinson, Mark and Lee 1992.
39. Mark and Dickinson 2003.
40. *Ibid.*; Mark and Dickinson 2004.
41. 'Pukerau Copper Tussock Scientific Reserve' would be a more accurate title. The name of the southern subspecies *cuprea* refers to the tussock's distinctive copper colour.
42. Mark 1990a.
43. Sly et al. 1977. This survey was part of a Lands and Survey assessment of a proposed skifield development.
44. Mark 1990a.
45. Author's personal archive.
46. Letter to the Editor, *Central Otago News,* 30 May 1991, from G.M. Eckhoff, Coal Creek, Roxburgh.
47. Mark, Dickinson, Patrick et al. 1989. Our 1987 study led to an addition of some 20,000 ha. to this park when it was established in 2003.
48. I was recently asked to document this expansion. See Mark 2012a.
49. Mark, Dickinson, Patrick et al. 1989.
50. Mark and McSweeney 1987.
51. Mark, Dickinson, Patrick et al. 1989.
52. Mark 2004. For the Hocken lecture I traced much of the history of our indigenous grasslands from the Quaternary Era through to Polynesian settlement about 800 years ago, when frequent extensive fires resulted in

NOTES

further expansion of the grasslands, which probably reached their greatest extent immediately prior to European settlement in the 1840s.

Seemingly lush and productive, the tussock grasslands obviously impressed Europeans with their apparent grazing potential. As with the grazing lands of Australia, those of the South Island high country remained under government ownership and control. All areas were leased in large blocks, including adjacent high-alpine areas and even permanent icefields, for extensive grazing. The government initially required high and rapidly increasing stocking rates; and so, with only very limited fencing and frequent, usually uncontrolled burning, 'exploitative pastoralism' began.

The combination of frequent burning and heavy and largely unregulated grazing by introduced mammals, an entirely new and unnatural phenomenon, caused serious degradation of the native grasslands and erosion of their soils. I traced the historical records documenting frequent expressions of concern by scientists and others about pastoral management. This management was initially largely dictated by a colonial government dominated by its masters in Britain. As early as 1868 botanist and artist John Buchanan, writing in the *Transactions of the New Zealand Institute*, had noted that 'nothing can show greater ignorance of grass conservation than the repeated burning which is so frequently practiced'. Despite the many attempts by government and others to address this serious situation, which were discussed, degradation has continued to the present. Current tenure reviews are now addressing the situation, hopefully more effectively.

53. This was largely in response to the Lake Manapouri development controversy.
54. Our proposal was fully supported in an audit by the Commission for the Environment and several other organisations.
55. Mackenzie 1979.
56. *Ibid.*
57. Mark 1982.
58. *Ibid.*
59. *Ibid.*
60. *Ibid.*
61. *Ibid.*
62. *Ibid.*
63. *Ibid.*
64. *Ibid.*
65. *Ibid.*
66. Pers. comm.
67. Pers. comm.
68. Pers. comm.
69. Baylis et al. 1970.
70. 'Report of the commission to inquire into the proposal to raise the level of Lake Manapouri for the purpose of generating electricity', Wellington, Government Printer, 1970.
71. *Press*, 7 November 1970; Mark, Johnson, Crush et al. 1972b.
72. Mark, Johnson, Crush et al. 1971; 1972b.

73. Mark, Johnson, Crush et al. 1972b.
74. Ibid.
75. Mark, Johnson and Wilson 1977.
76. Ibid.
77. Pers. comm.
78. Pickrill 1978.
79. Recorded in the 'Fifth annual report of the Guardians to the minister for the environment', 8 April 1978, Box 1, Hocken Collections.
80. Recorded in the 'Seventeenth annual report of the Guardians to the minister of conservation', 31 May 1990. Box 1, Hocken Collections.
81. Letter of 18 March 1987 from the minister of energy, sent to the Guardians by the minister of conservation and quoted in the 'Fourteenth annual report of the Guardians to the minister of conservation, 11 April 1987, Box 1, Hocken Collections.
82. Recorded in the 'Seventeeth annual report of the Guardians to the minister of conservation', 31 May 1990, Box 1, Hocken Collections.
83. Recorded in the 'Sixteenth annual report of the Guardians to the minister of conservation', 15 April 1989, Box 1, Hocken Collections.
84. Recorded in the 'Nineteenth annual report of the Guardians to the minister of conservation', 30 April 1992, Box 1, Hocken Collections.
85. Recorded in the 'Twenty-fourth annual report of the Guardians to the minister of conservation', 12 April 1997, Box 1, Hocken Collections.
86. Formal (undated) statement from ECNZ, headed: 'Executive summary, Manapouri Tailrace Investigation Project', appended to the Twenty-first annual report of the Guardians to the minister of conservation, 13 April 1994, Box 1, Hocken Collections.
87. Peat 1994.
88. Mark and Johnson 1985; Mark 1987; Mark and Kirk 1987; James et al. 2002.
89. Quin et al. 1987; Kelly et al. 1989; Tangney et al. 1990.
90. Mark 1975; Mark 1988a; Mark 1990b; Chapin et al. 2012.
91. Mark, Turner and West 2001.
92. The committee was chaired by geography professor Ron Lister, with Angus Black, Jolyon Manning, Gary Blackman, Basil Howard, Bill Landreth and myself as the remaining members, together with planner Donald Paterson.
93. Appendix A in 'Aramoana Land Use Investigation', Dunedin Metropolitan Regional Planning authority, 1975.
94. The Scientific Co-ordinating Committee on Beech Research was chaired by Colin Bassett, Director of Research in the Forest Service's Forestry Research Institute. Other members were: Eric Godley, Director of DSIR's Botany Division; Mike Leamy from the Soil Bureau of DSIR; Gordon Williams, director of the Department of Internal Affairs Wildlife Service (replaced, following his death, by Colin Ogle); Morgan Williams from the Ministry of Agriculture; Bob McDowall from the Fisheries Research Division of the Ministry of Agriculture and Fisheries; Harry Bunn, director of the Forest Service's Production Forestry Division; and Geoff Baylis and myself (replacing Colin Burrows in 1976) as nominees of the Royal Society of New Zealand. John Nicholls, senior ecologist

NOTES

with the Forestry Research Institute, was the technical advisor.
95. Scientific Co-ordinating Committee, 'Guidelines for selection of ecological areas', *Beech Research News* 8: 10, 1983.
96. See also Mark 1985a.
97. Mark and Smith 1975.
98. Dickinson and Mark 1994.
99. Wilkinson and Garrett 1977.
100. Mark 1998a; Mark 1998b.
101. The committee included Kevin O'Connor, Colin Burrows, Peter Wardle and others from whom advice was sought on the varied activities of this division of the Forestry Research Institute.
102. Mavora Lakes Pastoral Park, management plan (draft), 1984, Invercargill, Department of Lands and Survey.
103. Mavora Lakes Management Plan, 1985, series number C.L.29, Invercargill, Department of Lands and Survey.
104. Stephenson et al. 1983.
105. There were 59 terrestrial wetlands (19 in the North Island and 40 in the South Island) and 299 coastal wetlands (155 in the North Island, 138 in the South Island, and 6 on Stewart Island) classified.
106. Initially chaired by former High Court Judge Sir Clinton Roper of Christchurch, the Mountain Lands Committee was made up of John Bishop from Lands and Survey; Christchurch author Barry Brailsford; Methven high-country runholder and chair of the Federated Farmers High Country section, Hamish Ensor; John Holloway from DOC; Springfield high-country farmer and regional councillor Richard Johnson; George McMillan from Landcorp; Landcare Research CEO Andrew Pearce; Blenheim forestry consultant Jaquetta Smith; Christchurch businessman Peter Yeoman; and myself. Following his later resignation, Sir Clinton was replaced as chair by George McMillan.
107. The Hawkweeds Core Group comprised George McMillan as convenor, Hamish Ensor, Richard Johnson, Barney Foran, Jay Randall, Kevin O'Connor and me.
108. McMillan 1991.
109. New Zealand Mountain Lands Institute 1992. Guidelines on burning tussock grasslands. *Journal of the New Zealand Mountain Lands Institute Review* 49: 51–63.
110. *Ibid.*
111. The chinchilla is a South American rodent. The institute conveyed its concern to the minister of agriculture at their recent availability in the South Island.
112. McMillan 1992.
113. Fagan 1989. Following a reconnaisance of the *ca.* 165,000 ha. Manorburn Ecological District located east of the Clutha Valley in Central Otago, Brent made a detailed study of the most natural and diverse areas of native vegetation using a standard procedure involving fixed area plots. Landforms were described and species lists compiled. Fifteen areas were recommended for protection, ranging in size from 6 to 1970 ha. These totalled 5490 ha., or some 3.3% of the district's area. The recommended areas included wetlands, cushion vegetation, copper- and snow-tussock grasslands, shrublands and saline communities.
114. *Otago Daily Times*, 3 September 1993.

115. We stated as much in a joint scientific submission to the high country review panel. See Allan et al. 1994.
116. Connell 1998.
117. Author's personal archive.
118. Author's personal archive.
119. The Guardians of Fiordland Fisheries and Marine Environment consisted of two recreational fishers (Alan Key and Wayne Neiman), five commercial fishers (John Steffens, Ian Kennedy, Mark Peychers, Peter Young and Ian Leask), three charter/tourist operators (Peter Bloxham, Ian Buick and Gordon Johnson), a community representative (Irene Barnes) and two Ngāi Tahu representatives (Stewart Bull and Gail Thompson). John Steffens was elected chair.
120. Guardians of Fiordland Fisheries 1999.
121. Guardians of Fiordland Fisheries 2001.
122. Hon. Marion Hobbs, 12 April–19 May 2005. Third reading: Fiordland (Te Moana o Atawhenua) Marine Management Bill. New Zealand Parliamentary Debates 625: 19892–19897.
123. The committee was made up of four Marine Guardians (John Steffans, Mark Peychers, Alan Key and me), plus representatives from Te Rūnanga o Ngāi Tahu, MfE, the Ministry of Fisheries, DOC, the Marine Safety Authority and Environment Southland, with MfE the lead agency. It was established in December to guide the process through to completion by 2005.
124. 'Guardian Angels', *North & South*, July 2004: 70–78.
125. 'I must say that one thing that really concerned me was the appointment of Professor Alan Mark to the guardians. Professor Mark is well known to me and to the high-country community, because he has alienated virtually every farmer in the high country over his top-down approach to the whole process. Quite frankly, Alan Mark is a bad appointment to have made to that group. I concur totally that in order for these sorts of organisations to succeed, there has to be a bottom-up approach, which is exactly what we have in the guardians group at this time. But we cannot have people like retired emeritus Professor Alan Mark believe that people from Dunedin or Wellington are the appropriate people to have as the guardians of this most remarkable area of our country. Professor Mark stated in *North and South* magazine that he was 'marginally acceptable to Forest and Bird'. Well, the only thing I can say to that is 'Yeah, right'.

Professor Mark is well known as New Zealand's foremost preservationist. I make the distinction between conservation and preservation, because this bill should be about conservation, not preservation. Conservation would be welcomed, I am sure, by everybody in this House, including me and members of the ACT party. Irrespective of who it is, conservation is what we are about – perpetuation of the species, if one likes. Preservation, especially in remote areas, is all about creating a haven for poachers. If Government members and other members have not worked that out yet, they should come and talk to me, and I will point them in the right direction towards the people who understand that'. Gerard Eckhoff, 'Fiordland Marine Management Bill – First Reading: NZ Parliamentary Debates (Hansard), Vol 622, 18122.

The following was presented to Alan on 10 June 2015, by the Hon. Nick Smith

NOTES

at the Fiordland Marine Guardians' special function to celebrate 10 years since the passage of the Fiordland Marine Management Act:
Presented to Sir Alan Mark in recognition of his outstanding contribution to the management of the Fiordland (Te Moana o Atawhenua) Marine Area. As an original appointee to the Fiordland Marine Guardians, his ongoing involvement and commitment has contributed significantly towards the success of the Fiordland (Te Moana o Atawhenua) Marine Management Act 2005. The Act facilitates and promotes cooperation between the Fiordland Marine Guardians and management agencies and gives recognition to their visions. 'That the quality of Fiordland's marine environment and fisheries, including the wider fishery experience, be maintained or improved for future generations to use and enjoy'.

126. The other Marine Guardians appointed were Ian Buick, manager of South West Helicopters; Stewart Bull, chair of the Ōraka-Aparima Rūnaka; NIWA marine scientist Ken Grange of Nelson; Alan Key of the Southland Marine Recreational Fishers Association; prominent Te Anau commercial fisher John Steffens; and Laurel Tierney of Dunedin (who had been facilitator for the earlier guardians group). See Chapin et al. 2012.
127. Fiordland Marine Guardians, annual reports for 2006 onwards: www.fmg.org.nz.
128. Fiordland Marine Guardians 2008.
129. As well as the chair, Dr Margriet Theron, the review team consisted of John Craig from the University of Auckland; Maurice Te Whiti Love of Raukura Consultants; Ian Naumann from CSIRO's Division of Entomology; forestry consultant Colin O'Loughlin; Morgan Williams of the Ministry of Agriculture and Forestry; and me.
130. 'Land use, flora and fauna research: A review of science in New Zealand', Wellington. Ministry of Research, Science and Technology, 1993.
131. Mark 2012b.
132. The society now has over 50,000 members.
133. Pers. comm.
134. Mark 1980b.
135. Mark 1985b.
136. Molloy 1978; 1983; 1987.
137. McSweeney and Molloy 1984.
138. Mark 1984.
139. Mark 1985b.
140. Forest and Bird Protection Society 1994.
141. Balantine 1988.
142. Other aspects of the South Island high country were described in the February 1994 and August 1995 issues of *Forest & Bird*. The August 2002 issue was largely devoted to the South Island high country.
143. Mark 2012a.
144. The West Coast community also received $120 million in compensation.
145. McSweeney 1989.
146. *Ibid.*
147. South Westland Forests Working Party 1988.
148. Hutching and Potton 1987.

149. Authors were Gerry McSweeney (introduction to the World Heritage Concept), Craig Potton (geology and European history), Kevin Smith (vegetation), Colin O'Donnell (wildlife), Keri Hulme (Māori history) and Guy Salmon (the politics of preservation).
150. South Westland Forests Working Party 1988.
151. Mark 1998b.
152. Forest & Bird interview: Lady Peg Fleming. *Forest & Bird* 21(1): 32–33.
153. Mark and McSweeney 1990.
154. Hager and Burton 1999.
155. *Ibid.*
156. Author's personal archive.
157. Author's personal archive.
158. Author's personal archive.
159. *The Press*, 8 February 2000.
160. Author's personal archive.
161. Author's personal archive.
162. Debs Martin, pers. comm.
163. www.nzffa.org.nz/system/assets/1287/principles_plantation_forest_2004.pdf.
164. Otago-Southland Wilding Tree Accord 1998.
165. National Radio news item, following an interview with reporter Ian Telfer.
166. *NZ Wilderness* article in the issue October 2000.
167. Wardle 1963.
168. Baylis and Mark 1963.
169. Mark and Baylis 1963.
170. Baylis et al. 1963.
171. Wardle et al. 1970; Wardle and Mark 1970.
172. Mark and Baylis 1975.
173. Mark and Baylis 1982.
174. *Ibid.*
175. Mark, Baylis and Dickinson 1991.
176. Mark, Scott, Sanderson et al. 1964.
177. Mark, Dickinson and Fife 1989.
178. Sommerville et al. 1982.
179. The Hollyford Valley, (Mark and Sanderson 1962); Lake Hankinson (Scott et al. 1964); Secretary Island (Mark 1963).
180. Wells and Mark 1966.
181. Wardle et al. 1973.
182. Johnson et al. 1977.
183. Similar catastrophes befalling 19th- and early 20th-century plant collectors in various parts of the world have been documented recently by Australian Philip Short in his book *In Pursuit of Plants* (Timber Press, Portland, 2004).
184. Mark 1977
185. Mark 1979a.
186. Mark 1989.
187. Mark 1999a.
188. Mills and Mark 1977.

NOTES

189. Mills et al. 1980.
190. Mark, Rawson and Wilson 1979.
191. So described by renowned soil scientist Hans Jenny in 1969–80
192. Ward 1988; Mark, Grealish, Ward et al. 1988.
193. Mark and Lee 1985.
194. Dickinson et al. 1994.
195. Hofstede et al. 2001.
196. Dickinson and Mark 1994.
197. Robertson et al. 1991.
198. Dickinson and Mark 1999.
199. Dickinson et al. 1998.
200. Mark, Johnson, Dickinson et al. 1995.
201. McGlone et al.1995.
202. Dickinson et al. 2002; Chagué-Goff, Mark and Dickinson 2010.
203. Mark, Dickinson and Fife 1989.
204. Yin et al. 1984.
205. Cook et al. 1980.
206. Bond et al. 2004.
207. Mark and Dickinson 1997; Mark, Dickinson and Hofstede 2000.
208. Mark and Bliss 1970.
209. Bliss and Mark 1974.
210. Talbot et al. 1992.
211. Billings and Mark 1961; Mark and Bliss 1970; Grab et al. 2008.
212. Mark 1994b.
213. Stanley et al. 1998; Dickinson et al. 2007.
214. Mark and Adams 1973, 1979, 1986, 1995.
215. Mark 1970.
216. Mark 2012b.
217. The full text of the Maruia Declaration ran as follows:
    Native forests where they remain, need recognition and protection in law. To date, four and a half million acres of lowland forest can potentially be logged, chipped, pulped or burnt and converted to exotics; of this, barely ten per cent has any form of legal protection ...
    The wholesale burning of indigenous forests and wildlife has no place in a civilised country. Almost a million acres of our remaining native forest lands are considered suitable for conversion to exotics under the new planting programme. But ample quantities of timber for New Zealand's domestic and export needs can be produced by planting open land outside indigenous forests, especially land that was unwisely cleared in the past.
    The logging of virgin forests (with certain exceptions) should be phased out by 1978. Westland is an exception: there the regional economy still depends on some indigenous sawmilling, which must decline over a longer period while alternative industries, including the exotic forest industries, are urgently developed. Again, there are a few places where it may be possible to produce high quality, decorative woods in perpetuity. But elsewhere, the logging of virgin native forests is an episode that belongs to history. Today, society's wood

needs can be supplied from plantations established outside native forests. Yet indigenous sawmills and chip mills, contributing only nine per cent to our total wood production, are still being allowed to devastate more than 10 000 acres of beautiful virgin forests every year. This must be stopped. Such forests are unique and irreplaceable: those we can save now are all we shall ever have.

Our remaining publicly owned native forests should be placed in the hands of an organisation that has a clear and undivided responsibility to protect them. It is too much to expect Departments mainly concerned with wood production or land clearance to adequately protect these forests. The organisation we need could be formed by taking the Parks and Reserves Division of the Lands Department and the Environmental Forestry Division from the Forest Service, and combining these divisions into a new Nature Conservancy charged with safeguarding all of our remaining native forests.

To reduce commercial pressures on native forests, the growing of fine quality exotic and native timbers on land not presently forested should be given encouragement. Such timbers should not be wastefully used as they are at present, but conserved for their highest uses …

It is prudent to be conservative in our consumption and export of those forest products, especially newsprint and packaging paper, which make heavy demands on our precious resources of land, energy and water. If, on their maturity, we were to convert into newsprint just half the pines that were planted last year, we would have to consume for this purpose alone more electric power and water than was used last year by the entire country. Surely we must distinguish between people's real needs, and what the forest industries tell us we need. Let us conserve our resources wisely, and recycle them wherever we can.

218. 'Management Policy for New Zealand Indigenous State Forests', 1977, Wellington, New Zealand Forest Service.
219. *Ibid.*
220. The consortium consisted of Fletcher Challenge with Alusuiss and an Australian company, CSR.
221. The departments of Agriculture, Forestry, Lands and Survey and the Ministry of Works.
222. Roxburgh et al. 1988.
223. *Otago Daily Times*, 19 January 1977; Mark 1978.
224. Mark 1978.
225. *Ibid.*
226. Otago Catchment Board report and recommendation: Application for water rights for DG3, Clutha River, Clyde, 25 October 1977; Mark 1978.
227. Mark 1978.
228. *Ibid.*
229. *Ibid.*
230. *Ibid.*
231. *Otago Daily Times*, 23 June 1982.
232. Water Conservation (Kawarau) Order, 1997.
233. The out-of-town speakers at the afternoon event were Auckland University economist Tim Hazledine; Massey University freshwater ecologist Mike Joy;

NOTES

Otago University (Wellington Campus) orthopaedic surgeon Russell Tregonning; Victoria University glacial-climatologist Peter Barrett; and Canterbury University systems engineer Susan Krumdieck. Among the locals we had Hoani Lansbury, Neville Peat, Jean Fleming, Maree Baker-Galloway and Louis Chambers. Our evening meeting took a similar format as the afternoon launch but Royden Somerville QC stood in for Maree Baker-Galloway.

234. Sir Geoffrey Palmer, speech to the 350.org group in Wellington on 16 February 2015.
235. One of the most persistent critics has been runholder Gerry Eckhoff of Mt Benger Station, Roxburgh. On May 15 1988 he wrote to the university's registrar: *Dr Alan Mark is quoted a lot by groups associated with the conservation and recreation lobbies and also his work is used as reference material by DoC, etc. Dr Mark enjoys a very high profile and is held in high regard throughout the country, however, I do feel it is necessary to establish that his work is totally value free as I'm sure all scientific work should be. To this end would you please forward to me a list of Dr Mark's work from, say, the last 10 years that has been published in international scientific journals that would of course be independently refereed. I believe that while the local scientific community is very capable I also feel that it is very closely connected, hence the need for overseas botanists to referee this material. Would it be possible to receive a list of organisations that Dr Mark is associated with that are connected with the conservation issues?*

In response, Professor P. Bannister, Head of the Botany Department, replied (May 23): *In response to your letter of 5 May inquiring into the professional standing in the field of tussock grasslands research of Professor A.F. Mark of this Department, the most appropriate response is to forward you a copy of Dr Mark's curriculum vitae. I believe it speaks for itself.*

In response, Mr Eckhoff wrote (June 21): *Thank you for your letter of 23rd May which enclosed Professor Mark's curriculum vitae. There are some further specific questions I would like answered about Professor Mark's standing. Very few of Professor Mark's publications have the status of being published in journals which have overseas referees. Perhaps numbers 3, 4, 5, 6, 15, 28, 55, 61, 64, 79, 80 and 83 come into this category. Amongst a small group, such as NZ ecologists, there is danger that within-group refereeing may not be very rigorous. Is this number of papers in overseas refereed journals normally sufficient for a promotion to a personal chair at your university? Professor Mark is the president of the Royal Forest & Bird Protection Society which fulfills an active political role in the conservation camp. Is the University of Otago worried about; (i) The reduced teaching and research that is implied by this extra curriculum activity? (ii) The possibility that association with a propaganda pressure group (or groups) may reduce the scientific credibility of Professor Mark, the Botany Department and the University of Otago? (iii) The possibility that enthusiasm for his credo may reduce the flow of information between teacher and students who may be apprehensive about the effect on their marks from expressing contrary ideas to those held by Professor Mark. PS. I would be obliged if Dr Irvine would comment on the above points raised also.*

Professor Bannister replied (23 June): *Thank you for your letter of 21 June. I* shall endeavour to answer the points that you raised. I have passed a copy of your letter and my reply to the Vice-Chancellor. 1. Many of Professor Mark's papers have been published in local journals, but merely because they are mainly of local interest. Many local journals (e.g. the various DSIR publications) have an international distribution and standing, and I have no reason to believe that the standard of refereeing differs from that abroad. Many academic referees from within New Zealand have themselves come from abroad or been trained abroad. 2. Professor Mark was appointed to a personal chair before I took appointment in New Zealand. Recommendations for personal chairs are evaluated by specially constituted sub-committees of the Academic Staffing Committee and subject to external as well as internal assessment. His record of publication was quite evidently judged adequate for the award of a personal chair. 3(i). Professor Mark's extra-curricular activities have not reduced his contribution to teaching and research. He takes a full teaching load and his research output has not diminished. His uninterrupted list of publications shows this. (ii). I am unaware that the scientific credibility of Professor Mark, the Botany Department, or the University of Otago has been diminished by Professor Mark's association with conservation groups. (iii). I am satisfied that Professor Mark's views have not affected his marking of student's questions. Apart from the fact that I have received no complaints on that score, I should emphasise that Professor Mark's teaching within the Department of Botany is concerned with the scientific study of plant ecology and not with eco-politics. I trust this answers your enquiries satisfactorily.

BIBLIOGRAPHY

Allan, R., Dickinson, K., Espie, P., Floate, M., Hewitt, A., Lee, B., Mark, A., Mason, C., McIntosh, P., Meurk, C., Nordmeyer, A., O'Connor, K., Scott, D., and Tate, K., 1994, 'Review of South Island high country land management issues: Joint submission to the Ministerial High Country Review Committee from the New Zealand Ecological Society and the New Zealand Society of Soil Science', *New Zealand Journal of Ecology* 18: 69–81.

Balantine, B., 1988, 'Marine protected areas: The only enemy is indifference', *Forest & Bird* 19 (1): 2–4.

Baylis, G.T.S., and Mark, A.F., 1963, 'Vegetation studies on Secretary Island, Fiordland, part 4: Composition of the beech–podocarp forest, *New Zealand Journal of Botany* 1: 203–07.

Baylis, G.T.S., Johnson, P.N., and Mark, A.F., 1970, 'The vegetation and flora of the islands and shoreline of Lake Manapouri', Botany Department, University of Otago.

Baylis, G.T.S., Wardle, P., and Mark, A.F., 1963, 'Vegetation studies on Secretary Island, Fiordland, part 8: Vascular plants recorded from Secretary Island', *New Zealand Journal of Botany* 1: 236–42.

Billings, W.D., and Mark, A.F., 1957, 'Factors involved in the persistence of montane treeless balds', *Ecology* 38: 140–42.

—— 1961, 'Interactions between alpine tundra vegetation and patterned ground in the mountains of southern New Zealand', *Ecology* 42: 18–31.

Bliss, L.C., and Mark, A.F., 1974, 'High-alpine environments and primary production on the Rock and Pillar Range, Central Otago, New Zealand', *New Zealand Journal of Botany* 12: 445–83.

Bond, W., Dickinson, K.J.M., and Mark, A.F., 2004, 'What limits the spread of fire-dependent vegetation? Evidence from geographic variation of serotiny in a New Zealand shrub', *Global Ecology and Biogeography* 13: 115–27.

Brown, C.S., Mark, A.F., Kershaw, G.P., and Dickinson, K.J.M., 2006, 'Secondary succession: 24 years disturbance of a New Zealand high-alpine cushionfield', *Arctic, Antarctic and Alpine Research* 38: 325–34.

Bulloch, B.T., 1973, 'A low altitude snow tussock reserve at Black Rock, eastern Otago', *Proceedings of the New Zealand Ecological Society* 20: 41–47.

Chagué-Goff, C., Mark, A.F., and Dickinson, K.J.M, 2010, 'Hydrological processes and chemical characteristics of low-alpine patterned wetlands, south-central New Zealand', *Journal of Hydrology* 385: 105–19.

Chapin, F.S. III, Mark, A.F., Mitchell, R.A., and Dickinson, K.J.M., 2012, 'Design principles for socio-ecological transformation toward sustainability: Lessons for New Zealand sense of space', *Ecosphere* 3: 1–22.

Connell, J (ed.), 1998, 'Otago Conservation Management Strategy', volumes I–III and appendices, Dunedin, Department of Conservation.

Cook, J.M., Mark, A.F., and Shore, B.F., 1980, 'Responses of *Leptospermum scoparium* and *L. ericoides* (Myrtaceae) to waterlogging', *New Zealand Journal of Botany* 18: 233–46.

Dickinson, K.J.M., Chagué-Goff, C., Mark, A.F., and Cullen, L., 2002, 'Ecological processes and trophic status of two low-alpine patterned mires, south-central South Island, New Zealand'. *Austral Ecology* 27: 369–84.

Dickinson, K.J.M., Kelly, D., Mark, A.F., Wells, G., and Clayton, R., 2007, 'What limits a rare alpine species? Comparative demography of three endemic species of *Myosotis* (Boraginaceae)', *Austral Ecology* 32: 155–68.

Dickinson, K.J.M., and Mark, A.F., 1994, 'Forest-wetland vegetation patterns associated with a Holocene dune-slack sequence, Haast Ecological District, South Westland', *Journal of Biogeography* 21: 259–81.

Dickinson, K.J.M., and Mark, A.F., 1995, 'Parallel dune and wetland swales: A South Westland coastal landscape', *Forest & Bird* 215: 38–41.

—— 1999, 'Interpreting ecological patterns in an intact estuary, South West New Zealand World Heritage Area', *Journal of Biogeography* 26: 913–32.

Dickinson, K.J.M., Mark, A.F., Barrett, B.I.P., and Patrick, B.H., 1998, 'Rapid ecological survey, inventory and implementation: A case study from the Waikaia Ecological Region, New Zealand', *Journal of the Royal Society of New Zealand* 28: 83–156.

Dickinson, K.J.M., Mark, A.F., and Dawkins, B., 1994, 'Ecology of lianoid/epiphytic communities in coastal podocarp rain forest, Haast Ecological District, New Zealand', *Journal of Biogeography* 20: 687–705.

Dickinson, K.J.M., Mark, A.F., and Lee, W.G., 1992, 'Long-term monitoring of non-forest communities for biological conservation purposes', *New Zealand Journal of Botany* 30: 163–79.

Fagan, B., 1989, 'Protected Natural Areas Survey of the Manorburn Ecological District', unpublished MSc thesis, University of Otago.

Fahey, B.D., Davie, T., and Stewart, M., 2011, 'The application of a water balance model to assess the role of fog in water yields from catchments in the east Otago uplands, South Island, New Zealand', *Journal of Hydrology (New Zealand)* 50: 279–92.

Fahey, B.D., Murray, D.L., and Jackson, R.M., 1996, 'Detecting fog deposition to tussock by lysimetry at Swampy Summit near Dunedin, New Zealand', *Journal of Hydrology (New Zealand)* 35: 87–104.

Fiordland Marine Guardians, 2008, 'Beneath the reflections: A user's guide to the Fiordland (Te Moana o Atawhenua) Marine Area', Wellington, Ministry for the Environment.

Forest and Bird Protection Society, 1994, 'The Tongariro Declaration: A charter for national parks and protected natural areas for the next 100 years', 'Forest and Bird Policy Booklet', Wellington, Forest and Bird Protection Society: 53–54.

Grab, S.W., Dickinson, K.J.M., Mark, A.F., and Maegli, T., 2008, 'Ploughing boulders on the Rock and Pillar Range, south-central New Zealand: Their geomorphology and alpine plant associations', *Journal of the Royal Society of New Zealand* 38: 51–70.

BIBLIOGRAPHY

Guardians of Fiordland Fisheries, 1999, 'A characterisation of Fiordland's fisheries', Dunedin, Ministry of Fisheries.
—— 2001, 'Fiordland's fisheries and the marine environment: A bibliography', Te Anau, Department of Conservation.
Hager, N., and Burton, B., 1999, *Secrets and Lies: The anatomy of an anti-environmental PR campaign*, Nelson, Craig Potton.
Halloy, S.R.P., and Mark, A.F., 2003, 'Climate-change effects on alpine plant biodiversity: A New Zealand perspective on quantifying the threat', *Arctic, Antarctic and Alpine Research* 35: 248–54.
Hofstede, R.G.M., Dickinson, K.J.M., and Mark, A.F., 2001, 'Distribution, abundance and biomass of epiphyte/lianoid communities in a New Zealand lowland *Nothofagus*-podocarp temperate rain forest: Tropical comparisons', *Journal of Biogeography* 28: 1033–49.
Hofstede, R.G.M., Dickinson, K.J.M., Mark, A.F., and Narvaez, E., 2014, 'A broad transition from cloud forest to paramo characterizes an undisturbed treeline in Parque Nacional Llanganates, Ecuador', *Arctic, Antarctic and Alpine Research* 46: 975–86.
Holdsworth, D.K., and Mark, A.F., 1990, 'Water and nutrient input:output budgets: Effects of plant cover at seven sites in upland snow tussock grasslands of Eastern and Central Otago, New Zealand', *Journal of the Royal Society of New Zealand* 20: 1–24.
Hutching, G., and Potton, C. (eds), 1987, *Forest, Fiords and Glaciers: New Zealand's World Heritage: The case for a South-West New Zealand World Heritage Site*, Wellington, Royal Forest and Bird Protection Society.
Ingraham, N.L., and Mark, A.F., 2000, 'Isotopic assessment of the hydrological importance of fog deposition on tall tussock grass on southern New Zealand uplands', *Austral Ecology* 25: 402–08.
Ingraham, N.L., Mark, A.F., and Frew, R.D., 2008, 'Fog deposition by snow tussock on the Otago uplands: Response to a recent review of the evidence', *Journal of Hydrology (New Zealand)* 107: 107–22.
James, M., Mark, A.F., and Single, M., 2002, *Lake Managers' Handbook: Lake level management*, Wellington, Ministry for the Environment.
Johnson, P.N., Mark, A.F., and Baylis, G.T.S., 1977, 'Vegetation at Ajax Hill, south-east Otago, New Zealand', *New Zealand Journal of Botany* 15: 209–20.
Kelly, B.J., Wilson, J.B., and Mark, A.F., 1989, 'Causes of the species-area relation: A study of islands in Lake Manapouri, New Zealand', *Journal of Ecology* 77: 1021–28.
Kelly, D., Geldenhuis, A., James, A., Holland, E.P., Plank, M.J., Brockie, R.E., Cowan, P.E., Harper, G.A., Lee, W.G., Maitland, M.J., Mark, A.F., Mills, J.A., Wilson, P.R., and Byrom, A.E., 2013, 'Of mast and mean: Differential-temperature cue makes mast seeding insensitive to climate change', *Ecology Letters* 16: 90–98.
Kepner, W.G., Ramsey, M.M., Brown, E.S., Jarchow, M.E., Dickinson, K.J.M., and Mark, A.F., 2012, 'Hydrologic futures: Using scenario analysis to evaluate impacts of forecasted land use change on hydrologic services', *Ecosphere* 3: 1–25.
Lough, T.J., Wilson, J.B., Mark, A.F., and Evans, A.C., 1987, 'Succession in a New Zealand alpine cushion community: A Markovian model', *Vegetatio* 71: 129–38.

McGlone, M.S., Mark, A.F., and Bell, D., 1995, 'Late Pleistocene and Holocene vegetation history, Central Otago, South Island, New Zealand', *Journal of the Royal Society of New Zealand* 25: 1–22.

Mackenzie, T.D., 1979, 'Land development and water quality', in 'The agricultural industry and its effects on water quality', Hamilton, International Conference, 15–18 May 1979: 42–43

McMillan, G., 1991. 'Hawkweed report', *Journal of the New Zealand Mountain Lands Institute* 48: 8-31.

—— 1992, 'Institute to close', *Journal of the New Zealand Mountain Lands Institute* 49: 74.

McSavaney, M.J., and Whitehouse, I.E., 1988. 'Snow tussocks and water yield: A review of the evidence', Christchurch, Soil Conservation Group, Department of Scientific and Industrial Research.

McSweeney. G., 1989, 'The greening of a forest giant', *Forest & Bird* 20 (3): 10–13

McSweeney, G., and Molloy, L., 1984, 'New Zealand's tussockland heritage', *Forest & Bird* 15 (4): 2-5.

Mark, A.F., 1955, 'Grassland and shrubland on Maungatua, Otago', *New Zealand Journal of Science and Technology* A37: 349–66.

—— 1958, 'The ecology of the southern Appalachian grass balds', *Ecological Monographs* 28: 293–336.

—— 1959, 'The flora of the grass balds and fields of the southern Appalachian Mountains', *Castanea* 24: 1–21.

—— 1963, 'Vegetation studies on Secretary Island, Fiordland, part 3: The altitudinal gradient in forest composition, structure and regeneration', *New Zealand Journal of Botany* 1: 189–202.

——1965a, 'Vegetation and mountain climate', in R.G. Lister (ed.), *Central Otago*, New Zealand Geographical Society Special Publication: 69–91.

—— 1965b, 'Flowering behaviour in a New Zealand mountain grass', *Die Naturwissenschaften* 52: 157–58.

—— 1965c, 'The environment and growth rate of narrow-leaved snow tussock, *Chionochloa rigida*, in Otago', *New Zealand Journal of Botany* 3: 73–103.

—— 1965d, 'Flowering, seeding and seedling establishment of narrow-leaved snow tussock, *Chionochloa rigida*', *New Zealand Journal of Botany* 3: 180–93.

—— 1965e, 'Ecotypic differentiation in Otago populations of narrow-leaved snow tussock, *Chionochloa rigida*', *New Zealand Journal of Botany* 3: 277–99.

—— 1965f, 'Effects of management practices on narrow-leaved snow tussock, *Chionochloa rigida*', *New Zealand Journal of Botany* 3: 300–19.

—— 1968, 'Factors controlling irregular flowering in four alpine species of snow tussock', *Proceedings of the New Zealand Ecological Society* 15: 55–60.

—— 1969, 'Ecology of snow tussocks in the mountain grasslands of New Zealand', *Vegetatio* 18: 289–306.

——1970, 'Floral initiation and development in New Zealand alpine plants', *New Zealand Journal of Botany* 8: 67–75.

—— 1974a, 'Environment in crisis', *New Zealand's Nature Heritage* 1: 4–8.

—— 1974b, 'The Old Man Range', *New Zealand's Nature Heritage* 19: 524–31.

—— 1974c, 'The snow tussock grasslands', *New Zealand's Nature Heritage* 35: 976–81.

BIBLIOGRAPHY

—— 1975, 'Lakes Manapouri and Te Anau', *New Zealand's Nature Heritage* 103: 2877–84.

—— 1977, 'Vegetation of Mt Aspiring National Park', New Zealand National Parks Authority Scientific Series, no. 2.

—— 1978, 'Continuing saga of Clutha Valley development', Editorial, *Soil & Water* 14 (2): 3–7.

—— 1979a, 'Mount Aspiring National Park vegetation survey: Permanent photographic points for following vegetation changes', *Tussock Grasslands & Mountain Lands Institute Review* 37: 38–45.

—— 1979b, 'Environmental issues and New Zealand scientists', in Wren Green (ed.), *Focus on Social Responsibility in Science*, Wellington, New Zealand Association of Scientists: 191-202.

—— 1980a, 'Cockayne Memorial Lecture 1980: Progress in tussock grasslands research since Cockayne's day', *Proceedings of the Royal Society of New Zealand* 108: 122–42.

—— 1980b, 'A disappearing heritage: Tussock grasslands of the South Island rain shadow region', *Forest & Bird* 13 (8): 18–24.

—— 1982, 'The tussock grassland struggle: A case study from Otago', *Soil & Water* 18 (3): 4–9.

—— 1984, 'Dramatic landforms of the Central Otago uplands', *Forest & Bird* 15 (4): 8–9.

—— 1985a, 'The botanical component of conservation in New Zealand', *New Zealand Journal of Botany* 23: 789–810.

—— 1985b, 'Forgotten habitats: Conservation challenges of the future', *Forest & Bird* 16 (4): 30–32.

—— 1987, 'Lake level control', in Henriques, P.R. (ed.), *Aquatic Biology and Hydroelectric Power Development in New Zealand,* London, Oxford University Press: 113–23.

—— 1988a, 'Manapouri-Te Anau: Case study of its hydro-electric development from conflict to resolution', Proceedings of 'Ecopolitics' Conference, University of Waikato, Hamilton: 126–29.

—— 1988b, 'Political and public conscience-raising for reservation of New Zealand's tussock grasslands: An historical perspective', Proceedings of 'Ecopolitics' Conference, University of Waikato, Hamilton: 130–33.

—— 1988c, 'The role of snow tussocks in maximising water yield from upland snow tussocklands of the Taieri Catchment and its relevance for land management', in J. Hamel (ed.) 'Research in the Taieri Catchment', *University of Otago Ecology Research Group Occasional Paper,* 1: 28–32.

—— 1989, 'Responses of indigenous vegetation to contrasting trends in utilization by red deer in two southwest New Zealand National Parks', *New Zealand Journal of Ecology* 12 (supp.): 103–14.

—— 1990a, 'Ecological and nature conservation values: The case for a conservation park', in Fitzharris, B.B., and Kearsley, G.W., (eds), *Southern Landscapes: Essays in honour of Bill Brockie and Ray Hargreaves*, Dunedin, University of Otago: 233–73.

—— 1990b, 'The Guardians of Lake Manapouri and Te Anau', *New Zealand Environment* 63: 4–8.

—— 1992, 'Managing Lakes Manapouri and Te Anau for conservation and hydro-electric generation: A case study in conflict resolution to integrate conservation with development', in *Perspectives on a History of Sciences in Otago: A series of public lectures*', Dunedin, University of Otago, Division of Sciences: 30–72.
—— 1993a, 'Indigenous grasslands of New Zealand', in Coupland, R.T., and Goodall, D.W., (eds), *Natural Grasslands: Eastern hemisphere,* Ecosystems of the World 8B, Elsevier, Amsterdam: 372–410.
—— 1993b, 'Ecological degradation', guest editorial in *New Zealand Journal of Ecology* 17: 1–4.
—— 1994a, 'Effects of burning and grazing on sustainable utilisation of upland snow tussock (*Chionochloa* spp.) rangelands for pastoralism in South Island, New Zealand', *Australian Journal of Botany* 42: 149–61.
—— 1994b, 'Patterned ground activity in a southern New Zealand high-alpine cushionfield', *Arctic and Alpine Research* 26: 270–80.
—— 1995, 'Environmental synergism through collaboration between engineers and ecologists: The second Murray Sweetman Memorial Lecture', *Institution of Professional Engineers of New Zealand Transactions* 22 (1/Gen.): 20–26.
—— 1998a, 'Te Wahipounamu: South-West New Zealand World Heritage Area: Ecological research and conservation history', An essay in honour of Dr Peter Wardle, *Royal Society of New Zealand Miscellaneous Series* 48: 39–68.
—— 1998b, 'Te Wahipounamu: South-West New Zealand World Heritage Area: Ecological research and conservation history', *Journal of the Royal Society of New Zealand* 28: 657–84.
—— 1998c, 'The role of snow tussocks in maximising water yield from upland snow tussocklands of the Taieri Catchment and its relevance to land management', *University of Otago Ecology Research Group Occasional Paper* 1: 28–32.
—— 1999a, 'The botany of Otago and Southland', in Sorrell, P., (ed.), *The Cyclopedia of Otago and Southland*, Dunedin, Dunedin City Council: 1004–07.
—— 1999b, 'Guardians of the lakes', in Sorrell, P., (ed.), *The Cyclopedia of Otago and Southland*, Dunedin, Dunedin City Council: 1153–55.
—— 2000, 'Integrating conservation with hydro-electric development of Lakes Manapouri and Te Anau, New Zealand: An exercise in complexity', in Halloy, S., and Williams, T., (eds), *Applied Complexity: From neural nets to managed landscapes*, Christchurch, Crop and Food Research: 88–103.
—— 2004, 'Our Golden Landscapes: An historical perspective of the ecology and management of our tussock grasslands and associated mountainlands', Hocken Lecture.
—— 2005, 'Fifty years of snow tussock grassland research applied to high country landscape management', *Proceedings of Otago Regional Council's High Country Landscape Management Forum*, Queenstown: 43–52.
—— 2012a, 'Recent progress with the conservation and protection of temperate indigenous grasslands in New Zealand', *Parks* 18.1: 1–11.
—— 2012b, *Above the Treeline: A nature guide to alpine New Zealand*, Nelson, Craig Potton.
—— 2015, 'The 2015 Banks Memorial Lecture: Advocating for nature conservation in New Zealand: Is there a dilemma?', *New Zealand Garden Journal (Journal of the Royal New Zealand Institute of Horticulture)* 18 (1): 18–32.

BIBLIOGRAPHY

Mark, A.F., and Adams, N.M., 1973, *New Zealand Alpine Plants*, A.H. & A.W. Reed, Wellington. Revised and reprinted 1979, 1986 and (by Godwit, Auckland) 1995.

Mark, A.F., Barratt, B.I.P., and Weeks, E., 2013, 'Ecosystem services in New Zealand's indigenous tussock grasslands: Conditions and trends', in Dymond, J.R., (ed.), *Ecosystem Services in New Zealand*, Lincoln, Manaaki Whenua Press: 1–33.

Mark, A.F., and Baylis, G.T.S., 1963, 'Vegetation studies on Secretary Island, Fiordland, part. 6: The subalpine vegetation', *New Zealand Journal of Botany* 1: 215–20.

—— 1975, 'Impact of deer on Secretary Island, Fiordland, New Zealand', *Proceedings of the New Zealand Ecological Society* 22: 19–24.

—— 1982, 'Further studies on the impact of deer on Secretary Island, Fiordland, New Zealand', *New Zealand Journal of Ecology* 5: 67–75.

Mark, A.F., Baylis, G.T.S., and Dickinson, K.J.M., 1991, 'Monitoring the impacts of deer on vegetation condition of Secretary Island, Fiordland National Park, New Zealand: A clear case for deer control and ecological restoration', *Journal of the Royal Society of New Zealand* 21: 43–54.

Mark, A.F., and L.C. Bliss, 1970, 'The high-alpine vegetation of Central Otago, New Zealand', *New Zealand Journal of Botany* 8: 381–451.

Mark, A.F., and Dickinson, K.J.M., 1997, 'New Zealand alpine ecosystems', in Weilgolaski, F.E., (ed.), *Alpine and Polar Tundra*, Ecosystems of the World 3, Elsevier, Amsterdam: 311–45.

—— 2003, 'Temporal responses over 30 years to removal of grazing from a mid-altitude snow tussock grassland reserve, Lammerlaw Ecological Region, New Zealand', *New Zealand Journal of Botany* 41: 655–68.

—— 2004, 'South Island high country in transition: Issues, options and initial outcomes with the tenure review process', in Kearsley, G.W., Fitzharris, B.B., (eds), *Glimpes of a Gaian Earth: Essays in honour of Peter Holland*, Dunedin, University of Otago: 285–308.

—— 2008, 'Maximizing water yield with indigenous non-forest vegetation: A New Zealand perspective', *Frontiers in Ecology and the Environment* 6: 25–34.

Mark, A.F., Dickinson, K.J.M., Allen, J., Smith, R., and West, C.J., 2001, 'Vegetation patterns, plant distribution and life forms across the alpine zone in southern Tierra del Fuego, Argentina', *Austral Ecology* 26: 423–40.

Mark, A.F., Dickinson, K.J.M., and Fife, A.J., 1989, 'Forest succession on landslides in the Fiord Ecological Region, southwestern New Zealand', *New Zealand Journal of Botany* 27: 369–90.

Mark, A.F., Dickinson, K.J.M., and Hofstede, R.G.M., 2000, 'Alpine vegetation, plant distribution, life forms, and environments in a perhumid New Zealand region: Oceanic and tropical high mountain affinities', *Arctic, Antarctic and Alpine Research* 32: 240–54.

Mark, A.F., Dickinson, K.J.M., Maegli, T., and Halloy, S.R.P., 2006, 'Two GLORIA long-term alpine monitoring sites established in New Zealand as part of a global network', *Journal of the Royal Society of New Zealand* 36: 111–28.

Mark, A.F., Dickinson, K.J.M., Patrick, B.H., Barratt, B.I.P., Loh, G., McSweeney, G.D., Meurk, C.D., Timmins, S.M., Simpson, N.C., and Wilson, J.B., 1989, 'An ecological survey of the central part of the Eyre Ecological District, northern Southland, New Zealand', *Journal of the Royal Society of New Zealand* 19: 349–84.

Mark, A.F., Fetcher, N., Shaver, G.R., and Chapin, F.S. III, 1985, 'Estimated ages of mature tussocks of *Eriophorum vaginatum* along a latitudinal gradient in central Alaska, U.S.A.', *Arctic and Alpine Research* 17: 1–5.

Mark, A.F., Grealish, G., Ward, C.M., Wilson, J.B., Tangney, R.S., Ogle, C.C., Patrick, B.H., and Mason, G.M., 1988, 'Ecological studies of a marine terrace sequence in the Waitutu Ecological District of southern New Zealand', parts 1–5, *Journal of the Royal Society of New Zealand* 18: 29–90.

Mark, A.F., and Johnson, P.N., 1985, 'Ecologically derived guidelines for managing two New Zealand lakes', *Environmental Management* 9 (4): 355–63.

Mark, A.F., Johnson, P.N., Crush, J.R., and Meurk, C.D., 1971 , 'Vegetation of the Lake Te Anau shoreline with special reference to the implication of proposed lake level alterations', unpublished report, Botany Department, University of Otago.

—— 1972a, 'Applied ecological studies of shoreline vegetation at Lakes Manapouri and Te Anau, Fiordland', *Proceedings of the New Zealand Ecological Society* 19: 100–57.

—— 1972b, 'Lake Te Anau', *New Zealand Environment* 2: 14–30.

Mark, A.F., Johnson, P.N., Dickinson, K.J.M., and McGlone, M.S., 1995, 'Southern hemisphere patterned mires, with emphasis on southern New Zealand', *Journal of the Royal Society of New Zealand* 25: 23–54.

Mark, A.F., Johnson, P.N., and Wilson, J.B., 1977, 'Factors involved in the recent mortality of plants from forest and scrub along the Lake Te Anau shoreline, Fiordland', *Proceedings of the New Zealand Ecological Society* 24: 34–42.

Mark, A.F., and Kirk, R.M., 1987, 'Lake levels and lakeshore erosion', in Vant, W.N., (ed.), *Lake Managers' Handbook,* Hamilton, Ministry of Works and Development: 215–22.

Mark, A.F., Korsten, A.C., Guevara, D.U., Dickinson, K.J.M., Humar-Maegli, T., Michel, P., Halloy, S.R.P., Lord, J.M., Venn, S.E., Morgan, J.W., Whigham, P.A., and Nielsen, J.A., 2015 (in press), 'Ecological responses to 52 years of experimental snow manipulation in high-alpine cushionfield, Old Man Range, south-central New Zealand', *Arctic, Antarctic and Alpine Research*.

Mark, A.F., and Lee, W.G., 1985. 'Ecology of hard beech (*Nothofagus truncata*) in southern outlier stands in the Haast Ecological Region, South Westland, New Zealand', *New Zealand Journal of Ecology* 8: 97–121.

—— 2003, 'Tussock grasslands and associated mountainlands', in Darby, J., Fordyce, R.E., Mark, A.F., Probert, K., and Townsend, C. (eds), *The Natural History of Southern New Zealand*, Dunedin, University of Otago Press: 191–236.

Mark, A.F., and McLennan, B., 2004, 'The conservation status of New Zealand's indigenous grasslands', *New Zealand Journal of Botany* 43: 247–70.

Mark, A.F., and McSweeney, G.D., 1987, 'Eyre-Cairnard: Biological treasure trove', *Forest & Bird* 18 (2): 10–12.

—— 1990, 'Patterns of impoverishment in natural communities: Case history studies in forest ecosystems – New Zealand', in Woodwell, G.W. (ed.), *The Earth in Transition*, New York, Cambridge University Press: 152–77.

BIBLIOGRAPHY

Mark, A.F., Michel, P., Dickinson, K.J.M., and McLennan, B., 2009, 'The conservation (protected area) status of New Zealand's indigenous grasslands: An update', *New Zealand Journal of Botany* 47: 53–60.

Mark, A.F., Molau, U.,Whigham, P., Little, L., and Nielson, J. 2015, 'A periglacial tarn on the Rock and Pillar Range crest, south-central New Zealand, and its surrounding snowbank ecosystem', *Austral Ecology* (in press).

Mark, A.F., Porter, S., Piggott, J.L., Michel, P., Maegli, T., and Dickinson, K.J.M., 2008, 'Altitudinal patterns of vegetation, flora, life forms, and environments in the alpine zone of the Fiord Ecological Region, New Zealand', *New Zealand Journal of Botany* 46: 205–37.

Mark, A.F., Rawson, G., and Wilson, J.B., 1979, 'Vegetation pattern of a lowland raised mire in eastern Fiordland, New Zealand', *New Zealand Journal of Ecology* 2: 1–10.

Mark, A.F., and Rowley, J., 1976, 'Water yield of low-alpine snow tussock grassland in Central Otago', *Journal of Hydrology (New Zealand)* 15: 59–79.

Mark, A.F., Rowley, J., and Holdsworth, D.K., 1980, 'Water yield from high-altitude snow tussock grassland in Central Otago', *Tussock Grasslands and Mountain Lands Institute Review* 38: 21–33.

Mark, A.F., and Sanderson, F.R., 1962, 'An altitudinal gradient in forest composition, structure and regeneration in the Hollyford Valley, Fiordland', *Proceedings of the New Zealand Ecological Society* 9: 17–26.

Mark, A.F., Scott, G.A.M., Sanderson, F.R., and James, P.W., 1964, 'Forest succession on landslides above Lake Thomson, Fiordland', *New Zealand Journal of Botany* 2: 60–89.

Mark, A.F., and Smith, P.M.F., 1962, 'A frost-tolerant porous-pot evaporimeter', *Proceedings of the New Zealand Ecological Society* 9: 13-14.

—— 1975, 'A lowland vegetation sequence in South Westland: Pakihi bog to mixed beech–podocarp forest, part 1: The principal strata', *Proceedings of the New Zealand Ecological Society* 22: 76–92.

Mark, A.F., Turner, K.J., and West, C.J., 2001, 'Integrating nature conservation with hydro-electric development: Conflict resolution with Lakes Manapouri and Te Anau, Fiordland National Park, New Zealand', *Lake and Reservoir Management* 17: 1–16.

Mark, A.F., and Whigham, P.A., 2011, 'Disturbance-induced changes in a high-alpine cushionfield community, south-central New Zealand', *Austral Ecology* 36: 581–92.

Mark, A.F., and Wilson, J.B., 2005, 'Tempo and mode of vegetation dynamics over 50 years in a New Zealand alpine cushion/tussock community', *Journal of Vegetation Science* 16: 227–36.

Mark, A.F., Wilson, J.B., and Scott, C., 2011, 'Long-term retirement of New Zealand snow tussock rangeland: Effects on canopy structure, hawkweed (*Hieracium* spp.) invasion and plant diversity', *New Zealand Journal of Botany* 49: 243–62.

Mills, J.A., Lee, W.G., Mark, A.F., and Lavers, R.B., 1980, 'Winter use by takahe (*Notornis mantelli*) of the summer-green fern *Hypolepis millefolium* in relation to its annual cycle of carbohydrates and minerals', *New Zealand Journal of Ecology* 3: 131–37.

Mills, J.A., and Mark, A.F., 1977, 'Food preferences of takahe in Fiordland National Park, New Zealand, and the effect of competition from introduced red deer', *Journal of Animal Ecology* 46: 939–59.

Molloy, L., 1978, 'Red Mountain – national park or asbestos mine?', *Forest & Bird* 210, supplement.
—— 1983, 'How much longer before Red Hills is protected?', *Forest & Bird* 14 (8): 17–24
—— 1987, 'The Red Hills – The final round?' *Forest & Bird* 18 (1): 16–19
Moore, L.B., 1955, 'The plants of tussock grasslands', *Proceedings of the New Zealand Ecological Society* 3: 7–8.
New Zealand Mountain Lands Institute, 1992, 'Guidelines on burning tussock grassland', *Journal of the New Zealand Mountain Lands Institute* 49: 51–63.
Onipchenko, V., Mark, A.F., and Wells, G., 2005, 'Floristic richness of three perhumid New Zealand alpine plant communities in comparison with other regions', *Austral Ecology* 30: 518–25.
Payton, I.J., Lee, W.G., Dolby, R., and Mark, A.F., 1986, 'Nutrient concentrations in narrow-leaved snow tussock (*Chionochloa rigida*) after spring burning', *New Zealand Journal of Botany* 24: 529–37.
Payton, I.J., and Mark, A.F., 1979, 'Long-term effects of burning on the growth, flowering, and carbohydrate reserves in narrow-leaved snow tussock (*Chionochloa rigida*)', *New Zealand Journal of Botany* 17: 43–54.
Peat, N., 1994, *Manapouri Saved! – New Zealand's first great conservation success story*, Dunedin, Longacre Press.
Pickrill, R.A., 1978, 'Beach and nearshore morphology of Lakes Manapouri and Te Anau, New Zealand: Natural models of the continental shelf', *New Zealand Journal of Geology and Geophysics* 21: 229–42.
Quin, S.L., Wilson, J.B., and Mark, A.F., 1987, 'The island biogeography of Lake Manapouri, New Zealand', *Journal of Biogeography* 14: 569–81.
Robertson, A.W., Mark, A.F., and Wilson, J.B., 1991, 'Ecology of a coastal lagoon to dune forest sequence, South Westland, New Zealand', *New Zealand Journal of Botany* 29: 17–30.
Roxburgh, S.H., Wilson, J.B., and Mark, A.F., 1988, 'Succession after disturbance of a New Zealand high-alpine cushionfield', *Arctic and Alpine Research* 20: 230–36.
Scott, G.A.M., Mark, A.F., and Sanderson, F.R., 1964, 'Altitudinal variation in forest composition near Lake Hankinson, Fiordland', *New Zealand Journal of Botany* 2: 310–23.
Sly, B.K., Hislop, W.F., Chalmers, W.I., and Mark, A.F., 1977, 'The Remarkables and Hector Mountains, Otago, New Zealand: A management study', Dunedin, Lands and Survey Department.
Smith, B., Mark, A.F., and Wilson, J.B., 1995, 'A functional analysis of New Zealand alpine vegetation: Variation in canopy roughness and functional diversity in response to an experimental wind barrier', *Functional Ecology* 9: 904–12.
Sommerville, P., Mark, A.F., and Wilson, J.B., 1982, 'Plant succession on moraines of the upper Dart Valley, southern South Island, New Zealand', *New Zealand Journal of Botany* 20: 227–44.
South Westland Forests Working Party, 1988, 'South Westland, south of the Cook River: Resource management study', Wellington, Ministry for the Environment.
Stanley, R.J., Dickinson, K.J.M., and Mark, A.F., 1998, 'Demography of a rare *Myosotis*: Boom and bust in the high-alpine zone of southern New Zealand', *Arctic and Alpine Research* 30: 227–40.

BIBLIOGRAPHY

Stephenson, G.K., Card, B., Mark, A.F., McLean, R., Thompson, K., and Priest, R.M., 1983, 'Wetlands: A diminishing resource', a report for the Environmental Council, Water & Soil Miscellaneous Publication No. 58, Wellington.
Talbot, M.J., Mark, A.F., and Wilson, J.B., 1992, 'Vegetation-environment relations in snowbanks on the Rock and Pillar Range, Central Otago, New Zealand', *New Zealand Journal of Botany* 30: 271-301.
Tangney, R.S., Wilson, J.B., and Mark, A.F., 1990, 'Bryophyte island biogeography: A study in Lake Manapouri, New Zealand', *Oikos* 59: 21-26.
Ward, C.M., 1988, 'Marine terraces of the Waitutu district and their relation to the late Cenozoic tectonics of the southern Fiordland region, New Zealand', *Journal of the Royal Society of New Zealand* 18: 1-28.
Wardle, P., 1963, 'Vegetation studies on Secretary Island, Fiordland, part 2: The plant communities', *New Zealand Journal of Botany* 1: 171-87.
Wardle, P., and Mark, A.F., 1956, 'Vegetation and climate in the Dunedin district', *Transactions of the Royal Society of New Zealand* 84: 33-44.
—— 1970, 'Vegetation studies on Secretary Island, Fiordland, part 10: Vascular plants recorded from Secretary Island', *New Zealand Journal of Botany* 8: 22-29.
Wardle, P., Mark, A.F., and Baylis, G.T.S., 1970, 'Vegetation studies on Secretary Island, Fiordland, part 9: Additions to parts 1, 2, 4 and 6', *New Zealand Journal of Botany* 8: 3-21.
—— 1973, 'Vegetation and landscape of the West Cape District, Fiordland, New Zealand', *New Zealand Journal of Botany* 11: 599-626.
Wells, J.A., and Mark, A.F., 1966, 'The altitudinal sequence of climax vegetation on Mt Anglem, Stewart Island, part 1: The principal strata', *New Zealand Journal of Botany* 4: 267-82.
Wilkinson, G.B., and Garrett, K.J., 1977, 'South Westland Land Use Study', Wellington, New Zealand Forest Service and Department of Lands and Survey.
Yin, R., Mark, A.F., and Wilson, J.B., 1984, 'Aspects of the ecology of the indigenous shrub *Leptospermum scoparium* (Myrtaceae) in New Zealand', *New Zealand Journal of Botany* 22: 483-507

INDEX

Page numbers in **bold** refer to illustrations.

A & T Burt 13
acclimatisation societies 174
Aciphylla spedenii (speargrass) 80
Acromanthus (*Leucopogon*) *colensoi* 69
Adams, Amy 246
Adams, Nancy **224**, 224–25
Ahuriri Conservation Park 78, 177
Ahuriri Valley 174
Alabaster, Lake 21
Alabaster Pass 21
Alexandra 34, 35, 52, 55, 155, 248
Allan, John 55
Allan, Ralph 17
Allen, Ralph 231
Allendale Station 64, 65
alpine vegetation 26, 80, 137, 143, 200, 208; *New Zealand Alpine Plants* (Mark and Adams) 170, **224**, 224–25, **225**; New Zealand vegetation in global context 221–25; *see also* specific vegetation types and species, e.g. cushionfields
Alta, Lake **155**
aluminium smelters: Aramoana 134, 230–34; Tiwai Point 94–95, 96, 101, 112
Anderson, David 199
Anderson, Peter 191
Angelm, Mount 204
Anthosachne (*Elymus*) *solandri* (blue wheatgrass) 80
Apodasmia (*Leptocarpus*) *similis* (jointed rush) **231**

Appalachian Trail 27
Appleyard, Jo 191
Aramoana 134
Aramoana Ecological Area 234, **234**
Aramoana saltmarsh 149, 193, 230–34, **231**, **232**, **234**
Arawhata River 140, 214
Arawhata Valley 205–06, **206**
Armstrong, Mount 221
Arthur's Pass National Park 140
Asplenium bulbiferum (hen and chickens fern) 201
Athenaeum, Dunedin 14
Australian Ecological Society, *Austral Ecology* 59
Awarua Point 164

Bain Conservation Area 160
Balantine, Bill 177
Bambery, Colin 101
Barkla, John **207**
Barrett, Peter 255
Bassett, Colin 64–65, 134, **135**
Bathurst Resources 189, 191–92
Baumgart, Ian 103
Baylis, Geoff 19, **20**, 21, 38–39, **39**, 70, **135**, 199, 204, 224
Beanland, Sarah 120
bears 27
Beattie, John **155**
Beaumont Road, Dunedin 14, **15**
Beaumont Station 151

INDEX

Beech Action Committee (BAC) 227
beech forest 73, 74, 80, 184, 185–86; Burmeister Ecological Area 136; hard beech (*Fuscospora* [*Nothofagus*] *truncata*) 213–14; Mavora area 143, 145; Nardoo catchment 82; North Westland Beech Project Area 136; Scientific Co-ordinating Committee on Beech Research 134–37, **136**, 230; Secretary Island **200**; silver beech (*Lophozonia* [*Nothofagus*] *menziesii*) 82, 143, **200**, 202, **203**, 214, 215; South Island Beech Utilisation Scheme 134, 227, 228; South Westland 213–14; Te Anau 103, 113–14, **114**
Behrend, Fred 30
Bell Hill 19
Bellamy, David 180, 211, **211**
Ben Nevis Station 245
Benger, Mount, and district 33
Bertram, Geoff 254
Billings, Dwight **20**, 22, **25**, 26
Billings, Shirley **20**
Binney, Don, *Puketotara, Twice Shy* 233
biosystematics research and collections 169, 170
Birch, Bill 231, 232
Birch Island 158
Black Rock Scientific Reserve 67–69, **68**
Blair Trust fellowship 20
Blakely, Roger 178
Bliss, Larry **25**, 222
Blue Mountains 16
Blue Ridge, Southern Appalachian Mountains 26, 27
Blue Spur gold mine 14
blue wheatgrass (*Anthosachne* [*Elymus*] *solandri*) 80
boardwalks and viewing platforms 193, 217, **231**, 234
Boffa Miskell 187, 188
bog pine 20, 64, **65**
Bond, William 221
Booth, Kay 165
Borland Mire 210–11

Borrell, Arthur 59–60, 62
Bowmar, Erskine 72
Bradshaw, Peter 231
Breaksea Island 202
Bretton, Wiremu 196
Briden, Keith 198
Broad, Allison **195**
Brockie, Bill 74
broom 71
Bruce, Don 223
Bull, Stewart **165**
Bulloch, Bruce 68–69
Bunn, Harry **135**
Burke, Mervyn 204
Burmeister Ecological Area 136–37
burning of tussock grassland *see* fire
Burrows, Colin 188
Burrows, Larry 196
Burton, Bob 184–85
Burwood Station 72, 73–74, **74**, 142–43
Bycroft, Chris 70, 71

Cainard pastoral farming block 79–80
Cairngorm Mountains 46
Caldwell, David 70
Caltha obtusa 225
Campbell, Wilson 108, **108**, 115, **121**
Card, Bernard 147
Carex pyrenaica 36
Carey, Peta 163
Cargill, Mount 19, 52, 133
Carter, Chris **156**
Cascade forest 180
Catlins Coastal Rainforest Park 158, **159**
Catlins region 16, 17, 134, **159**, 193, 221; debate about logging Māori land 157; vegetation sequences 204
cattle 66, 73, 78, 143–46
Caversham, Dunedin 28
Caversham Valley, Dunedin 193
Celmisia (alpine daisies): *philocremna* 80; *semicordata* 66; *thomsonii* 80; *viscosa* 51
Central Otago 32, 33, 34, 36, 173, 220, 221, 222; *see also* names of towns, mountains/ranges and rivers

Central Otago Conservation Park, proposed 74–78
Central Otago District Council 155, 243, 246
Central Otago Environmental Society 243, 244, 246
Central Otago News 55, 77
Chamberlain, Jenny 60
Chambers, Louis 250
Chandler, David **167**
Child, John 227
Chionochloa: crassiuscula 209; *flavescens* (later *rigida* subsp. *amara*) 209; *macra* 40, 43; *pallens* 209, **210**; *rigida* 40, 43; *rubra* subsp. *cuprea* (red/copper tussock) 69–74, **72**, 143, 155; *teretifolia* 210
Chou Shim, Jimmy 14
Civilian Land Settlement Scheme 86
Clarence/Kaikoura/Ka Whata Tu o Rakihouia Conservation Park 78, 177
Clark, David 250
Clark, Helen 182
Clark, Mark **155**, 161
Cleland, Ray 205
Cleveland, Les **155**, 160, 161
climate change 12, 194–95, 224, 251, 252, 255–57
Climate Change Response Act 2002 194
climate stations and records: Alexandra 34, 35; Old Man Range 33, 34–36
Clinton River 102
Clutha River: Contact Energy plans for third dam 242, 243, 246, 248; Rongahere Gorge 158; Upper Clutha area 238, 239, 240–42
Clyde High Dam 237–42, **241**
Coal Creek, Roxburgh 77
coal mining 189, 191–92, **192**
Coates, Gerry 254
Cockayne, Leonard 26, 171, 183
Cocks, John 249
Cole Creek 214
Collingwood, David 231–32
Comalco (NZ) Ltd 98, 100, 116,

118–19; DOC Southland conservation award 182; sponsorship of kākāpō 181–82
Commission for the Environment 82, 144
Connell, Jeff 60, 81, **155**, 160, 161
Connell, Sandra 161
Conning, Linda **167**
Conservation Act 1987 109, 168
Conservation Authority *see* New Zealand Conservation Authority
conservation coalitions 174
conservation covenants 157, 178
Conservation Law Reform Act 1990 121
conservation parks and areas 75, 76, 78; Ahuriri Conservation Park 78, 177; Bain Conservation Area 160; Central Otago Conservation Park, proposed 74–78; Eyre Mountains/Taka Rā Haka Conservation Park 78, 81, 177; Flat Top Hill Conservation Area 160; Gorge Hill Red/Copper Tussock Conservation Area **72**, 71–74, **74**; Hakatere Conservation Park 78, 177; Hawea Conservation Park 78, 178; Ka Whata Tu o Rakihouia/Kaikoura/Clarence Conservation Park 78, 177; Kopuwai Conservation Area 78, 154; Korowai/Torlesse Conservation Park 78; Mavora Lakes Park 146; Oteake Conservation Park 78, **177**, 178; Pisa Conservation Park (proposed) 78; Remarkables Conservation Park (proposed) 78; Rock and Pillar Conservation Park (proposed) 78; Ruataniwha Conservation Park 78, 177; Te Kahui Kaupeka Conservation Park 177; Te Papanui Conservation Park 60, **61**, 78, 93, 154–55, **156**, 177, 196
Consolidated Zinc Pty Ltd 94
Contact Energy 158, 242, 246, 248
Cook River 139
Cooper, Michael 232
Cooper, Warren 238
COP 21 conference 2015, Paris 256, 257
Coprosma cheesemanii 69

INDEX

Coronet Peak 40–41
Council of Outdoor Recreation Associations of New Zealand (CORANZ) 174
covenants, conservation 157, 178
Craigieburn Range 137
Craigroy Station 245
Craspedia lanata 36
Cromwell Gorge 237, **237**, 238, 239, 240, 242
Crowe, Bill 17
Crush, Jim 103, 105
Cumberbeach, Jim 18
cushionfields 20, 36, **37**, 64, 66, 204, 222, **222**, **223**, 235–36, **236**

Dacrycarpus dacrydioides (kahikatea) 100, 139, 214–16, **215**
Dagg brothers 40
Dansereau, Pierre 21–22
Dart valley 21; Upper Dart plant succession study **203**, 204
Davie, Arthur 28, **32**
Davie, Helen **32**
Davie, Ivy 28, **32**
Davie, Patricia *see* Mark, Patricia (née Davie)
Davie, Tim 60, 61
Davis, Gwenny 227
Davis, Jack 18
Dawson, Laura 166
Day, Colin 196
Deep Cove, Doubtful Sound 96, 126, 127
deer 168; decline in commercial hunting 168, 208; Mount Aspiring National Park 204, 206–07, 208; Murchison Mountains 209–10; recreational shooting 16, 21; Secretary Island, impact of browsing 199–202, **200**, **201**
Denniston Plateau 183, 189–92, **190**, **191**, **192**
Department of Conservation (DOC): Aramoana saltmarsh 231, 232; boardwalks and viewing platforms 193, 217, **231**; and

Conservation Authority 167; conservation boards 154; Crown land allocation 79, 80, 81, 93; and Denniston Plateau 192; emergency grazing on DOC land 160–61; Eyre Mountains survey 80; forest protection and management 178, 179, 180, 184, 185; formation 93; and Guardians of Fiordland Fisheries and Marine Environment 162, 164; and Guardians of Lakes Manapouri and Te Anau 120–21, 123; and Otago Conservation Board 154–61; Scientific Co-ordinating Committee recommendations 136; Secretary Island deer control **201**; Southland, conservation award to Comalco 182; Threatened Species Trust 181–82; tussock grassland protection and management 70–71, 76, 77, 78, 146, 175; Waitutu marine terrace sequence management 213; wilding tree control 194, 196, 197, 198
Department of Lands and Survey *see* Lands and Survey Department
Department of Scientific and Industrial Research (DSIR) 53, 54–55, 103, 107, 110, 179; Biological Resources Centre 141; Botany Division 28, 71, 80, 92, 96, 101, 111, 134; Protected Natural Areas Programme 141; *see also* Geological Survey; Soil Bureau
Depression, 1930s 13
Devine, Kieran 130
Dickinson, Katharine 62, **79**, **166**, 166–67, **167**, 214, 215, 216, 218, 221
Dicksonia squarrosa (wheki) 202
Dodd, Jack 98
Dome Burn 218, 220
Dominion Museum 103
Donaldson, John 73
Doubtful Sound 96, 126, 127; Hall Arm **162**
Douglas fir (*Pseudotsuga menziesii*) 196
Dracophyllum: longifolium (inaka) 66, 69; *muscoides* 36

Duke University 10, 22–28, **23**, **25**, 30
Dunedin 13–14; *see also* names of suburbs and streets
Dunedin City Corporation, Transport Department 13
Dunedin City Council 50, 232, 233, 235
Dunedin Regional Planning Authority, Technical Advisory Committee on Reserves and Scenic Amenities 133–34
Dunedin Town Belt 133
dune/swale systems, Haast–Okuru **216**, 216–17, **217**, 220
Dunnett, Barry 174
Dunstan Mountains 223–24

Earnscleugh Station 154
earthquake, Te Anau, 1988 120
East Cape Ecological District 141
Eckhoff, Gerry 77, 160, 164
Eco-Action 196
Ecologic Foundation 230
ecological areas: Aramoana Ecological Area 234, **234**; Burmeister Ecological Area 136–37
ecological regions and districts: East Cape Ecological District 141; Mackenzie Ecological Region 141; Manorburn Ecological District 155, 157, 160; Nokomai Ecological District 75; Old Man Ecological District 75, 141; Remarkables Ecological District 75; Rodney Ecological District 141; Umbrella Ecological District 75
Ecological Society of America 62
Ecology Action, Dunedin 226
ecopolitics 258
eco-tourism 75, 76, 180
Eden, Chris **155**
Edmonds, Alan 172, 173
Eichelbaum, Thomas 98, 100
Electricity Corporation of New Zealand (ECNZ) 118, 119, 120, 122, 123–24, 125, 126, 128, 158; *see also* Ministry of Energy, Electricity Department; New Zealand Electricity Department (NZED)

Ell, Gordon 180
Ellesmere, Lake 149
Ellis, Jim 54–55
Ellis, Tony 173
Elworthy, Jonathan 89, 139
Engineers for Social Responsibility 254
English, Bill 128
Entrance Island Marine Reserve 162
Environment and Conservation Organisations of New Zealand (ECO) 174
Environment Canterbury 188
Environment Court 189, 191, 243, 244, 245, 246
Environment Southland 162, 164, 196
Environmental Council, Working Party on the Environmental Movement in New Zealand 132
Environmental Non-Governmental Organisations (ENGOs) 132, 171, 226–27
Environmental Protection Agency (US) (EPA) 62
epiphytic communities on rainforest trees 214–16, **215**
Erewhon Station **176**
erosion 76, 83, 134
estuary, Hapuka 217–18
Evans, Allan 92, 142, **143**
Excell, Jerry **165**, 166
Eyre Creek pastoral farming block 79–80
Eyre Mountains land allocation 78, **79**, 79–81
Eyre Mountains/Taka Rā Haka Conservation Park 78, 81, 177

Fagan, Brent 155, 156
Fahey, Barry 60, 61
falcon, New Zealand 81
Falla, Robert 103
Farewell Spit 148, 149
farming *see* pastoral farming
Farrant, Ted 18
Fauna Protection Advisory Committee 73

INDEX

Federated Farmers 84, 89, 141, 142, 147; High Country 52–53, 194; Southland 72–73
Federated Mountain Clubs (FMC) 92, 139, 142, 174
Festuca novae-zelandiae (hard tussock) 80
Fiordland Flyer 120
Fiordland Marine Area 163–64
Fiordland Marine Guardians *see* Guardians of Fiordland Fisheries and Marine Environment
Fiordland (Te Moana o Atawhenua) Marine Management Act 2005 163–64
Fiordland National Park 94, 102, 107, 109, 140; Board 199
Fiordland Travel 123, 130
fire: burning of tussock before tree planting 196; cattle grazing to reduce risk 144, 145–46; Māori, early occupation of Otago 218; pastoral farmland burning 33, 43–45, **44**, 55, 63, 68, 73, 85, 86, 87, 145, 152, 153, 155; and serotiny 221; tussock management 43, 76, 153; unauthorised burning 235
fish and fisheries 83–84, 145, 148; Fiordland 161–66
Fish and Game New Zealand 245–46
five-finger (*Pseudopanax colensoi* var. *fiordensis*) **200**, 201
Flagstaff 19
Flagstaff Scenic Reserve 133, **166**
Flat Top Hill 155
Flat Top Hill Conservation Area 160
Fleming, Sir Charles 131, 173, 182, 227
Fletcher Challenge 233
Fletcher, Hugh 233
fog: Old Man Range 34, 35; water production from 49, **49**, 51–62, **52**
Forest & Bird articles 173–74, 176
Forest & Bird Society *see* Royal Forest and Bird Protection Society of New Zealand
Forest Research Institute (FRI) 50
Forest Service (NZ): administration of protected forests 63; deer control 201; exotic plantings 50, 64, 227, 229; Eyre Mountains land allocation 79; Land Use Study of South Westland 137; Management Policy for New Zealand Indigenous State Forests 229; Mount Aspiring National Park vegetation monitoring 207–08, 209; National Forest Survey 19, 21; Protected Areas Scientific Advisory Committee (PASAC) 136; Protected Natural Areas Programme 141; Protection Forestry Division 137; replacement by ForestCorp 93, 147; Scientific Co-ordinating Committee on Beech Research 83, 134–37, **136**, 230; South Island Beech Utilisation Scheme 134, 227; Te Anau vegetation survey 103; Waitutu Forest area 211
Forest Service (US) 28
Forestcorp 79, 93
Forestry Stewardship Council 179
forests: Cascade forest 180; exotic 50, 64, 134, 193–98, 227, 229; Joint Campaign on Native Forests 174, 230; Maungatua area 20–21; Mavora area 143; mixed exotic–native 134; Paparoa Forest 174; podocarp forest, buried 69–70; podocarp–broadleaf forest 20, 26, 136, 218; 'Principles for Plantation Forest Management in New Zealand' 194; Protection Forestry Research Advisory Committee 137; replacement by tussock grassland 26; reserves 134–37, 229–30; Secretary Island 200, **200**; Snowden State Forest 144; Station Creek Experimental Forest, Maruia valley **228**; succession studies 202, **203**, 204; swamp forest 102; Waikukupa and Okarito forests 138–39, 174; Waitutu State Forest 140, 211; West Coast indigenous forest protection 178–81, 184–87; Whirinaki Forest 140, 174;

see also beech forest; logging; Maruia Society; Native Forest Action Council (NFAC)
Forests, Fiords and Glaciers: New Zealand's world heritage (Forest & Bird) 179
Forests (Permanent Forest Sink) Regulations 2007 194
forget-me-knot, high alpine (*Myosotis oreophila*) 223–24
Fountain, Harold 17
France, Mark 125, 129
Franks, Stephen 250, 251
Fraser catchment 33
Frew, Russell 60
Frontiers in Ecology and the Environment 62
Fulbright Travel Grants 22
Fuscospora (*Nothofagus*): *cliffortioides* (mountain beech) 214; *truncata* (hard beech) 213–14

Galaxias gollumoides 245
Gardner, John 99, **108**
Garrett, Keith 137
Garvie Mountains 174, 218
Gaston, Frank 18
Gaultheria macrostigma 69
Geddes, Peter **167**
Geering, Lloyd 254
Generation Zero (GenZero) **249**, 250, 253, 254
Geological Survey 131
Gilbert, Tommy and Patsy 28–29, **29**
Gillespie, Neil 246, 248
glasswort (*Sarcocornia quinquifolia*) **231**
Glendhu 50, 57
Godley, Eric **39**, **135**
gold mining 14
Gore High School 70
Gorge Hill Red/Copper Tussock Conservation Area **72**, 71–74, **74**
gorse control 132–33
Gould, Bryan 254
Governor-General 171–72
Graham, Kennedy 250, 254
Grange, Ken 162, **165**

grass balds 26–28, 29, 30
grazing impacts of pastoral farming 33, 43–44, **44**, 45, 63, 68, 73, 76, 85, 86, 139, 143–46, 152, 160–61
Great Depression 13
Great Moss Swamp 149
Great Smoky Mountains 24–25, 27, 29
Green, F.W.H. 46
Green Party 249, 250, 254
Greenall, Alan 34
greenhouse gas emissions 251, 255, 256; *see also* climate change
Grono, Mount 200
Groser, Tim 256
Guardians of Fiordland Fisheries and Marine Environment 161–66, **165**, 183; *Characterisation of Fiordland's Fisheries, A* 162; Draft Integrated Management Strategy for Fiordland's Fisheries and Marine Environment 162–63; *Users Guide to the Fiordland Marine Area* 166
Guardians of Lakes Manapouri and Te Anau 11, 71, **108**, 108–31, 132, 181; 21st anniversary **121**, 123; addition of Lake Monowai 121–22; lake-operating guidelines 111, 112, 113, 114, 115–16, 117–18, 120, 122–23, 124, 126–27; second tail-race for West Arm, Manapouri 126–27, 130; silver jubilee 128, **129**; Waiau River Working Party 123–25

Haase, Peter 214
Haast 181
Haast–Okuru parallel dune/swale systems **216**, 216–17, **217**
Haast Range 140
Hager, Nicky 184–85
Hakatere Conservation Park 78, 177
Halwyn Station 155
Hamel, Jill 160
Hands Off Wanaka Lake (HOWL) 106
Hapuka estuary 217–18
hard beech (*Fuscospora* [*Nothofagus*] *truncata*) 213–14

INDEX

hard tussock (*Festuca novae-zelandiae*) 80
Hargreaves, Ray 74
Harris, Jocelyn 249
Harty, Joe 73
Hawea Conservation Park 78, 178
hawkweed (*Hieracium*) 152–53; mouse ear hawkweed (*Hieracium pilosella*) 69
Hawkweeds Core Group, Mountain Lands Institute 152–53
Hayward, John 51, 52
Head, Nicholas 188
Hebe odora 68
helicopters 204–05, 206, 208–09, 211
Hellaby, Arthur **39**
Hellaby Indigenous Grasslands Research Trust 38–62, **39**, 63, 84, 92
Hellaby, Lily 39, **39**
hen and chickens fern (*Asplenium bulbiferum*) 201
herbfields 80, 222, **222**, **223**
Herlihy, Gavan 160
Heron, Lake 148
Hieracium (hawkweed) 152–53; *pilosella* (mouse ear hawkweed) 69
High Country Federated Farmers 52–53
high country, Forest & Bird activities 174
High Country Public Lands Coalition 174
High Country Trustees 77
Highlands Biological Station, North Carolina 27
Hikurangi Farm Settlement 145
Hill, John 32, 34, 36–37, 38
Hilliard, Dave 185, 186
Hislop, Bill 66
Hocken Lecture, 2004 81
Hodgson, Pete 162
Hofstede, Robert 215, 221
Holdsworth, David 50
Holloway, Jack 21, 26, 103, 137
Hollyford River 106
Hollyford Valley 21; Monkey Flat **17**
Holyoake, Keith 100
Hore, Brian 218, 220
Horsehoof Station 64, 65

Howard, Basil 19
Hughes, Tony **211**
Hunter Mountains 96
Hurunui Water Project 187–89
Hutchings, Gerard 179
Hutchins, Brian **167**
Hutchins, Les 108, **121**, 123, 174, 211, **211**
Hutchison, James 98, 100
hydroelectric schemes and proposals 133, 158, 187, 235, 244, 245–46, **247**, 248; *see also* Clyde High Dam; Guardians of Lakes Manapouri and Te Anau; Manapouri, Lake; Manapouri power station; Te Anau, Lake
Hypnum cupressiforme 69
Hypolepis millefolium (thousand-leaved fern) 210

inaka (*Dracophyllum longifolium*) 66, 69
Ingraham, Neil 58–59, 60
Invermay Research Centre 80, 86
Ireland, Len 34
Irvine, Robin 97
Irving, Paul 163

Jacks Blowhole (Tunnel Rocks Scenic Reserve) 193
Jackson, Jon 244, 245, 246
Jackson, Mark 249
James B. Duke fellowship 30
Jepson, Robin **155**
Joe valley **207**
Johnson, Peter 71–72, 73, 92, 96–97, 103, 105, 106, 122
Joint Campaign on Native Forests 174, 230
jointed rush (*Apodasmia* [*Leptocarpus*] *similis*) **231**
Jollies Spur, Mid Dome **195**
Jones, Ali 251
Jones, Hector **108**
Jones, Norman 115
Journal of Hydrology 59
June, Selwyn 213

kahikatea (*Dacrycarpus dacrydioides*) 100, 139, 214–16, **215**
Kahurangi National Park 190
Kaikorai Stream 13, 235
Kaikoura ranges 174
Kaikoura/Clarence/Ka Whata Tu o Rakihouia Conservation Park 78, 177
kākāpō, sponsorship by Comalco 181–82
Katrine, Loch 187
Kawarau River 245
Kean, Geoff **195**
Kelleria childii 36
Kember, David 130–31
Kepler Mire 149, **151**
Kepler Track **138**
Kerr, Chris 150
Key, Alan **165**
Key, John 189
Kilmory Run 47
Kirk, Bob 112, 115, 120–21, 122, 125–26
Kirk, David 242
Kirk, Norman 106, 107–08, 235
Kneebone, John 142
Kofoed, Bill 21
Kopuatai Dome 148, 149
Kopuwai Conservation Area 154
Kopuwai Conservation Park (proposed) 78
Körner, Christian **72**
Korowai/Torlesse Conservation Park 78
Kramer, Paul 31

Labour governments: *1972–75* 107–08, 109–10, 112, 114–15, 118–19, 235; *1984–90* 92, 93, 142, 147, 180–81, 233, 234; *1999–2008* 161, 162, 163, 165, 184, 185
Labour Party 106, 107, 142, 185, 250, 254
Laidlaw, Chris 251
Lake ... *see* name of lake, e.g. Manapouri, Lake
Lake and Reservoir Management 130
Lake Guardians *see* Guardians of Lakes Manapouri and Te Anau
Lake Wanaka Preservation Act 1973 108

Lammerlaw Range **48**, 50, 51, 58–59, 62, 82, 174; Black Rock Scientific Reserve 67–69, **68**; Deep Stream catchment 57–58, 61, **61**; Mahinerangi Wind Farm proposal 242, 243; Teviot Swamp **151**
Lammermoor Range **46**, 50, 174; Project Hayes wind farm proposal 242, **243**, 243–45
lancewood (*Pseudopanax crassifolius, P. lineare*) 202
Land Act 1948 150, 152
Land Information New Zealand (LINZ) 78, 197
Land Settlement Board 67, 82, 84–85, 86–89, 92, 93, 141–47, **143**; 'Conservation, Education and Research' policy statement 90–91
Land Use Capability classes 75–76, 80
Landcare Research 60, 146, 169, 186–87, 196; Land Management Division 56
Landcorp 79, 80, 81, 93, 146, 196
Lands and Survey Department: Black Rock Scientific Reserve 67–68, **68**; conflict between land development and nature conservation 93, 146–47; environmental impacts of land development 82–83, 142–46; farmland development 67, 70, 72, 142–46; Gorge Hill Red/Copper Tussock Conservation Area 71–72; land allocation 79; Land Use Study of South Westland 137; Maungatua Reserve 63–65, **65**, 66–67; Mount Aspiring National Park vegetation survey/monitoring 204–09, **206**, **207**; Nardoo catchment reservation 84, 85–86, 87, 88, 89, 90, 92–93; and National Parks and Reserves Authority 138, 139, 146–47; Protected Areas Scientific Advisory Committee (PASAC) 136; Protected Natural Areas Programme 141; Pukerau Red/Copper Tussock Scientific Reserve 70; Reserves Section 144; wetlands management 149, 210; *see*

INDEX

also Land Settlement Board
Lange, David 180
Lauder, Glen 129
Lawrence 14
Lawson, Malcolm **165**, 166
Leamy, Mike **135**
Ledingham, Janet **247**
Lee, Bill 137, 210, 213–14
Lee, Sandra 161, 180, 182–83
Leptospermum scoparium (manūka) ecology 220–21
Libby Flat, Medicine Bow Mountains 26
Libocedrus bidwilli (mountain cedar, pāhautea) 204
Lincoln College Council 150
Lincoln University 152, 154, 157
Linn, Bob **25**
Lister, Ron 98, 133
Little Valley conservation issue 155–57
Lloyd, Bob 249, 254
Lloyd, Kelvin 190
lodgepole pine (*Pinus contorta*) 194, 197–98
logging: Buller District 178; state-owned indigenous forest 174, 227, 229; sustainable management 186–87; Tasman Forest Accord 178–79; Timberlands 178, 184–87; West Coast Forest Accord 178, 179, 184, 185
Loh, Graeme **79**
Longslip Station 55
Lophozonia (*Nothofagus*) *menziesii* (silver beech) 82, 143, **200**, 202, **203**, 214, 215
Lucas, Bing 92, 138, 139, 142

Mackenzie Basin 16
Mackenzie Ecological Region 141
Mackey, Moana 254
MAF Qual, Advisory Panel on the Biological Control of Gorse 132–33
Mahinerangi, Lake 84
Mahinerangi Wind Farm 242, 243
Mahitahi Maori Committee 179
Mai Mai Research Area 134
Manapouri Commission of Inquiry 98, 100–01, 181
Manapouri, Lake 10–11, 94–98, **95**, 100–01, 106, 109, **117**, **151**, 171–72, 252; catamaran and launch impacts on shoreline 120–21; control structure and gates 113, 116, 117, 119, 124–25; Hope Arm **95**, 98, 110; islands **95**, 96, 100, 131; Lookout Beach **111**; MANTAray model use 123, **124**; rainfall and flood impacts 113, 119–20, 125; sandy beach assessment 115; shoreline monitoring 110, 112, 124, 125–26, 128; slumping of lakeshore at Surprise Bay 106–07, 110; South Arm 97, 106, **107**; vegetation survey 96–98, **99**, 102, 111; West Arm 96, 126–27; *see also* Guardians of Lakes Manapouri and Te Anau; Save Manapouri Campaign
Manapouri Officials Committee 103
Manapouri power station 94–96, 98, 109, 111–13, 116, 117, 118–19, 120, 123, **127**; second tail-race for West Arm 126–27, 130
Manapouri Tailrace Amended Discharge Project (MTAD) 130
Manapouri–Te Anau Development Act 1963 109, 115; Amendment Act 1981 109, 117–18
Manapouri township 106, 109
Maniototo Environmental Society 243–44
Manorburn Ecological District 155, 157, 160
MANTAray model, Fiordland lakes management 123, **124**
manūka (*Leptospermum scoparium*) ecology 220–21
Māori: debate about logging on Māori land in Catlins 157; fires, early occupation of Otago 218; in research and research management 169; role of Māori as land-owning stakeholders 169

Māori Party 250
Mararoa River and catchment 116–17, 125, 143, 145
marine conservation 177
Marjorie Barclay Trust 193, 238
Mark, Sir Alan
  conference and other presentations: The Agricultural Industry and its Effects on Water Quality and Quantity, 1979 83; Ecological Society of America Millennium Conference 62; Ecosystems Center, Massachusetts, 1987 182; International Conference on Lake Ecosystem Conservation and Management, 5th, 1993 129–30; North American Lake Management Society, 18th International Symposium, 1998 130; papers on ecopolitics 258
  conservation and ecological work: memberships: Ecology Action, Dunedin 226; Forest Service Scientific Co-ordinating Committee 83; Guardians of Fiordland Fisheries and Marine Environment 161–66, **165**; Guardians of Lakes Manapouri and Te Anau 11, 71, **108**, 108–31, 132, 181; Land Settlement Board 141–47, **143**; National Parks and Reserves Authority 89, 137–41, **138**, **140**, 166; Native Forest Action Council 227–30; New Zealand Conservation Authority 166–68, **167**, 183; New Zealand Mountain Lands Institute 150, 152–54; Otago Catchment Board 227, 235–42; Otago Conservation Board 154–58, **155**, **156**, 160–61; Protection Forestry Research Advisory Committee 137; Review Panel on Flora, Fauna and Land Use, MoRST 168–70; Royal Forest and Bird Protection Society 11–12, 93, 137, 161, 166, 171–98, **183**, **195**, **197**; Save Aramoana Campaign 230–34, **231**, **232**, **234**; Scientific Co-ordinating Committee on Beech Research 83, 134–37, **136**; Task Force on Wetlands, New Zealand Environmental Council 147–49; Technical Advisory Committee on Reserves and Scenic Amenities 133–34; Wise Response 12, 248–54, **249**, **253**
  conservation and ecological work: specific areas and issues: Black Rock Scientific Reserve 67–69, **68**; Central Otago Conservation Park, proposed 74–78; Central Otago proposed energy projects 242–48; Clyde High Dam 237–42, **241**; Denniston Plateau 183, 189–92, **190**, **191**, **192**; Eyre Mountains land allocation 78, **79**, 79–81; Gorge Hill Red/Copper Tussock Conservation Area **72**, 71–74, **74**; Hurunui Water Project (Lake Sumner) 183, 187–89; Little Valley conservation issue 155–57; Manapouri and Te Anau lakes 10–11, 94–131, **105**, **107**, **108**, **121**, **129**; manūka ecology 220–21; Maukaatua (Maungatua) Scenic Reserve 63–67, **65**; Mavora Lakes (Pastoral) Park 142–46, 174; Mount Aspiring National Park vegetation survey and monitoring 204–09, **206**, **207**; Nardoo catchment debate 82–93, **91**, 136, 171; New Zealand alpine vegetation in global context 221–25; Nokomai patterned wetlands 218, **219**, 220; Otago Conservation Management Strategy (CMS) 78, 157–58, 160–61; Pukerau Red/Copper Tussock Scientific Reserve 69–71; Secretary Island, impact of

INDEX

deer browsing 199–202, **200**, **201**; South Westland ecological studies 213–18, **215**, **216**, **217**; Southland ecology and conservation 209–11, **210**; vegetation succession studies 202, **203**, 204; Waitutu marine-terrace sequence **211**, 211–13, **212**; water production from fog 49, **49**, 51–62, **52**; wilding tree control 193–94, **195**, 196–98, **197**

early years and influences: family background 13–14; holidays 14, 16; influences 10, 16–17; photographs **15**, **16**

education: correspondence school 18; Duke University 10, 22–28, **23**, **25**, 30; Mornington School 13; Mosgiel District High School 10, 17–18; Otago Boys' High School 18; University of Otago 10, 18–22, 25, 28

employment: Hellaby Indigenous Grasslands Research Trust 38–62, **39**, 63; Otago Catchment Board 32–37, 63; University of Otago 11, 39, 54, 76

lectures: Hocken Lecture, 2004 81; Sanderson Memorial Lecture, 1972 171–72; Sanderson Memorial Lecture, 1985 174–75

marriage and family: birth and baptism of Jenifer 32, **32**; family photo on 80th birthday **259**; family support 258–59; wedding and later reception 10, 28–29, **29**, 32; *see also* Mark, Patricia (née Davie)

recognition 12, 258; Forest & Bird Distinguished Life Membership 183

travel: Scotland, 1966 study leave 46; US, following study at Duke University 30–32

Mark, Alastair 259, **259**

Mark, Bridget 259, **259**

Mark, Cyril 13, 14, 16, **16**, **17**, 19, **32**

Mark, Elaine 13, 14, **15**, **16**, **17**

Mark, Emma 14, **15**

Mark, Eva 13, 14, **16**, **17**, 19, **32**

Mark, Jenifer 32, **32**, 259, **259**

Mark, Patricia (née Davie): children 32, **32**, 259, **259**; conservation activities 28, **247**, **253**; engagement 22, 28; family background 28; family photo **259**; travel around US 30–31; at University of Otago 19, 28; wedding and later reception 10, 28–29, **29**, 32

Mark, Stephen 259, **259**

Mark, Tom 14, **15**

Marlborough, Inland 174

Marples, Brian 19

Marshall, Denis 123, 234, **234**

Marshall, Frank 14, **15**, 17

Marshall, Jack 106

Marshall, Jane 14, **15**

Marshall, Kerry **167**

Martin, Debs 192

Martin, Tom 127

Maruia Society 178, 228, 230; *see also* Native Forest Action Council (NFAC)

Mason, Bruce 174

Matheson, Doug 47

Maungarakau, Golden Bay 19

Maungatua (Maukaatua) 20–21, 22, 39–41, **41**; Maukaatua (Maungatua) Scenic Reserve 63–67, **65**

Mavora Lakes (Pastoral) Park 142–46, 174

McArthur, Alastair 157

McCambridge, John 40

McCaskill, Lance 68, 69

McCrae, Jack 34

McDermott, Anne **165**, 166

McDonald, Kerry 119, 181, 182

McDonald, Stafford 236

McFarlane, Dave 196, **197**

McFarlane, Jim 108, **108**, **121**

McFarlane Mound 214

McGuigan, Tom 112

McKellar, Ian 236

McKenzie, Bruce 97, 106, 128
McLean, Jean 233
McLean, Jill 108
McLean, Roger 147
McLean, Ron 108, **108, 121**, 123, 250
McClelland, Teri 129
McMillan, George **143**, 154
McNab, Ross 199–200
McSavaney, Morrie 53, 54, 55, 56, 60, 62
McSweeney, Gerry **79**, 142, 173, 174, 180, 182, 183, **183**, 232
MacTavish, Dugald 249, 252
Meridian Energy 127, 128, 130, 131, 242, 244–45, 248
Meurk, Colin 103, 105
Mid Dome Wilding Trees Charitable Trust **195**, 197–98
Mill Creek–Waipori Gorge scenic reserve 67
Millar, Rhys 196
Miller, John 54, 55, 56, 57, 76
Milligan, Bob 114
Mills, Jim 209
Ministry for the Environment (MfE) 162, 163, 164, 197, 245
Ministry of Energy, Electricity Department 118; *see also* Electricity Corporation of New Zealand (ECNZ); New Zealand Electricity Department (NZED)
Ministry of Fisheries 162, 164
Ministry of Forestry 179
Ministry of Research, Science and Technology, Review Panel on Flora, Fauna and Land Use 168–70
Ministry of Works and Development (MWD): Clyde High Dam report 240; Manapouri and Te Anau electricity development 97–98, 100, 101, 110, 115; Water and Soil Division 50, 83
Miranda wetland 149
Mitchell, Rob **155**
Mitchell, Stuart 84
Mixed Ownership Model Bill 131
moa gizard stones (gastroliths) 21
Molau, Ulf **159**

Molesworth Station 78, 168, 174
Molloy, Les 139, 174
Monkey Flat, Upper Hollyford Valley **17**
Monowai, Lake 121–22, 128
Monowai Power Station 122
Moore, John 108, **108**, 110, 112–13, **121**
Moore, Lucy 45
Mora, Jim 250–51
Mornington School 13
Morris, John 137
Morris, Rod 190
Morton, John 173
Mosgiel Borough Council 235
Mosgiel District High School 10, 17–18
Mount ... *see* name of mountain, e.g. Cargill, Mount
Mount Aspiring National Park 137, 139–40, 174, 204; Board 28, 207; vegetation survey and monitoring 204–09, **206**, **207**
Mount Cargill Scenic Reserve 133
mountain beech (*Fuscospora* [*Nothofagus*] *cliffortioides*) 214
mountain cedar (*Libocedrus bidwilli*, pāhautea) 204
Mulberry Lane, Dunedin 13, **15**, **16**
Muldoon, Rob 115, 238
Munro, J.B. 113
Murchison Mountains 73, 209–10, **210**
Murray, Jas 199, 200
Myosotis oreophila (high-alpine forget-me-not) 223–24

Nankervis, John **167**
Nardoo catchment debate 82–93, **91**, 136, 142, 155, 171
National Development Act 1979 9, 231
National Film Unit 116
National governments: *1960–72* 94–95, 100, 101, 104–05, 106–07, 171–72; *1975–84* 115–18, 138, 139, 227, 229, 231, 232, 237–39, 240, 241; *1990–99* 123, 124, 128, 153, 154, 155–56, 157, 158, 160–61, 184, 185; *2008–* 131, 178, 189, 192, 252,

INDEX

256–57
national parks 63, 75, 76, 167, 168; Arthur's Pass National Park 140; Fiordland National Park 94, 102, 107, 109, 140, 199; Kahurangi National Park 190; Mount Aspiring National Park 28, 137, 139–40, 174, 204–09, **206**, **207**; Paparoa National Park 139, 173, 178; Te Urewera National Park 140; Tongariro Declaration 175–76; Westland National Park 138–39; Whanganui National Park 139, **140**
National Parks Act 1980 138, 168
National Parks and Reserves Authority 75, 89, 90, 137–41, **138**, **140**, 146–47
National Party 115, 250
National Water and Soil Conservation Authority 238
Native Forest Action Council (NFAC) 171, 172, 174, 178; Maruia Declaration, 1975 227–30; *see also* Maruia Society
Nature Conservancy, Scotland 46
Nature Conservation Council 236
nature tourism 75, 76, 180
Neill, Geoff 231
Nelson region 134; northwest 19, 21
Nelson, Wendy **167**
Nevis catchment 75
Nevis River dam proposal 242, 243, 245–46, **247**
New Zealand Alpine Plants (Mark and Adams) 170, **224**, 224–25, **225**
New Zealand Conservation Authority 137, 158, 160–61, 166–68, **167**, 183; *see also* New Zealand National Parks and Reserves Authority
New Zealand Ecological Society 59, 60, 84; *Proceedings* 102
New Zealand Electricity Department (NZED) 96, 97, 98, 101, 103, 104, 106, 109, 110, 111–12; *see also* Electricity Corporation of New Zealand (ECNZ); Ministry of Energy, Electricity Department

New Zealand Entomological Society 90
New Zealand Environmental Council, Task Force on Wetlands 147–49
New Zealand Federation of Freshwater Anglers 174
New Zealand First Party 250, 254
New Zealand Forest Owners Association 194, 196
New Zealand Institute of Agricultural Scientists 90
New Zealand Mountain Lands Institute 150, 152–54
New Zealand National Parks and Reserves Authority 75, 89, 90, 137–41, **138**, **140**, 166
New Zealand Wild Rivers Day 247
Newhook, Laurie 191
Ngāi Tahu 180
Ngāi Tahu Māori Trust Board 181
Ngāi Tahu Settlement Act 1997 67
Nicholls, John 134, **135**
Nissan Hill 214
NIWA 162
Nokomai Ecological District 75
Nokomai patterned wetlands 218, **219**, 220
North and South 59–60, 163
North Westland Beech Project Area 136

O'Connor, Kevin 174, **175**
Official Information Act 1982 60, 132
Ogle, Colin **135**
Ohinemaka forest block 137
Okarito Forest 138–39, 174
Okarito region 173
Old Dunstan Road 244
Old Man Ecological District 75, 141
Old Man Range 33, 75, 154, 174, **224**; climate stations and records 33, 34–36; cushionfield 235–36, **236**; Obelisk rock tor outcrop 235, 236; road for TV translator tower 235–36; snow fence 33, 36, **37**; snow tussock 35, 39–41, **41**, 42, 45; soil hummocks, stripes and solifluction terraces **222**, 222–23, **223**

Oliver, Anton 242
Olivine Valley 21
Ombudsman 84–89, 142, 196
orchids 96
Otago Boys' High School 18
Otago Catchment Board 227, 235–42; High Country Survey (initially Research) Team 32–37, 63; Water Resources Committee 235
Otago Central Electric Power Board 245
Otago Conservation Board 28, 78, 154–58, **155**, **156**, 160–61, 194
Otago Conservation Management Strategy (CMS) 78, 157–58, 160–61
Otago Daily Times 55, 70, 105, 160, 242
Otago Harbour Board 230, 232, 233
Otago Metals Ltd 230–31
Otago National Parks and Reserves Board 89–90, 203
Otago Regional Council 55–56, 153, 155, 242, 243, 246; Environmental Award **197**; Plant Pest Strategy 194
Otago University *see* University of Otago
Oteake Conservation Park 78, **177**

pāhautea (*Libocedrus bidwilli*, mountain cedar) 204
pakihi wetland 136
palaeoecology: Maungatua area 20–21; wetlands 148
Palmer, Sir Geoffrey 180, 182, 254, 255, 257
Paparoa Forest 174
Paparoa National Park 139, 173, 178
parataxonomic surveys 170
parks and reserves: Black Rock Scientific Reserve 67–69, **68**; Catlins Coastal Rainforest Park 158, **159**; Entrance Island Marine Reserve 162; Flagstaff Scenic Reserve 133; forest reserves 134–37, 229–30; Maukaatua (Maungatua) Scenic Reserve 63–67, **65**; Mavora Lakes (Pastoral) Park 142–46, 174; Mount Cargill Scenic Reserve 133; Nardoo Scientific Reserve 155; Pukerau Red/Copper Tussock Scientific Reserve 69–71; Rock and Pillar Scenic Reserve 160; Stoney Creek Tussockland Scenic Reserve 196; Tautuku Scenic Reserve 193; Te Rere Yellow-eyed Penguin Reserve 193; Tunnel Rocks Scenic Reserve 193; *see also* conservation parks; ecological areas; national parks
Parliamentary Commissioner for the Environment 250, 252
pastoral farming: Benger district 33; burning impacts 33, 43–45, **44**, 55, 63, 68, 73, 85, 86, 87, 145, 152, 153, 155; Cainard and Eyre Creek blocks 79–80, 81; grazing concession, Westland National Park 138, 139; grazing impacts 33, 43–44, **44**, 45, 63, 68, 73, 76, 85, 86, 139, 143–46, 152, 160–61; heritage features and conservation values, pastoral leasehold land 174; Hikurangi Farm Settlement 145; introduced grasses 85, 86, 87; land degradation 37, 44, 46, 80; Land Use Capability Class VIIe 75–76, 80; Maungatua area 21; Mavora Lakes (Pastoral) Park 142–46; Nardoo catchment 82, 83, 84–93, **91**; ploughing 92; runholders' responses to water yield studies 50–62; sustainable practices 36–37; tenure review of pastoral leases 76, 150, 152, 177–78; top-dressing 68, 85, 86, 87, 89; water quality issues 83
Patrick, Brian 174
Patterson, Rodney 55–56
Payton, Ian 45
Peake, Rex and Winnie 28, 29
Pearce, Andy 186
Pearce, Lindsay 199
Pearl Harbour 121
Peat, Neville 123, 131
perching plants on rainforest trees 214–16, **215**
Permanent Forests Sink Initiative (PFSI) 194

INDEX

Petrie, Donald 223
Pew Environmental Group, Te Papa Symposium 182–83
Peychers, Mark **165**, 166
Phyllachne rubra 36
Pickrill, Dick 115
pink pine 20, 64, **65**
Pinus: contorta (lodgepole pine) 194, 197–98; *radiata* forest, water yield 50
Pioneer Generation 122, 242, 243, 245–46
Pisa Conservation Park (proposed) 78
Planning Tribunal 233–34
plant ecology 10, 19–20; Maungatua area 20–21; Southern Appalachian Mountains 26–28; vegetation succession studies 202, **203**, 204; *see also* names of specific plants and areas, and also under Mark, Alan: conservation and ecological work
Poa colensoi 47
podocarp–broadleaved forest 20, 26, 136, 218
podocarp forest, buried 69–70
Polystichum vestitum (prickly shield fern) 202
Porters Pass **175**
Potton, Craig 179, 183, **183**
Powell, Conway **99**, 204
Powelliphanta: patrickensis (giant snail) 191; *spedeni spedeni* (giant snail) 81
Powles, Sir Guy 84–89
precipitation: Glendhu 50, 57; Lammerlaw Range 51, 57–59, 61, 62; Mount Cargill 52; Old Man Range 34–36; Otago high country (generally) 46, 52–54, 60, 61–62, Rock and Pillar Range 49, 52, 58–59; Swampy Summit 57, 58–59; Torlesse catchment 51, 52; *see also* fog
prickly shield fern (*Polystichum vestitum*) 202
Priest, Bob 147
Project Hayes 242, 243–45
Protected Areas Scientific Advisory Committee (PASAC) 136

Protected Natural Areas Programme 140–41
Protected Natural Areas (PNA) Survey 75, 141, 155, 156
Protection Forestry Research Advisory Committee 137
Pseudopanax: colensoi var. *ternatum* (three-finger) 201; *colensoi* var. *fiordensis* (five-finger) **200**, 201; *crassifolius* (lancewood) 202; *lineare* (lancewood) 202
Pseudotsuga menziesii (Douglas fir) 196
Public Access New Zealand (PANZ) 174
Pukerau Red/Copper Tussock Scientific Reserve 69–71

Quasi-Autonomous Non-Governmental Organisations (qangos) 132–33
Queenstown 196, 246
Queenstown Lakes District Council 196
Question of Power, A: The Manapouri Debate 116

rabbits 152
Radio New Zealand 196, 250–51
Radio New Zealand, 'Rural Report' 53
rain 52, 53, 58, 59, 61; Manapouri–Te Anau 112–13, 119–20
Raleigh, North Carolina 23
Ramsar International Wetland Convention 148, 149, 190–91
Ranunculus scrithalis (scree buttercup) 80
Red Hills 137, 139–40, 180
red/copper tussock (*Chionochloa rubra* subsp. *cuprea*) 69–72, **72**, 143
Reeve, Richard 242
Reid, Archie 21, 40, 64, 65–66
Reid, Ken 21, 64, 65, 66
Reid, Ron 21
Remarkables 174
Remarkables Conservation Park 78
Remarkables Ecological District 75
remote experience areas 76
renewable energy 242–43, 251
research management 168–70
reserves *see* parks and reserves
Reserves Act 1977 138, 141

Resource Management Act (RMA) 1991 9, 55, 124, 155; Amendment Act 2004 256; proposed amendments 256–57
Rhododendron catawbiense natural gardens, Roan Mountain 27
Riddell, Dave 129
Riddell, Jan 125
Rio Tinto Alcan 182; *see also* Comalco (NZ) Ltd
Roan Mountain 27, 28–30
Roaring Lion Mire 218, **219**, 220
Roaring Lion Stream 218
Roberts, Patricia 23
Robertson, Brian 150
Rock and Pillar Conservation Park (proposed) 78
Rock and Pillar Range 47, 49–50, 51, **52**, 58–59, 222
Rock and Pillar Scenic Reserve 160
rock wren 81
Rocklands Station 155
Rodda, Julian 139
Rodney Ecological District 141
Rogers, Geoff **207**
Rongahere Gorge, Clutha River 158
Roslyn Woollen Mills 13
Rotorua, Lake 108
Rowley, Jennifer 47
Royal Forest and Bird Protection Society of New Zealand 11–12, 80, 93, 100, 137, 142, 161, 163, 171–73, 226, 231, 244; ambassadors 183, **183**; Aramoana saltmarsh boardwalk 234; Charles Fleming Environmental Award 182; Comalco sponsorship of kākāpō 181–82; council meeting, Erewhon Station, 1988 **176**; Distinguished Life Membership to Alan Mark 183; Distinguished Life Membership to Sandra Lee 182; diversification of activities 173–78; Dunedin Branch activities 193–94, **195**, 196–98, **197**; *Forests, Fiords and Glaciers: New Zealand's world heritage* 179; Hurunui Water Project 187–89; Sanderson Memorial Lectures 171–72, 174–75; Save the Denniston Plateau 183, 189–92, **190**, **191**, **192**; Tongariro Declaration 175–76; West Coast indigenous forests protection 178–81, 184–87; wilding tree control 193–94, **195**, 196–98, **197**

Royal Society of New Zealand 84, 134, 167, 184, 186, 212, 255; Otago Branch 98
Ruataniwha Conservation Park 78, 177
Rural Bank and Finance Corporation 141
Ryan, Kathryn 251

Salmon, Guy 227, 230
Salmon, Peter 1889
Sanders, Lyndon 157
Sanson, Lou **129**
Sarcocornia quinquifolia (glasswort) **231**
Savage, Richard 98
Save Aramoana Campaign 230–34, **231**, **232**, **234**
Save Central 243, 248
Save Manapouri Campaign 108, 115, 123, 130–31, 250; silver jubilee 128, **129**
Savoy tearooms, Dunedin 14
Sawyer, Duncan 92
Scaife, Arthur 142
Scales, Sid 105
Scientific Co-ordinating Committee on Beech Research, Forest Service 134–37, **136**
Scott, David 69
Scott, Pat 249
scree buttercup (*Ranunculus scrithalis*) 80
Secretary Island **167**; impact of deer browsing 199–202, **200**, **201**
Secrets and Lies (Hager and Burton) 184–85
serotiny 221
Sewell, Alan 18
Shandwick NZ Ltd 184, 186
Shattky, Graye 242
Shaw, Chris 129
Shaw, Willie 190

INDEX

sheep 21, 44, 85, 152
Shipley, Jenny 158, 185
Shotover River 60
shrublands 20, 21, 64, **65**, 68, 69, 80, 136, 137, 143, 189, 204, 208, 217
silver beech (*Lophozonia* [*Nothofagus*] *menziesii*) 82, 143, **200**, 202, **203**, 214, 215
Silver Peaks 20
Simpson, Barbara **79**
Simpson, Neil **79**, **155**
Skerrett, Michael **195**
Slatyer, Ralph 31
Smith, Kevin 181
Smith, Nick 128, **129**, 160, 161, 192, 256–57
Snag Burn 102
snails, giant (*Powelliphanta spedeni spedeni*, *P. patrickensis*) 81, 191
snow (precipitation) 53
snow fence, Old Man Range 33, 36, **37**
snow tussock: burning impacts 43–45, **44**; Coronet Peak 40–41; deer impacts **206**, 209–10; Eyre Mountains 80; flowering (masting) **41**, 42–43, 44, 45; germination 43, 44; grazing impacts 43–44, **44**, 45, **206**, 209–10; growth rates 45–46; Lammerlaw Range 67–69, **68**; Lammermoor Range **46**; Maungatua area 20, 21, 39–41, **41**, 63–64; Mavora area 143; Mount Aspiring National Park **206**, **207**, 208; Murchison Mountains 209–10, **210**; narrow-leaved snow tussock **156**; Old Man Range 35, 39 41, **41**, 42, 45; reciprocal transplanting experiment 40–43, **41**; research for Hellaby Trust 39–62; slim snow tussock 42; and water production 46–47, **48**, **49**, 49–62, **52**
snowbank plants 36, **37**, 80, 222, **223**, 225
Snowden State Forest 144
Snowdon, Edward 187, **188**

Soil Bureau 134
Soldanella minima 225
Solid Energy 248
Soper, Frederick 39
South Island Beech Utilisation Scheme 134, 227, 228
South Okarito State Forest 138–39
South Pacific Aluminium Ltd 231, 232, 233
South West New Zealand World Heritage Area (Te Wāhipounamu) 137, 146, 149, 179–81, 182, 213, 217
South Westland Working Party 179–81
Southern Appalachian Mountains 26–28, 30
Southland 146; ecology and conservation 209–11, **210**; western 134
Southland Catchment Board 110, 144
Southland Conservation Board 194
Southland Conservation Management Strategy 146, 166
Southland Electric Power Supply 122
Southland Fish and Game Council 122
Southland Regional Council 122, 123–24, 125
speargrass (*Aciphylla spedenii*) 80
St Bathans Range **44**
St James Station 78
State Owned Enterprises Act 1986 118
Station Creek Experimental Forest, Maruia valley **228**
Stebbins, G. Ledyard 22
Steffans, John 162
Stephenson, Gordon 147
Stephenson, Loraine **167**
stewardship land 192
Stewart, Mike 60, 61
Stitt, Greg 116
Stoney Creek Tussockland Scenic Reserve 196
Stretch, Mason 129
Sumitomo 119
Sumner, Lake 183, 187–89, **188**
Sunnybrae, Otago Peninsula 32
Sustainable Dunedin City 249

Sutherland Falls 106
Sutton, Roger **129**
swale/dune systems, Haast–Okuru **216**, 216–17, **217**, 220
swamp forest 102
Swampy Summit 20, 57, 58–59
Swiss Aluminium Ltd 230–31
Sydney, Grahame 161, 242

Taieri River 235
takahē 73–74, **74**, 209, 210
Talbot, Joy 222
Talboys, Brian 101
Tararua Wind Farm 244
Tasman Agriculture 70
Tasman Forest Accord 178–79
Tasman Forestry Ltd 178, 179
Tautuku Scenic Reserve 193
Taylor, Stan 34, 36
Te Anau, Lake 10–11, 94, 95, 96, 106, 107, 109; control structure and gates 101, 113, 116, 120, 125; Delta Burn chase **114**; earthquake, 1988 120, 125; rainfall and flood impacts 112–13, 119–20, 125; sandy beach assessment 115; shoreline monitoring 110, 112, 113–14, 125–26, 128; vegetation survey and report **99**, 101–05, 111; *see also* Guardians of Lakes Manapouri and Te Anau
Te Anau township 73, 94, 100, 101, 109, 113, 120, 127, 162, 163
Te Kahui Kaupeka Conservation Park 177
Te Papanui 'Waterlands' Conservation Park 60, **61**, 78, 93, 154–55, **156**, 177, 196
Te Rere Yellow-eyed Penguin Reserve 193
Te Urewera National Park 140
Te Wāhipounamu–South West New Zealand World Heritage Area 137, 146, 149, 179–81, 182, 213, 217
Technical Advisory Committee on Reserves and Scenic Amenities,

Dunedin Regional Planning Authority 133–34
Telfer, Ian 196
Templeton, Hugh 101
tenure review, high-country pastoral leases 76, 150, 152, 154, 177–78
Teviot Swamp **151**
Theron, Margriet 168
Thom, David 137
Thompson, Keith 147
Thomson, Lake, forest succession studies 202, **203**, 204
Thomson, Matt 196
thousand-leaved fern (*Hypolepis millefolium*) 210
Threatened Species Trust 181–82
three-finger (*Pseudopanax colensoi* var. *ternatum*) 201
Tierney, Laurel 162, 164, 166
Timberlands 178, 184–87
Timmins, Susan **79**
Timms, Ali **195**, 196
Tiwai Point aluminium smelter 94–95, 96, 101, 112
Todd, Chris 187, 189
Tongariro Declaration 175–76
top-dressing impacts 68, 85, 86, 87, 89
Torlesse catchment 51, 52
tourism 101, 109, 113; *see also* eco-tourism
Tourist and Publicity Department 179
Treaty of Waitangi 152, 169
trout fishing 16, 145
TrustPower 122, 128, 242–43, 244
Tunnel Rocks Scenic Reserve 193
Turnbull, Ian 120
Turner, Brian 242
Turner, Keith 130
Turner, Sukhi 234
tussock grassland: Alastair McArthur's criticism of research 157; blue tussock (*Poa colensoi*) 47, **48**, 49, 51, 52; Denniston Plateau 189–90; DOC protection and management 175; Eyre Mountains 80; Forest & Bird

INDEX

activities 173, 175; hard tussock (*Festuca novae-zelandiae*) 80; Lammermoor Range **243**, 244–45; Maungatua area 20, 21; Nardoo catchment 83, 87, 88, **91**, 93; Otago high country 33, 35, 173; red/copper tussock (*Chionochloa rubra* subsp. *cuprea*) 69–74, **72**, 143, 155; replacement of forest 26; research 157; *see also* snow tussock
Tussock Grasslands and Mountain Lands Institute 51, 150
Tussocklands Resource Users Association 76

ultramafic belt 143
Umbrella Ecological District 75
Undaria pinnatifida 165
UNESCO 'Man and the Biosphere' programme 84
United Future Party 250
Universal Declaration of Human Rights 251
University of Auckland, Geology Department 58
University of Canterbury 112, 115
University of Otago 10, 18–22, 24, 25, 28, 55, 76, 97, 162; and Aramoana smelter proposal 232; Botany Department 11, 19, 21, **38**, 39, 40–43, **41**, 54, 77, 80, 83, 96, 97, 104, 166–67, 205, 209, 249; Chemistry Department 60, 232; Economics Department 232; Geography Department 74–75; Hocken Lecture, 2004 81; Zoology Department 83, 84
Upland Landscape Protection Society 243
Upton, Simon 153

Van der Goes, Marion **167**
Van Moeseke, Paul 232
van Reenen, Gilbert **155**, 242
vehicle access to high country 157
Verduyn-Cassels, Louis 248

'Vote for the Environment' campaign 174

Waiatoto River 140, 213–14
Waiatoto Valley 207
Waiau River, Lower 112, 116, 117, **117**, 120, 121, 122–23, 124–25, 127, 164
Waiau River Working Party 123–25
Waihola, Lake 149
Waikato Valley Authority 147
Waikukupa Forest 138–39, 174
Waikukupa region 173
Waipori, Lake 149
Waipori Station 82, 83, 84–93, 196
Wairarapa, Lake 149
Wairau hydro proposal 244
Waitohi Irrigation and Hydro Scheme (WIHS) 187, 189
Waituna wetland 149
Waitutu Māori Trust Board 213
Waitutu marine-terrace sequence **211**, 211–13, **212**
Waitutu State Forest 140, 211
Wakatipu Wilding Tree Group 196
Walding, Joe 109, 110
Walker, Mabel and Bob 14
Wallace County Council 120
Wanaka, Lake 106, 108, 205
Ward, Chris 211, **211**
Wardle, Peter 19–20, 21, 24, 25, 33, 136, 199, 214
Water and Soil Conservation Act 1967 237, 241
water production: blue tussock (*Poa colensoi*) 47, **48**, 49, 51, 52; from fog 49, **49**, 51–62, **52**; snow tussock 46–47, **48**, **49**, 49–62, **52**; *see also* precipitation
water quality: cattle impacts 144; and intensification of agriculture 9; Mosgiel Borough Council 235; nutrient status 84; and wetlands 148
Water Resources Council 50
Watt, Jim 199
Weatherall, Alan 63, 64, 66
Webb, Alf 190

Webb, Marilynn 242
weeds 69, 76, 85, 86, 87, 116, 133, 139, 152–53, 240
West Cape, Fiordland 204
West, Carol 130
West Coast: Forest & Bird activities 172, 173, 178–81; Land Use Study of South Westland 137; National Forest Survey 19, 21; North 134; North Westland Beech Project Area 136; protection for indigenous forests 178–81, 184–87; South 136, 137, 179; South Westland ecological studies 213–18, **215**, **216**, **217**
West Coast Forest Accord 178, 179, 184, 185
Westland National Park 138–39
Wetere, Koro 92, 141, 142
wetlands: Borland Mire 210–11; definition 147; Denniston Plateau 189, 190–91; Kepler Mire 149, **151**; Nokomai patterned wetlands 218, **219**, 220; pakihi wetland 136; Ramsar International Wetland Convention 148, 149, 190–91; swale/dune systems, Haast–Okuru **216**, 216–17, **217**, 220; Task Force on Wetlands, New Zealand Environmental Council 147–49; Teviot Swamp **151**
Weyden Stream 71
Whangamarino Swamp 148, 149
Whanganui National Park 139, **140**
Whanganui River 139
whekī (*Dicksonia squarrosa*) 202

Whirinaki Forest 140, 174
White Hill wind farm 244
Whitehouse, Ian 53, 54, 55, 56–57, 60, 62
Whitewater New Zealand 246
wilding tree control 193–94, **195**, 196–98, **197**
Wildland Consultants 190
Wildlife Service 103, 134, 209
Wilkie, Lake **159**, 193
Wilkinson, George 137
Williams, Andrew 250
Williams, Gordon 103
Williams, Morgan **135**
Williamson Flat, Arawhata Valley 205–06
Williamson, John 55, 56
Wilmot Pass 96
wind farms 242–45
Windpower Maungatua Ltd 67
Wing, Steve 162, 165
Wise Response 12, 248–54, **249**; petition to parliament **253**, 253–54
Woodhouse, Michael 250
Woodside scenic reserve 67
World Conservation Union, World Heritage Committee 181
World Heritage Convention 190; *see also* Te Wāhipounamu–South West New Zealand World Heritage Area
Wright, Jan 250, 252

Yardley, Dave 70
Yellow-eyed Penguin Trust 28
Yin Ronghua 72–73, 220–21
Young, Venn 229